The Essential

It's a Wonderful Life

The Essential

IT'S A WONDERFUL LIFE

A SCENE-BY-SCENE GUIDE TO THE CLASSIC FILM

75th Anniversary Edition

MICHAEL WILLIAN

Library of Congress Control Number: 2021921571
ISBN: 978-0-9762429-2-5

Publisher's Cataloging-in-Publication data

Names: Willian, Michael, author.
Title: The essential It's a Wonderful Life, 75th anniversary edition : a scene-by-scene guide to the classic film / Michael Willian.
Description: 3rd edition. | Chicago, IL: Kerpluggo Books, 2021.
Identifiers: LCCN: 2021921571 | ISBN: 978-0-9762429-2-5
Subjects: LCSH It's a wonderful life (Motion picture) | BISAC PERFORMING ARTS / Film / Guides & Reviews | PERFORMING ARTS / Film / History & Criticism | HISTORY / United States / 20th Century
Classification: LCC PN1997.I7583 W55 2021 | DDC 791.43/72--dc23

Book design by Carlene Vitale

Bedford Falls downtown and residential set illustration by Richard Thompson
Downtown Bedford Falls and Pottersville map line drawings by Midwest IP LLC
Building & Loan and 320 Sycamore line drawings by Brian Daniel
RKO Encino Ranch photos on pages 184-191 courtesy of Bison Archives and HollywoodHistoricPhotos.com
Wonderful Life Lamanda Park train depot set photo (p. 192) courtesy of Stan Kistler
1931 Lamanda Park depot photo courtesy of the Springer Archives, Temple, Texas
Jimmy Stewart photos courtesy of The Jimmy Stewart Museum
Photos on pages 27, 36, 45, 61, 70, 94, 105, 124, 133, 150, 160, 170 and cover courtesy of USC Cinema-Television Library and Archives of Performing Arts
Photos on pages 77, 180 courtesy of The Academy of Motion Picture Arts and Sciences
Photos on pages 6, 13, 98, 118 courtesy of Richard Goodson
Images on page 137, top of pages 193–196, and top two on page 197, from Liberty Films' 1946 *It's a Wonderful Life*
Images on bottom of pages 196, 197 from RKO Radio Picture's 1947 *The Bachelor and the Bobby-Soxer*

Remaining photos by Michael Willian

Published by Kerpluggo Books

Visit www.michaelwillianbooks.com for more *It's a Wonderful Life* features and inside stories about my research for this book.

For my parents

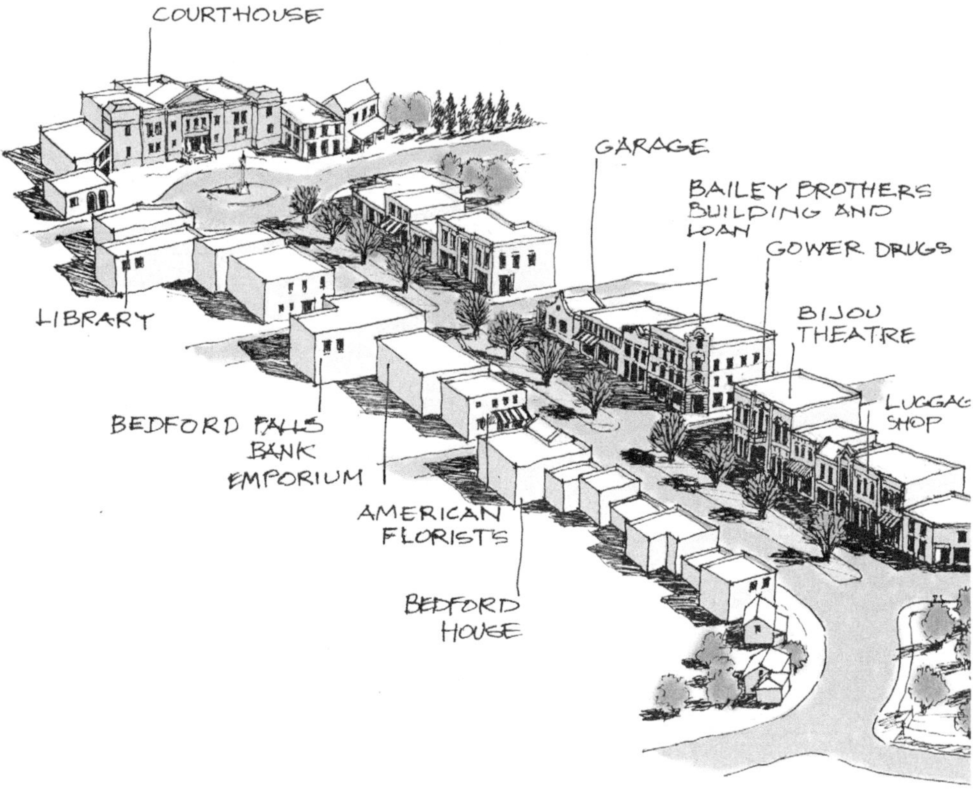

This illustration is an enhanced rendering of the Bedford Falls downtown and residential set areas as they were configured on the RKO Encino Ranch backlot. As shown, these downtown and residential sets actually connected and could be presented on film as a cohesive section of town. While the

IT'S A WONDERFUL LIFE

BEDFORD FALLS—DOWNTOWN AND RESIDENTIAL AREAS
FILMED AT RKO ENCINO RANCH, 1946
ENCINO, CALIFORNIA

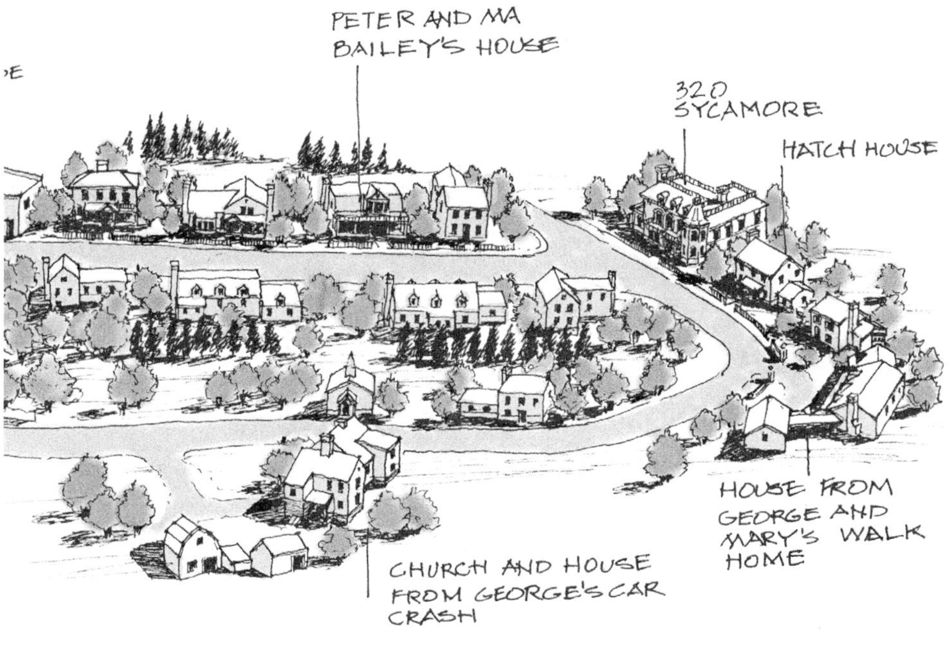

nearness of sets in *Wonderful Life* is due to backlot realities and filming necessity, it's fun to think about Mary Hatch growing up next to 320 Sycamore, George growing up half a block from Mary, and George and Mary raising their family just steps from downtown.

CONTENTS

INTRODUCTION

What is it about this film? There's no denying it's a classic. But over the past seventy-five years, *It's a Wonderful Life* has somehow managed to transcend mere artistic expression, weaving its way into the very fabric of our holiday ritual. For so many of us, getting into the proper holiday spirit goes hand in hand with watching George Bailey's epic struggle to find love, contentment, and his purpose in life.

But what exactly makes this film so alluring? On the most basic level, sheer exposure has certainly played a role. This film led a rather unheralded existence until the mid-1970s when the studio that owned the film forgot to file the requisite copyright renewal papers. This administrative oversight led television stations across the country to believe that they could show the film gratis. And show it they did, over and over again. It didn't take long before Pavlovian forces had us associating *It's a Wonderful Life* with our holiday experience.

Probing deeper, several of the film's themes speak to us on varying levels. The time-honored story of Good triumphing over Evil, using love, friendship, and old-fashioned values to defeat the Potters of the world. George and Mary's romantic journey, one that, in the end, has us yearning for the very things that George wants to throw away. The film's honest portrayal of the common man's pursuit of the sometimes elusive "American dream." Is that sympathy or empathy we feel for George as his life's dreams go unpursued?

But perhaps the film's greatest gift is its central message. *It's a Wonderful Life* serves as a much-needed annual reminder of the profound and positive impact that each of us has on the lives of others. At a time of year when perspective is at a premium, the film gently forces us to concede yet again that, hey, life really ain't all that bad after all!

Whatever the allure, one thing is certain: with each December viewing, the film seems as familiar to you as an old friend. And why shouldn't it? After all, you've seen it enough times. You know most of the lines. And you surely know an amusing anecdote or two about the film or have a favorite scene detail that you keep an eye out for each year.

But how well do you really know it? Well, trust us—there is much, much more to learn about this film. With this guide, our goal is to breathe new life into this friend, clueing you in to the veritable treasure trove of anecdotes and items of intrigue that have managed to elude you all these years. We do this by walking you through the film, scene by scene, in a fun, insightful, and occasionally offbeat manner. We provide in-depth discussions of film details, curiosities, gaffes, anecdotes, historical tie-ins, strange lines, and countless other things you've never noticed before. In the end, we assure you, you will come away with a newfound appreciation for the film and its cast and crew.

So if you think you know this film, we invite you take another look with us. Fire up the film, with remote at the ready, and join us as we put *It's a Wonderful Life* under the microscope for you.

USING THIS GUIDE

Before we dive headlong into the fun stuff, we recommend checking out the film chronology we pulled together for you. It clarifies the sequence and timing of events in the film, which can be a little hard to keep straight given the number of years covered. With this overview fresh in your mind, you'll be ready to start your scene-by-scene review.

We have organized the film into chapters based on the relation of scenes either temporally or from a plot standpoint. Each chapter begins with an overview of the scenes covered. Each scene overview is followed by topics relating to events occurring in the chapter, organized sequentially under one of these headings: Closer Looks, Did You Know?, History Lesson, Just Wondering, Film Anecdotes, Cast Anecdotes, Music Notes, Random Thoughts and Explanation Required.

The guidebook makes for a great read all by itself. We provide plenty of context for the items discussed, so you'll have no trouble understanding what we're talking about. Of course, if you want instant gratification just keep the film handy and use the digital bookmarks we provide to help you pinpoint some of the harder to find items. (Keep in mind that film versions can vary by a few seconds, so you may need to adjust for this.)

You will definitely want to examine, early and often, the array of set illustrations we created in the spirit of providing you with a more immersive experience. Trying to orient yourself in the film's settings through casual viewing is no easy thing, particularly for the downtown scenes, which are spread out over three and a half blocks and covered through a dizzying array of shot angles. So we have done the heavy lifting for you, painstakingly analyzing and reconstructing the sets so that you can see for the first time the location of key set features. Even better, the maps and floor plans are annotated to enable you to see where key scenes occur in relation to one another. Inside you'll find:

- Maps of downtown Bedford Falls and Pottersville, showing streets names and all known store locations, and pinpointing scene locations.
- Architectural floor plans for the Building & Loan offices and 320 Sycamore, showing offices, rooms, key set features and even furniture.

- A unique birds-eye view map showing how the Bedford Falls downtown and residential sets all fit together on the studio backlot. (Trust us, you will be surprised and amazed.)

These illustrations are completely original to this book and offer a level of insight into the film that cannot be found anywhere else. And be sure to examine the new collection of photos we've complied for additional insights into the backlot and on-location sets, and other items of intrigue.

Finally, the guidebook shines some light on the film's largely overlooked soundtrack, a hodgepodge of score cues and popular songs that, in the end, works quite well. In addition to the Music Notes that appear throughout the guidebook, we've provided the names of songs and cues and where they appear in the film.

FILM CHRONOLOGY

Following the film's storyline can be tricky given that it spans three decades, contains numerous jumps in time, and discloses a fair amount of background information through throwaway dialogue. Adding to the confusion is the fact that the film's director, Frank Capra, opted against using makeup to visibly age Jimmy Stewart and Donna Reed. Thus, George and Mary look just as fresh faced in December 1945 as they do at the graduation dance in 1928. Finally, while many scenes contain clues to the year and month they are set in, the timing of some scenes can be pegged only by referencing the film's production materials.

So to help give you a better perspective of how the story unfolds, we have put together a handy scene chronology. Nothing fancy here. Just a quick overview to get you oriented.

CHRISTMAS EVE 1945: The film picks up in Bedford Falls at 9:45 P.M., one hour before George arrives on the bridge contemplating suicide. The opening scenes cover the prayers of George's friends and family and the angels in heaven assigning Clarence the task of saving George.

WINTER 1919: The retrospective of George's life starts with a look back at the winter day in 1919 when George rescues Harry after he falls through the ice during a sledding excursion. George is twelve at the time of the accident; Harry is nine.

MAY 1919: Later that spring, George saves Mr. Gower from certain ruin by intercepting a prescription that Mr. Gower has accidentally filled with poison capsules.

JUNE 1928: Nine years later, George is preparing to leave the next day on a much-anticipated trip overseas. George, now twenty-one or twenty-two, deferred going to college and has spent the last few years helping his dad run the Building & Loan. Mary, now eighteen, is graduating from high school. This single day covers: George at the luggage shop, George visiting Mr. Gower at Gower Drugs, George walking through downtown Bedford Falls, George at home with his family, Harry's graduation dance, and George walking Mary home after the dance.

SEPTEMBER 1928: Three months late, George is scheduled to catch a train for college immediately after he attends a meeting of the Building & Loan's board of directors, at which a successor to George's father will be appointed.

JUNE 1932: Four years later, Harry returns from college. George, now twenty-five or twenty-six, has been waiting for Harry to come home and take over for him at the Building & Loan. Mary, now twenty-two, is just back from college. This single day covers: George and Uncle Billy meeting Harry at the train station, Harry's "welcome home" party at Mrs. Bailey's house, George encountering Violet downtown, and George calling on Mary.

OCTOBER 1932: Four months later, George and Mary get married. Their wedding day covers: the wedding send-off, the bank run scenes, and George and Mary in the "bridal suite."

JUNE 1934: Twenty months later, George and Mary help the Martinis move from Potter's Field to Bailey Park. This single day covers: the Martini move, Potter meeting with his rent collector, George meeting with Potter to discuss possible employment, and George returning home to learn that Mary is "on the nest."

JUNE 1934–SEPTEMBER 1945: The next eleven years are covered by montages—first a "Bailey family" montage and then a "war years" montage. George and Mary's first two children are born before World War II starts (meaning before September 1939). The youngest two Baileys arrive during the war, which officially ends in September 1945.

CHRISTMAS EVE 1945 (REPRISE): Still in flashback mode, we return to the day that George contemplates suicide. George is around forty; Mary around thirty-six. The daytime scenes cover: George spreading word of Harry's return from the war, Uncle Billy losing the bank deposit, Violet stopping by the Building & Loan for a favor from George, and George and Uncle Billy searching for the bank deposit.

George arrives home on Christmas Eve around 6:00 P.M. and storms out of the house fifteen minutes later. Between 6:15 P.M. and 10:45 P.M., George makes stops at Potter's office and Martini's. At precisely 10:45 P.M., George arrives on the bridge.

We are now officially back to the present. From 10:45 P.M. to around 11:45 P.M., George "rescues" Clarence and takes a whirlwind tour of Pottersville. George then returns to Bedford Falls, runs home from the bridge, and reunites with his family at five minutes to midnight.

THE ANGELS CONSPIRE TO SAVE GEORGE

"Please, God. Something's the matter with Daddy."

—JANIE BAILEY

We begin our journey by eavesdropping on the urgent prayers of several Bedford Fallsians this Christmas Eve 1945. In order, we hear from Mr. Gower, Mr. Martini, Mrs. Peter Bailey, Bert the cop, Ernie the taxi driver, Mary Bailey, Janie Bailey and Zuzu Bailey. The common theme of these prayers? George Bailey is in trouble and could use some help from above, and fast. For reasons that will be made known to us shortly, George has convinced himself that he's worth more dead than alive. And on his current course, he'll be putting this theory to the test just as soon as he can find a bridge suitable for jumping off of.

Enter the angels, who have heard this chorus of prayers and are now scrambling to come up with an intervention plan. The head angel and his assistant, Joseph, eventually assign good old Clarence to the project. Joseph doesn't have much confidence in Clarence's abilities, but we know better—Clarence is just the right man for the job. All Clarence needs is a little background on this Bailey character, and he and Joseph begin by reviewing a few defining moments from George's youth.

In the first of two such vignettes, we find George and his pals sledding down a riverbank during the winter of 1919. Everything is going swell until George's younger brother, Harry, eager to prove himself equal to the task, pushes off a little too hard, overshoots the bailout zone, and tumbles through an opening in the ice. George instantly jumps in after his brother and implores the other boys to help pull them out. Thanks to George's quick thinking, Harry will be around at the end of the film to toast his older brother.

The second vignette from George's youth is the infamous "poison capsules" incident at Gower Drugs. It is now late spring 1919, and George has recovered from last winter's sledding mishap, though he does have permanent hearing loss in one ear. George is working as Mr. Gower's store hand, and by all accounts he is an honest, hardworking young boy, if also a bit of a dreamer.

After getting scolded by old man Gower upon his arrival, George waits on two young girls, Violet Bick and Mary Hatch, both of whom will be vying for George's attention for years to come. There are some hints as to which girl will eventually win out, but it's going to be a while before George figures it out for himself.

While tending to Mary's order, George stumbles across a telegram containing news that Mr. Gower's son has died suddenly and under tragic circumstances. George suspects that all is not well with Mr. Gower in the back room and decides to investigate. Sure enough, Mr. Gower is stone drunk, and worse yet, he's filling prescriptions with poison capsules. This is not good. George is not sure how to handle this rather delicate situation, so he hightails it over to his dad's office at the Bailey Brothers Building & Loan Association.

Unfortunately, there's trouble brewing at the Building & Loan too. Henry F. Potter, the "meanest and richest man in town" and the Building & Loan's chief competition in the Bedford Falls real estate market, is in the house for a business meeting, and, invariably, these meetings are contentious. George slips into the meeting to find his father arguing with Potter about a loan that Potter is holding over the Building & Loan's head. The exchange gets more and more heated, and when Potter calls George's father a "miserable failure," George steps in with a few choice words—and a gratuitous shove—for the wheelchair-bound Potter. George is quickly shown the door by his father; and so ends the first of many skirmishes to come between George and Potter.

Forced to solve the drugstore dilemma on his own, George returns to the store, where he takes some serious heat from Mr. Gower for failing to deliver the prescription. But eventually he confronts his boss with the facts—"You put poison in those capsules, Mr. Gower!"

George's Friends and Family Pray For Him

CLOSER LOOK: We're not even ten seconds into the film and we already have a gem for you. Take a close look at the shot accompanying Mr. Gower's prayer. It shows the downtown Bedford Falls street that George runs down on his way home at the end of the film. After a few seconds, a man appears in the boulevard's median running wildly and waving his right hand. (1:29)

That, folks, is most definitely George Bailey. So what gives here? Did director Frank Capra purposefully and sublimely synchronize the prayers with George's triumphant return home? Are George's friends and family supposed to be praying for him at the very moment he's headed home to see them?

Um, no. In the next scene the angels respond to the various prayers at 9:45 P.M. (the head angel says George will be on the bridge at 10:45 P.M., prompting Clarence to remark that he only has "an hour to dress"). But George doesn't arrive home until 11:55 P.M. (the grandfather clock says so), which would place him downtown around 11:45 P.M.

This means George's appearance here is completely inadvertent. Capra needed a wintertime shot of the street in front of Gower Drugs to go with Mr. Gower's prayer and used an outtake snippet from his filming of George's run through downtown, perhaps unaware that the seemingly actionless footage actually captured Jimmy Stewart mid-run. Later on, we will show you this same type of editing mishap in a scene that takes place on Christmas Eve day.

CLOSER LOOK: Accompanying the prayer of George's mother is a shot of a local church. Look for this church later in the film across the street from where George crashes his car after leaving Martini's. (1:37:34) It's also visible when George returns to the scene of the accident in Pottersville (1:45:54), which is heartening news—it's nice to know that Pottersville has some churchgoers.

CLOSER LOOK: Bert's prayer is accompanied by a shot of a house, which, presumably is supposed to be his. Later on, we'll clue you in to the exact location of this house in Bedford Falls. For now, take a hard look at the very end of this clip—a mysterious man suddenly, and for no apparent reason, sprints off the front porch of the house next door. (1:43)

The Angels Talk in Heaven

FILM ANECDOTES: Although the "head angel" is never actually mentioned by name in the film, the script identifies this character as Franklin. This less-than-angelic-sounding name is a remnant of an earlier script that had Benjamin Franklin serving as the head angel and showed him talking to Joseph in heaven as he tinkered at a workbench with his latest invention. Thankfully, this cornball opening got the ax. This scene is just one of several that underwent late revisions for the better—we'll point out a few more along the way.

FILM ANECDOTES: Recognizing that the live-action "Ben Franklin" heaven scene wasn't the best fit, Capra eventually landed on using a celestial image with pulsing "stars" used to represent angels Franklin and Joseph, and, of course, Clarence. It's not exactly a visual thrill ride, and you would not be the first to wonder whether Capra, with his budget already blown, used this static scene to save a few nickels. Indeed, the hilariously-fake planet spinning across the screen—the purpose of which, we gather, is to sell us the notion that we are looking into deep space—makes it seem like the prop team cobbled this scene together over a set break.

But one should never underestimate Capra when it comes to his attention to detail. Spinning planet aside, the image Capra used here for heaven is an actual telescopic image of Stephan's Quintet, a cluster of five galaxies that can be found, albeit not without a pricey telescope, in the constellation Pegasus. When Franklin speaks, his voice is represented by the pulsing of one galaxy in Stephan's Quintet, while Joseph's voice is represented by two others.

FILM ANECDOTES: A few weeks before the film's premiere, word got out that Capra was so excited about his late-in-the-game solution for heaven that he swore the film's actors to secrecy. That sure sounds like him! Capra's inspiration for using Stephan's Quintet to depict heaven surely was born out of his lifelong passion for astronomy. Capra regularly insisted that had he not been in film he would have become an astronomer and worked for legendary astronomer Edwin Hubble. That's quite a bold statement. Hubble gets credit for two epic discoveries: there are galaxies beyond our Milky Way and the universe is expanding. All of that said, Capra's depiction of heaven in *Wonderful Life* essentially celebrates Hubble's "multiple galaxies" discovery.

Indeed, Capra forged a friendship with Hubble over the years. In 1931, Hubble famously hosted Albert Einstein at the Wilson Observatory outside Los Angeles for a star-gazing adventure and Capra convinced Hubble to let him to tag along to document it all. Years later, Capra invited Hubble and his wife to the 1937 Academy Awards. Capra was the president of the academy at the time, and that meant the couple sat at the head table with Capra and other A-listers. Early in the ceremony Capra gave a brief speech honoring Hubble and his discoveries, to the delight of the audience.

FILM ANECDOTES: After this scene, Franklin takes a back seat, allowing Joseph to quickly get Clarence up to speed on George's predicament. These "heaven" exchanges are mostly designed to help move things along, with Joseph providing key background on George's life. We will see Stephan's Quintet once more, just before the train depot scene.

DID YOU KNOW?: The creative seed for *Wonderful Life* was a short story called *The Greatest Gift.* The author, Philip Van Doren Stern, first printed the story in 1943 for distribution to his friends as a 24-page pamphlet-style Christmas greeting and later sold it to RKO Radio Pictures for $10,000. The story needed a lot of work, though. It began with "George Pratt" contemplating suicide on the bridge and had him masquerading as a door-to-door brush salesman in Pottersville as he investigated life in his absence.

While the RKO rewrites contributed several key scenes—George saving Harry, George at Gower Drugs, George and Mary on the night of the dance—they failed to capture the spirit of the original story. One script featured dueling Georges, with "good George" battling "bad George" to the death on the bridge. Another had Uncle Billy offing himself with a gun. Still, director Frank Capra was so convinced of the story's potential that he fronted his own money to buy it from RKO.

From there, the writing process was a bit bumpy, with Capra working with different writers in rough phases. He did engage some top talent, including the highly-regarded writing team of Frances Goodrich and Albert Hackett, who were behind the wildly popular *Thin Man* series. But that phase ended abruptly when the couple discovered that Capra was secretly rewriting their scenes with another Hollywood writer and long-time Capra collaborator, Jo Swerling. Undeterred, Capra pressed on with others while continuing to explore his own Capraesque ideas.

With so many contributors, credit for the screenplay ultimately had to be resolved through a Screen Writers Guild arbitration, with Goodrich, Hackett, Capra and Swerling prevailing to the exclusion of the RKO and other Capra-engaged writers.

FILM ANECDOTES: Although *Wonderful Life* received largely favorable reviews upon its release in December 1946, the film did not exactly take the box office by storm. According to Variety magazine, *Wonderful Life* failed to crack the top 25 grossing films for 1947, coming in on the list tied for 26th at $3.3 million, compared to $11.5 million for the top grosser, *The Best Years of Our Lives.*

The film's performance at the 1946 Academy Awards was also a bit of a letdown. While the film did receive five Academy Award nominations, including Best Director, Best Picture and Best Actor, it came away empty-handed, losing four of the five awards to that year's film juggernaut, *The Best Years of Our Lives.*

Wonderful Life was originally scheduled for release in January 1947, but at the last minute RKO leaned on Capra to move up the release date to December 1946. RKO, you see, had been banking on *Sinbad the Sailor* (1947) as its holiday season, um, anchor, but as the holidays neared it became clear that film prints would not be ready in time for a December release. Well, *Sinbad the Sailor* is not a Christmas movie, but *Wonderful Life* sure is, so it probably felt like a fortuitous no-brainer moving *Wonderful Life* into the 1946 holiday lineup. Unfortunately, for host of reasons, *Wonderful Life* fell short of being RKO's holiday season savior.

All of this strategic maneuvering had the effect of making *Wonderful Life* eligible for the 1946 Academy Awards. Many believe this worked against the film as the competition in 1947 was not quite as stiff. Whatever the case, a 1947 release date would have resulted in *Wonderful Life* going toe to toe for Best Picture with a rival of sorts in the holiday film genre, *Miracle on 34th Street.*

George, Harry and the Boys Go Sledding

CLOSER LOOK: As the boys prepare to sled down the river bank, check out the patch on each boy's toboggan cap. It's a rather ominous skull and crossbones, which no doubt signifies a gang that the boys all belong to. They sure look like they're having fun.

FILM ANECDOTES: Let's take a quick look at who's on the sledding hill. There are six boys in all. George, Marty, Sam and Harry are all identified by name, so that leaves two unnamed. One of them—the taller one—is actually Ernie. We know this from an earlier script in which Ernie went second. It was likely filmed that way, but his turn got cut in the editing room, no doubt to tighten up the scene.

But we have great news for Ernie fans—thanks to some editing slight-of-hand, he is in fact shown sledding. After George starts things off, Marty is next. Marty is shown at the beginning and end of his sled run, but the clip in between—showing the sledder mid-run—is actually footage borrowed from Ernie's turn. And indeed, when Marty gets to the bottom two boys—George and Ernie—are already down there. So George goes first, Ernie second and Marty third.

Moving right along, Sam sleds fourth and, while shoving off, introduces his signature "Hee Haw" donkey ears gesture—the first of many more to come. Next, of course, is Harry, who, despite his brother's unsupportive words, looks reasonably confident. That leaves a sixth sledder, who is not identified and who does not sled because Harry crashes. It's a fair guess that this is supposed to be young Bert; anyway, we like to think so.

CAST ANECDOTES: The closing credits have young Sam being played by Ronnie Ralph. But hold on. When we tried to do a basic visual identification of Ronnie Ralph, we discovered several things. First, Ronnie Ralph is not, in fact, the boy playing young Sam in the sledding scene. What?! Second, while Ronnie Ralph is in this film, he's nowhere to be found in the sledding scene. Third, Ronnie Ralph is in the upcoming Gower Drugs scene—as young George walks through downtown with his pals on their way to the store, Ronnie Ralph is on the far right.

With these revelations raising more questions than answers, we dug further and here's what we found:

- Ronnie Ralph was originally cast as young Sam, and was in fact playing young Sam in the Gower Drugs scene.
- The Gower Drugs scene was filmed several months before the sledding scene, and when it came time to film the sledding scene, Ronnie Ralph came down with the mumps.
- In the sledding scene, young Sam is played by Buz Buckley.

FILM ANECDOTES: Ronnie Ralph's illness created a rather unique continuity issue, with two actors playing the same character. But luckily Ralph did nothing in the Gower Drugs scene that revealed himself as playing young Sam. In the Gower Drugs scene, there's a "Hee Haw" reference, but it's yelled by all the boys, not just Ralph as young Sam. We're guessing both boys were disappointed at the time—Ralph for not being in the sledding scene and Buckley for not making the credits—but what really matters is that they got to be a part of the film.

EXPLANATION REQUIRED: The boys are actually having a contest—who can sled the farthest. As the boys finish their turn, they use tin-can markers and shovels to mark their distance.

CLOSER LOOK: As the boys sled, we spied an adult seated at the bottom of the hill on a stump. Unlike the boys, he's hatless. Look for him, all alone, when George heads down the hill (3:54). He's visible in the other three sled runs. For Marty's run you can see him in a blur as Marty whooshes past him at the end of the run. And when Marty goes, another likely adult appears at the top of the hill, just to the right of the remaining boys. If you think about it, the presence of adult spotters makes perfect sense—the sledding and water scenes easily qualify as stunt work.

CLOSER LOOK: The boys are actually trespassing as they sled, and, of course, the land just had to belong to the man that Bedford Fallsians love to hate, Henry F. Potter. No less than three of Potter's "No Trespassing" signs are visible in this scene. Look for the first one half way down the hill on the left as Marty (technically Ernie) takes his turn. The sign is legible but impossible to make out in real time. No worries, we've got you covered. It reads, "NO TRESPASSING. VIOLATORS WILL BE PROSECUTED TO THE FULL EXTENT OF THE LAW. HENRY F. POTTER." Well okay, Mr. Potter, message received.

Another one is visible (though in a blur) behind George, Marty and Sam at the end of their runs. Finally, a third sign is posted to a tree, right behind George as Harry sleds down the hill. (4:43) This one clearly reads, "NO TRESPASSING—HENRY F. POTTER."

CLOSER LOOK: Just after Harry shoves off, look for Marty standing down below and holding onto a shovel with his bare hands. Hmmm. He was wearing mittens a few seconds ago when he took his turn, and they are back on his hands when the boys pull Harry out of the water. Our guess? Danny Mummert, the boy who plays Marty, took them off between shots and no one noticed. Now, Sam is also without mittens, but at least he's barehanded throughout the scene. While it doesn't make much sense for any of the boys to be sledding without mittens, the production team may have had Sam go barehanded to highlight his "Hee Haw" gesture.

FILM ANECDOTES: An early version of this scene had Harry facing the same peril, but under different circumstances. In that version, the boys play ice hockey on the river as Potter watches with disdain from his house. An errant shot by George breaks Potter's "No Trespassing" sign, and the puck settles on his property. Seeing this, Potter becomes enraged. Moments later, the gardener releases Potter's attack dogs on the boys, and in the ensuing chase Harry falls through the ice.

Two thoughts here. The tough visual of guard dogs chasing boys, combined with the complexity of staging a hockey scene, no doubt drove the script rework. And eliminating Potter from the scene made good film sense. Having a Potter-George conflict here would have been redundant to the next scene, which was already in the can. Plus, it helped Capra shave a few seconds off the film's ballooning run time.

DID YOU KNOW?: George's technique for rescuing Harry is a bit unorthodox, though you sure can't argue with the results. George shouldn't have jumped in after Harry. The cold water is dangerously debilitating, and George now faces the same problems getting out that Harry does.

George should first have tried to pull him out with one of the shovels. That said, George's call for his pals to form a human chain (he yells, "Chain, gang!") was a good idea. Lying down near the breakthrough area distributed the boys' bodyweight and decreased the likelihood that they would break through the ice as well. By the way, if you ever find yourself alone and in Harry's predicament, all is not lost, but a game plan is critical. First and foremost, try to remain calm and breathe. Regaining a somewhat normal breathing pattern after the shock of hitting the cold water is a key to surviving. Next, go to the edge with the strongest ice, which, conveniently enough, is usually in the direction you approached from. Punch away any weak ice and find a solid edge.

Next grab any objects on you that can be used to claw into the ice (picture a polar bear clawing its way out of the water). Keys, a pen, a barrette, even a credit card, would come in handy here. Now, get those arms fully extended onto the ice, dig in with whatever you've got, let your body get horizontal in the water, start a swimmer's kick, and pull yourself up. Once you're out, to avoid an encore performance, don't forget to roll or slide away from the hole.

RANDOM THOUGHTS: Due to some ill-timed dubbing, Harry's second yell for help actually comes while he's underwater. What's more, we see what looks to be the very top of Harry's toboggan cap sticking out of the water, in which case there's a chance that someone's underwater in this shot.

CLOSER LOOK: Don't forget there's that last boy on the hill, set to sled right after Harry. That boy never takes his turn but he does run down to help rescue Harry. Harry and George are in the water, and four boys are in on the human chain. But in an interesting continuity twist, the actor playing that boy at the top of the hill is not the same one seen in the chain.

FILM ANECDOTES: All scenes in *Wonderful Life* were filmed either on an RKO studio soundstage, an RKO studio backlot or on location. If this sledding scene feels like it falls into the soundstage category, that's with good reason. This and other soundstage scenes were filmed at RKO's Culver Studios in Culver City. In 1928, RKO launched this studio and backlot, before leasing it to famed producer David O. Selznick in the mid-1930s. Selznick was still leasing the place the year Capra filmed *Wonderful Life*. The studio has changed hands through the years but some of the key stages used in *Wonderful Life* remain in use today.

Stage 14 at RKO's Culver Studios hosted the Christmas Eve gathering, Hatch house interiors, Martini's and Nick's, among others. The Building & Loan scenes were filmed on Stage 5. Stage 15 was one of the largest stages in Hollywood at around 33,000 square feet. For comparison, a football field is 57,600 square feet. The stage could also be flooded. Over the years Stage 15 hosted many films, including these large-scale numbers: *The Night of the Hunter* (river scenes), *The Bells of St. Mary's* (school grounds) and *Holiday Affair* (Central Park winter scenes).

Knowing this, you can probably guess that the sledding scene took place on Stage 15. It may have been balmy outdoors on the days this scene was filmed in mid-August 1946, but it was plenty cold inside Stage 15. While it's clear that this is an unusually large and involved set, the film does not reveal the set's true expanse. Potter's house (not visible) is on the hillside behind the boys as they cheer from the bottom. A cottage is on the river bank, visible screen left when Harry shoves off from the top. And then there's the hill—it's pretty good-sized, maybe around 35-40 feet, top to bottom. To some it's obvious that this is a set. In our view, the real tell is the audio—it just doesn't sound quite like they are outdoors.

George Waits on Mary and Violet at Gower Drugs

FILM ANECDOTES: The beginning of this scene gives us our first glimpse of one of the film's most important characters, downtown Bedford Falls. The downtown set consisted of three and a half full-scale city blocks, complete with a boulevard lined with trees. Different versions of the set were created to depict not only the aging of Bedford Falls (downtown scenes were set in 1919, 1928, 1932 and 1945), but also Bedford Falls' alter ego, Pottersville. We've reconstructed a map of downtown Bedford Falls and Pottersville from film footage, film stills and other sources. It does not appear that the production team ever documented the downtown layouts, so these maps offer never-before-seen insights into the downtown layouts. The maps will clue you in to the exact downtown location of various scenes as well as the location of various Bedford Falls and Pottersville businesses.

Also, we have updated the map to include some additional store names and a few newly discovered stores, such as a "U.S. Agriculture Department" storefront, a photography shop (next to the garage) and "Charm Beauty Studio" (squeezed in between the American Florists shop and the barber shop). We've also moved the luggage shop to the other side of the street after deciphering a few clues as to its exact location.

FILM ANECDOTES: In addition to soundstages, RKO's Culver Studios also had a fine backlot that Capra could have made use of. It was called Forty Acres and *Gone With the Wind* was filmed on it. But Capra, who did not like studio executives peeking over his shoulder on the set, instead chose to use a remote RKO backlot located way out in Encino, California. Encino is in the San Fernando Valley and back then it was pretty much out in the sticks. The ranch was a rectangular strip of land, not quite a hundred acres, surrounded by farmland and alfalfa fields. RKO purchased Encino Ranch in anticipation of its filming of the 1931 Western *Cimarron*. Practically the only thing out that way back then was a ranch owned by actor Edward Everett Horton, located on the other side of a dirt road from Encino Ranch.

The big draw for Capra was the ranch's huge main street set, which he transformed into Genesee Street and downtown Bedford Falls. And he didn't just use the main street set. Many other scenes were filmed in the ranch's open-air environs, including the 320 Sycamore and Hatch house exteriors, the Ma Bailey house exteriors, the Martini house in Potter's Field, George and Mary's post-dance stroll and George's car crash.

What's more, Encino Ranch also had interior shooting capabilities. For example, scenes inside Gower Drugs, the luggage shop and the bank lobby were all filmed on the ranch on working interior sets that were located on the main street set. This allowed Capra to stream live action past the windows. So when things like a horse-drawn delivery wagon go clip-clopping past Gower Drugs, it's easy for moviegoers to come away believing that Gower Drugs is a real drugstore in a real town.

FILM ANECDOTES: Film lore has it that the trees in downtown Bedford Falls were real oaks, transplanted for the shooting. We've always been skeptical—the trees are really big and transplanting just a single modest-sized tree is a huge undertaking, let alone a few dozen. Well, we are pleased to now have a definitive answer for you, thanks to the folks at the Seneca Falls *It's a Wonderful Life* Museum.

George Zermano was twenty-three when he worked on *Wonderful Life* as a part of the crew charged with managing greenery (real and artificial) and other natural settings called for in the set designs. Zermano confirmed for the museum that the downtown trees were not live; rather, the crew used the trunks of downed pepper trees. They attached the trunks to a platform running down the median and then built the trees out using, among other things, actual oak limbs nailed in place or secured with metal rods. So while these are not transplanted trees, we are looking at parts of actual trees.

CLOSER LOOK: We soon learn that George is headed to work at Gower Drugs, while his friends are headed to a baseball field. George is wearing a jacket and has a magazine tucked in the back pocket of his knickers. His friends on the other hand are wearing mismatched uniforms and a cool assortment of baseball equipment, including several mitts, a bat and a catcher's mask. They appear to be up to a bit of mischief, walking down the middle of the street, with arms locked, blocking a car that's trying to get through.

EXPLANATION REQUIRED: Given the baseball context, the B.B.C. on the one boy's sweatshirt may well stand for Base Ball Club. Through the early decades of baseball, the game mostly went by base ball and base-ball. But by the time the 1900s rolled around, the one-word version pulled ahead in popularity with baseball writers and was the standard by the 1910s. Still, out in the field, so to speak, there was some overlap for a spell.

CLOSER LOOK: Distracted by Potter, the boys miss a delivery truck headed the other way. It's a horse-drawn wagon for the Bedford Falls Bakery—you can just make out the name on the wagon's side, plus "Bread," "Pies" and "Cake" on its back panels. Too bad, they might have been able to finagle a handout.

RANDOM THOUGHTS: Bedford Falls must be a decent-sized town—it's busy enough to assign a traffic officer to the intersection outside the Building & Loan. Look for the officer standing next to his traffic signal as Potter's carriage whisks by. The signal is comprised of a pole stand, an umbrella and opposing "Stop" and "Go" signs attached to the pole beneath the umbrella. This umbrella-style traffic signal was an actual design, invented a few years before this scene is set. The officer changed signals by manually turning the pole a quarter turn.

CLOSER LOOK: Well, apparently pesky traffic laws do not apply to Potter—his carriage rumbles through the intersection even though he's got the "Stop" sign. No complaints from the officer, who knows what's good for him and obligingly waves Potter through.

The same traffic officer and stand appear in the next scene, set nine years later, as George waves to the Building & Loan gang. The four-way, three-colored traffic light had been invented well before then, but, hey, this is Bedford Falls, where, outside the luggage store, a horse-drawn wagon can be found navigating Genesee Street in 1928.

CLOSER LOOK: Potter's two-horse carriage is quite a ride. It's a Brougham-style carriage, and the size, lamps, monogram and detailing all bespeak nobility—even Clarence thinks this is the ride of a king. There's room for two drivers and four passengers in a closed compartment with three full sides of glass windows. There's a second passenger in the carriage, and that person does look like Potter's assistant.

CLOSER LOOK: Gower Drugs features bicycle delivery service. You can see the bicycle parked outside the store's front door as the boys fling George inside. A metal sign fitted to the inside of the frame advertises "Gower Drugs." We like the visual of George delivering prescriptions this way.

CLOSER LOOK: Check out the writing on the mirror behind the soda fountain counter. It's an advertisement for the "Gower Special," which sells for twenty cents. (6:12) No word on what this "Special" is, but given Mr. Gower's shaky mental state, we're recommending that customers ask Mr. Gower to take the first bite. Now, there's another item advertised on a mirror farther to the right. Almost all of it is blocked by a pole, but we can make out just enough to guess with confidence that it reads, "Banana Split 30 cents." Yes, please!

CLOSER LOOK: Young Violet has frequented Gower Drugs so often that George knows exactly what she's going to order—two cents' worth of shoelaces. Look for George actually ringing up two cents on the cash register. This looks to be an after school visit by the girls based on Mary's school books resting on the counter. And to our delight, we can read the title of the top book, Daily Lesson Plans. Hmmm. Isn't that book usually for the teacher?!

CAST ANECDOTES: As good as Jeanine Ann Roose (young Violet) and Jean Gale (young Mary) are in this scene, conveying at once their character's interest in George and disdain for one another, *Wonderful Life* was pretty much it in terms of their careers in film. Roose, though, acted for years on two very popular radio shows, including *The Jack Benny Program.* It's too bad Roose's role wasn't a little larger—it's fun to think about how things would have gone down had young Violet decided to stick around. Now, Gale was supposed to be in the sledding scene as well. She was even on the cast list for those shooting days. But young Mary got cut from the scene in a last-minute script change. A little later, we will share an interesting story about that cut and its consequences.

HISTORY LESSON: In this scene we learn that by the age of twelve George had already developed a fascination with travel and world geography. The subject of coconuts leads to George pontificating about the South Seas. His fascination with this area of the world was fairly typical for the era. Americans were introduced to the culture of the South Seas and Pacific Islands in the early part of the twentieth century, primarily through fairs and expositions such as the Panama-Pacific International Exposition in San Francisco in 1915. Beginning in the late teens, Americans were clamoring for anything related to Hawaiian culture, and were particularly obsessed with Hawaiian music and the exotic and dreamy sounds of the ukulele and the Hawaiian guitar.

CLOSER LOOK: The following products and advertisements appear in Gower Drugs during the "poison capsules" scenes—see if you can spot them:

- Coca-Cola
- Paterson tobacco pipes
- La Unica cigars
- Camel cigarettes
- Lucky Strike cigarettes
- Chesterfield cigarettes
- Vaseline hair tonic
- Penetro cough syrup
- Pepto-Bismol
- Bayer aspirin—"for colds and influenza"
- *The Saturday Evening Post*
- Gets-It corn remover
- St. Joseph aspirin
- LB hair tonic
- Mufti lighter fluid
- Dr. Scholl's Zino-pads—for "corns, callouses, bunions"
- Ingersoll watches

CLOSER LOOK: By far, the most prevalent advertising in Gower Drugs is for Coca-Cola, and it's well worth a deep dive on the drugstore's impressive array of Coca-Cola visuals. Outside, Gower Drugs boldly declares that it's a Coca-Cola establishment through large neon and banner Coca-Cola signs. The neon sign doubles as a sign for Gower Drugs; the banner fronts Genesee Street and reads, "Drink Coca-Cola Soda." That's right, Bedford Fallsians, no Pepsi served here!

The banner is visible in both 1919 Bedford Falls and 1945 Bedford Falls. The neon sign is visible in 1932 and 1945 Bedford Falls but not in 1919 Bedford Falls, owing to neon not being a thing until the mid-1920s. This is a nice example of how Capra and set designer Emile Kuri showed Bedford Falls aging through the years.

Inside, the theme continues with numerous Coca-Cola pieces. Most are prominently displayed, by design, as Kuri played on the brand's deep connection with American drugstores. First up, located behind the bar, is a thermometer with "Drink Coca-Cola—Delicious and Refreshing" at the top and a girl swigging a bottle of Coke at the bottom. Left of the register is a rectangular serving tray featuring a Coca-Cola calendar girl; it's known as the "Elaine" tray. Right of the register is an oval calendar girl tray known as the "Betty Girl" tray.

Farther right of the register, hanging on the wall, is a round Coca-Cola sign that reads, "Please Pay When Served—Thank You." Above the bar is a Tiffany-style Coca-Cola leaded glass ceiling light with beaded fringe. And two large Coca-Cola soda fountain syrup bottles hide among the array of items in the register area—see if you can find them.

Finally, atop the bar mirror hangs an over-sized cardboard Coca-Cola display known as the "Umbrella Girls Festoon," with three smiling beauties each holding a Coke in one hand and a sun umbrella in the other. It has adjustable arms, designed to fit the display to the contours of the bar. In the film you can only see part of two of the girls.

The thermometer is a bit out of place in this scene—it dates back to only 1939. The trays date to 1914 and 1916, the festoon to 1918. The light matches a known design from the 1920s and 1930s. All of the pieces are highly sought after, with the festoon being tops in value and quite possibly a five-figure auction item.

EXPLANATION REQUIRED: Are you impressed by George's pronouncement that he's been "nominated for membership" in the National Geographic Society? Here, he's referring to the rather formal, if low-bar, process for becoming a member of the society. The society technically was a club and joining is how you got your subscription to *The National Geographic Magazine.* A form in the 1919 version of the magazine simply called for a current member to provide a "recommendation for membership." So while George's claim that he had been nominated for membership was accurate, in all likelihood the person who nominated him was Uncle Billy.

CLOSER LOOK: With the scene calling for a fairly tight shot of such a popular magazine, the prop team's best play here was to go with a real issue. And we can confirm that they did just that. George has in his hands an actual issue from 1919, albeit the October issue instead of May. And interestingly, that particular issue includes an article relating to the South Seas. Still, the prop team was definitely aware of the May–October discrepancy—someone used a marker to obscure "October" on the front cover.

CLOSER LOOK: By the way, this is not the first time we have seen this magazine. George brought the magazine with him to the store—look for it rolled up in his back pocket as he and his pals gawk at Potter.

CLOSER LOOK: We watched this scene countless times without catching a sneaky move by George. After Mary says no to the coconuts he recommends, he turns to the back counter and proceeds to sprinkle a few spoonfuls of coconut onto her ice cream. Thank goodness this move wasn't an early deal breaker for Mary or we wouldn't have much to watch.

DID YOU KNOW?: When Mary leans over the counter to whisper in George's bad ear, do you know why there's a piece of tape on the edge of the counter? (7:00) It an actor's "mark," placed there to show Jean Gale and Bobby Anderson where to be when Jean leans over. Well, she hit her mark all right, but the film crew was either planning on Bobby's head blocking the tape or they meant to remove it before filming and forgot. Note that a few seconds earlier, in a wider shot from the same angle, the tape isn't there. This should have been caught during the daily footage review, but it happens so fast that it's easy to see how it slipped through.

CLOSER LOOK: Of course, Gower Drugs features a full-service soda fountain so you can order flavored sodas, with or without ice cream. We know for sure that Gower Drugs has orange soda because there's a Mission Orangeade syrup dispenser on the counter, visible when Mary sticks her tongue out at Violet. It's a super cool art deco piece that dates to the 1930s (so again just a bit off on timing), painted bright orange, naturally, with orange slices adorning the top. There's a spigot on the other side that George, serving as soda jerk, would draw from before adding the requisite carbonated water.

CAST ANECDOTES: Jimmy Stewart and Donna Reed both grew up in their own small-town versions of Bedford Falls. Stewart was born on May 20, 1908, in Indiana, Pennsylvania. He spent much of his youth helping his father run the family hardware store, not unlike young George working at Gower Drugs. By his own account, Stewart was not much of a student, and had an adventurous streak that found him as a little boy planning an African safari with the help of his indulgent father, and, later, creating an elaborate airplane model and diorama to track Charles Lindbergh's historic first non-stop solo transatlantic flight. Even with his creative mind, he could not possibly have imagined that thirty years later he would be starring as Lindbergh in the film *The Spirit of St. Louis* (1957).

Reed was born Donna Belle Mullenger on January 27, 1921, growing up on the family farm some seven miles outside of Denison, Iowa. The oldest of five, Donnabelle helped her parents keep order on the farm. A true midwestern farm girl, Donna was a 4-H member, and at the age of thirteen won a blue ribbon at the Iowa State Fair for a tasty batch of raised bread rolls. A few years earlier she dashed off a letter to a local paper, revealing that she was the proud owner of three cats and four ponies. And lest there be any doubt about her farmhand skills, here's a sampling of chores she handled back home: milking cows, feeding hogs and chickens, planting corn, gathering firewood, handling a tractor, churning butter, baking bread, pitching hay and painting barns. Yep, she definitely checks out as a farm girl.

FILM ANECDOTES: We originally included in the guidebook a well-circulated bit of *Wonderful Life* film lore that had Lionel Barrymore betting Donna Reed $50 during filming that she couldn't milk a cow, with Donna Reed winning the bet. It sounded like it could be a tale, but then again the RKO Encino Ranch was out in farmland, so the opportunity was at least there.

Well, we have since uncovered that this story first circulated in 1942 in connection with an MGM production, with a $25 war bond as the stakes. These accounts even included a photo of a beaming Reed sitting on a milking stool milking a cow. With that photographic proof, the story sure seems to check out, albeit several years before the filming of *Wonderful Life*.

But there's just one problem—a few years later, Reed intimated that maybe things didn't go down exactly as reported in the papers. Well, whatever the story, what we do know is that Reed would have won any bet along these lines. She had years of experience milking cows back home, and once explained, "Milking a cow is like riding a bike. Once you learn how, you can't forget."

Downtown Bedford Falls

1. Young George and his pals see Potter in his horse-drawn carriage (the carriage passes in front of the Building & Loan headed toward the courthouse).
2. The steps leading up to the Building & Loan.
3. George waves to Uncle Billy, Tilly and Eustace, who are all yelling to him from a Building & Loan window.
4. George, Bert and Ernie run into Violet after George picks up his suitcase (Violet crosses Jefferson Avenue walking toward the courthouse).
5. Violet spots George as she closes up shop on the night of Harry's "welcome home" party.
6. George and Violet discuss making a night of it (shot looking away from the courthouse).
7. George, Mary and Ernie observe a crowd gathering in front of the Bedford Falls Trust and Savings Bank on the day of the bank run.
8. Mr. Gower sells war bonds in front of the courthouse.
9. George hands Ernie and Mr. Gower newspapers on Christmas Eve announcing Harry's receipt of the Medal of Honor.
10. Uncle Billy salutes a military jeep on his way to the bank (shot looking toward the courthouse).
11. George and Uncle Billy retrace Uncle Billy's steps leading up to his visit to the bank (shot looking away from the courthouse).
12. George stands in front of "You Are Now in Bedford Falls" sign on his way home on Christmas Eve (shot looking toward the courthouse).
13. George wishes Potter a "Merry Christmas" on Christmas Eve as Potter sits in his office.

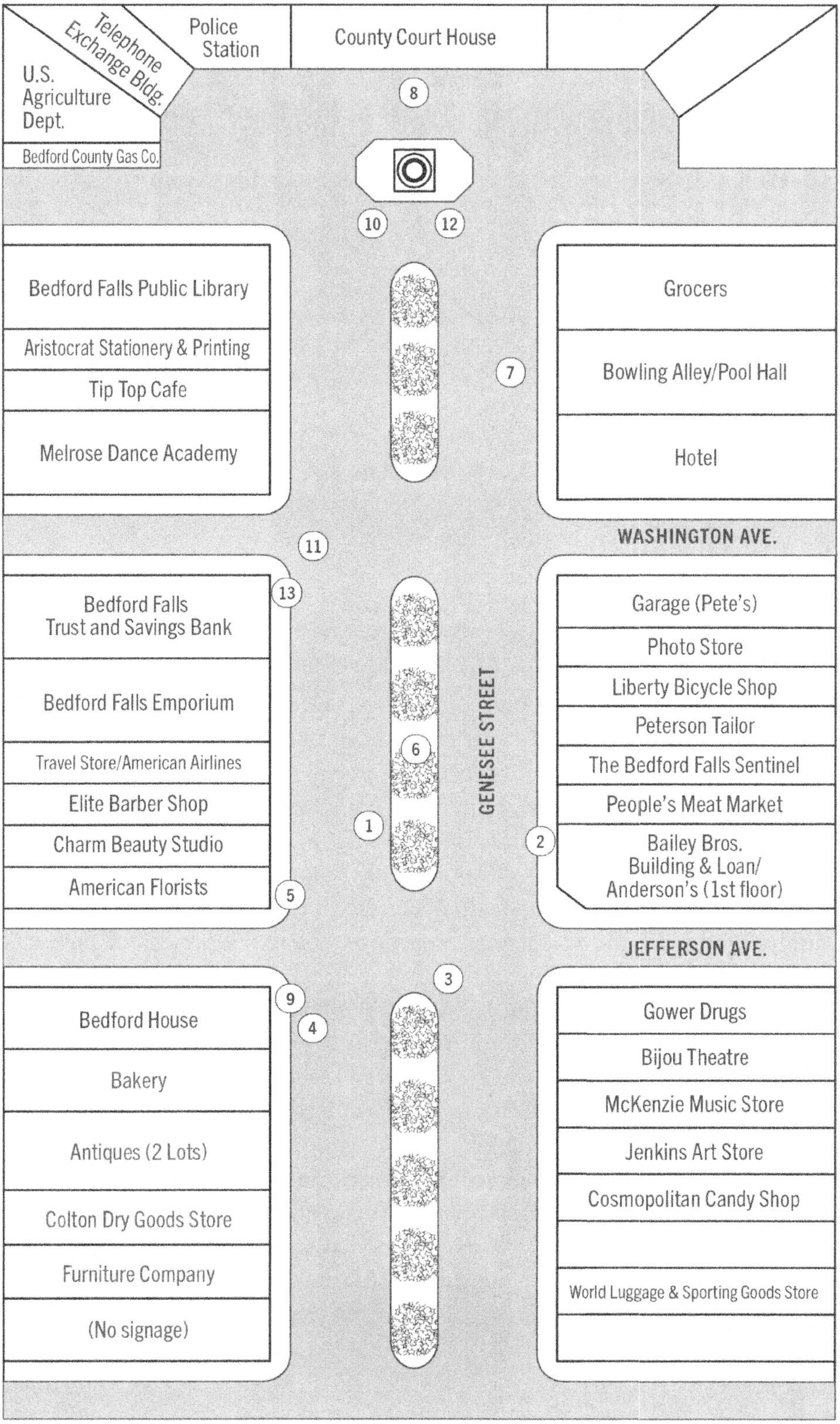
Telephone Exchange Bldg.
Police Station
County Court House
U.S. Agriculture Dept.
Bedford County Gas Co.
8
10
12
Bedford Falls Public Library
Aristocrat Stationery & Printing
Tip Top Cafe
Melrose Dance Academy
Grocers
7
Bowling Alley/Pool Hall
Hotel
11
WASHINGTON AVE.
13
Bedford Falls Trust and Savings Bank
Bedford Falls Emporium
Travel Store/American Airlines
Elite Barber Shop
Charm Beauty Studio
American Florists
5
1
6
GENESEE STREET
2
Garage (Pete's)
Photo Store
Liberty Bicycle Shop
Peterson Tailor
The Bedford Falls Sentinel
People's Meat Market
Bailey Bros. Building & Loan/ Anderson's (1st floor)
JEFFERSON AVE.
3
9
4
Bedford House
Bakery
Antiques (2 Lots)
Colton Dry Goods Store
Furniture Company
(No signage)
Gower Drugs
Bijou Theatre
McKenzie Music Store
Jenkins Art Store
Cosmopolitan Candy Shop
World Luggage & Sporting Goods Store

Trouble with Mr. Gower in the Back Room

CLOSER LOOK: Here's the text from the telegram that George finds by the register:

> BEDFORD FALLS NY QAB 605 31 3EX MAY 3 1919 1211AM
>
> MR EMIL GOWER
> BEDFORD FALLS NY
>
> WE REGRET TO INFORM YOU THAT YOUR SON ROBERT DIED
> VERY SUDDENLY THIS MORNING OF INFLUENZA STOP
> EVERYTHING POSSIBLE WAS DONE FOR HIS COMFORT STOP
> WE AWAIT INSTRUCTIONS FROM YOU STOP
>
> EDWARD MELLINGTON
> PRESIDENT HAMMERTON COLLEGE

HISTORY LESSON: While it may seem strange that Mr. Gower's college-aged son could die of the flu, such an occurrence was all too familiar to Americans back then. The Influenza Pandemic of 1918 was one of the most devastating plagues the world has ever seen. One of the virus's earliest appearances in America came in the spring of 1918 at a military training camp in Kansas. By fall, the virus was in full swing, with nearly 200,000 Americans dying in October alone. All told, the virus afflicted one in four Americans and accounted for an estimated 675,000 deaths. Worldwide the figures were staggering—one in five persons afflicted and, by some estimates, 50 million deaths.

While most strains of influenza are fairly mild and pose a death threat only to the elderly and very young, this particular strain proved most deadly for those between twenty and forty. Moreover, the strain struck with a quickness and severity not seen before or since. It was not uncommon for victims to develop fatal respiratory problems in a matter of hours. All of this means that Mr. Gower's son was a prime candidate for contracting the virus, and his sudden demise was entirely plausible. From a historical perspective, the timing of his son's death—early May of 1919—lands during a virus downturn after an early 1919 wave, though he certainly could have been among the tail-end victims.

CAST ANECDOTES: Director Frank Capra was one of the millions who fell ill during the 1918 pandemic, having contracted virus while serving in the military at San Francisco's Fort Point in the fall of 1918. By all accounts he should not have survived, laying exposed to a room full of infected men with no care and barely any food, before improbably rallying back to health.

CLOSER LOOK: Believe it or not, there are legitimate medicinal uses for poisons, so we will forgive Mr. Gower for having poison on hand. However, the specific type of poison that Mr. Gower filled the prescription with remains a mystery. On the back of the poison bottle several letters—*LYCYR*—are legible from a partially torn label. (8:19) These letters refer to the plant *Glycyrrhiza glabra,* which is better known as licorice.

Well, you don't need a degree in pharmacology to know that licorice is not a poison. Back then druggists used licorice root to flavor medicines as well as to treat a variety of common ailments. All of this means that the prop man may have just grabbed an old medicine bottle, slapped a poison label on one side and tried, with limited success, to peel off the licorice label on the other side.

CLOSER LOOK: As for the rest of the bottles in the back room, trying to read their labels is a frustrating exercise. Most of them are just a hair out of focus, and it doesn't help that these old apothecary bottles use arcane Latin abbreviations. Well, here are some of the bottles we can read—see if you can spot them and others: SULPHUR (antiseptic, antifungal), SALTPETRE, PV CINCH RUB and PV CINCH FLAV (cinchona; malaria medicine), R. ZINGIB (ginger), MYRISTICA (nutmeg), CAMPHORA (induces perspiration and coughing), CALAMUS (stomach, skin irritations), ZINC. OXID. (skin irritations).

HISTORY LESSON: George reveals that Mr. Gower is supposed to be filling a prescription for treating diphtheria. Mr. Gower undoubtedly spent a great deal of time treating this insidious disease, which was a leading cause of death for children during this era. While some strides were made treating and preventing diphtheria during the first two decades of the twentieth century, a surefire vaccine was not developed until the mid-1920s.

Take our word for it—this disease is not something you want to contract. Diphtheria typically takes hold in the nose and throat. Early symptoms are innocuous enough—fever, chills, sore throat, enlarged lymph nodes—but within a few days, a coating of gray matter begins to build in the upper respiratory tract. If left unchecked the buildup will result in death by asphyxiation. Also, the toxin produced by diphtheria can cause paralysis and death by heart failure. If this doesn't sound like something you'd care to experience, just remember to get that Td booster shot every ten years.

CLOSER LOOK: Keep an eye out for a minor film gaffe in this scene as Mr. Gower's cigar suddenly disappears from his mouth. (8:33)

CAST ANECDOTES: This is our first good look at old man Gower, Bedford Falls' town druggist, who, at least in 1919, has lost his way. The down-and-out Mr. Gower is played by H.B. Warner, who was a regular in films directed by Frank Capra, having appeared in no less than four of them prior to *Wonderful Life: Mr. Deeds Goes to Town* (1936), *Lost Horizon* (1937, nominated for Best Supporting Actor), *You Can't Take It With You* (1938) and *Mr. Smith Goes to Washington* (1939). Warner should have felt somewhat at home in the backroom of Gower Drugs given that he studied medicine in England before becoming an actor. Yes, Warner was an Englishman, accent and all, with fine manners and a dignified, courteous demeanor that served him well in film.

Early in his career, Warner had the distinction of playing Christ in Cecil B. DeMille's silent film classic and international sensation, *The King of Kings* (1927). Film lore has it that DeMille was so obsessed with protecting the sanctity of the film that he forced Warner to agree to various morality provisions regulating his lifestyle and restricting the types of film roles he could take on. Indeed, Warner was forever identified with the role and for decades his portrayal served as the public's main reference point for what Jesus Christ was like. It was for him, at times, a bit overwhelming. For years after the film, he'd be out for dinner enjoying a drink and someone would invariably crack something like, "What—Christ drinking a cocktail!?" And while he was not necessarily typecast, the role did send him down a career path cobbled with more serious characters.

Some twenty years later, though, Capra gave Warner the chance to show his true grit in *Wonderful Life*. And Warner delivered, playing not just one, but two drunks (one in Bedford Falls and one in Pottersville) to inebriated, stubble-faced perfection.

FILM ANECDOTES: As Mr. Gower grieves, we get a clear view of a framed photo of his son Robert. So who "plays" Mr. Gower's son in the photo? Well, turns out it's an actor named Glenn Vernon. Vernon was a rising young talent working at RKO at the time *Wonderful Life* went into production, so there's a studio connection that accounts for an RKO actor filling the frame. We'd love to know whether

RKO informed him in advance about this unusual cameo, and it's entirely possible he didn't get paid. If you want to see Vernon looking as youthful as he does in this photo, check out *Ding Dong Williams*, released by RKO the same year as *Wonderful Life*.

George Seeks His Dad's Advice

DID YOU KNOW?: As George wonders what to do about Mr. Gower and the poison capsules, he notices an advertisement in the drugstore that reads "Ask Dad, he knows," which prompts him to seek out his dad. This advertising slogan is for Sweet Caporal cigarettes and shows a fatherly figure puffing away on a smoke. It's unclear what "Dad" is supposed to "know," but whatever it is, it's obviously not that tobacco is bad for you.

Anyway, Sweet Caporal's chief claim to fame is its connection with what has long been considered the holy grail of baseball cards, the T206 Honus Wagner card. In the early 1900s, the American Tobacco Company ran an advertising campaign that involved inserting cards of major league baseball players into packs of its Sweet Caporal and Piedmont brand cigarettes.

Sometime later, Pittsburgh Pirates Hall of Famer Honus Wagner sought to have his card pulled from the promotion, some say over concerns that promoting tobacco products sent the wrong message to kids while others say he simply wanted more money. Whatever the reason, the company complied and the result was that relatively few Wagner cards made it into circulation. While it's not the rarest baseball card—more than fifty are known to exist—through the years it's consistently been the most coveted. Today, T206 Wagner cards regularly sell for several hundred thousand dollars, with one having sold for $6.6 million. Wow. Time to check your grandfather's attic.

CLOSER LOOK: Two editions of *The Saturday Evening Post* are visible in the store's "Daily Papers" rack as George rushes out the door for help. With *The National Geographic Magazine* edition in this scene being an actual 1919 edition, we expected nothing less with respect to the *Post* editions. Yep, both editions are real and, roughly, time appropriate. The edition on the top row is from May 24, 1919, with a cover illustration of a father and son decked out in fishing gear. Below that is an edition from March 22, 1919, with the cover featuring a young couple having a late-night visit on a couch.

Now, we just learned that the telegram George finds is dated May 3, 1919, which means the bottom edition is correct for the scene while the top one is just a few weeks off. It's nice to see another example of the prop team going the extra mile to source time-appropriate props.

FILM ANECDOTES: In the first shots inside Gower Drugs, the "Daily Papers" rack with the *Post* editions is several feet left of the front door. But here, as George heads out the door, the rack is quite close to the front door. This could have been an oversight resulting from some scene re-shoots that were required, but more likely the director had the rack moved, aware of the break in continuity, to allow the *Post* editions to fill in the frame.

CLOSER LOOK: On the stair risers leading up to the Building & Loan are the names of businesses located in the building—a cool, old-school building directory of sorts. (8:53) The list includes a jeweler, a veterinarian, an eye, ear, nose and throat doctor, and a collection service. Also, just to the right of the stairs is a women's department store called Anderson's. The Building & Loan is located on the second floor, directly above Anderson's. Here's a rundown of the riser directory, with presumed or illegible portions in parentheses.

STEN[OGRAPHY]
REAL ESTATE • JEWELERY
VETERINARIAN EST. 19[__]
EYE • EAR • NOSE • THROAT 3rd Fl.
BUILDING & LOAN ASSOCIATION 2nd Fl.
COLLECTION SERVICE Reasonable Rates

EXPLANATION REQUIRED: When George shows up at the office, Uncle Billy shouts, "Avast there, Captain Cook!" as he tries to prevent George from interrupting his father's meeting with Potter. *Avast* is an old nautical command that means "stop" or "cease." Uncle Billy uses the "Captain Cook" line again, years later, on the day George prepares for his overseas trip.

JUST WONDERING: Now, if you're a Building & Loan shareholder and you see Billy Bailey running around every day with strings tied around his fingers to remind him of his daily duties, wouldn't that make you just the slightest bit uneasy? Sure, today he just forgot to call the bank examiner, no big deal. But what will it be tomorrow or the next day? Misplacing Building & Loan shareholder funds? Stay tuned.

DID YOU KNOW?: Are you clued in to the fact that the two employees at the Building & Loan are actually George's cousins? If not, don't feel bad. This familial tie is revealed only through the closing credits and the film's final script. Their names are Tilly (short for Matilda) and Eustace Bailey. Tilly and Eustace's desk nameplates confirm that they are both Baileys. Look for Tilly's nameplate later in the film, just after George vaults over the counter during the bank run (53:08), and Eustace's as George searches the office vault on Christmas Eve after Uncle Billy loses the deposit (1:22:58).

We know that Tilly and Eustace are not Uncle Billy's children because they refer to him as Uncle Billy. So they must be the children of an undisclosed brother of Peter and Billy Bailey. As for Tilly and Eustace's responsibilities at the Building & Loan, the final script identifies Tilly as a telephone operator and Eustace as an office clerk.

CAST ANECDOTES: Mary Treen and Charles Williams, who play cousins Tilly and Eustace, were film regulars, each with over ninety films to their credit by the time they appeared in *Wonderful Life* (Treen racked up some twenty-two in 1935 alone). Both were cast in familiar roles in *Wonderful Life*. Treen typically played "plain Jane" types (nurses, phone operators, waitresses, secretaries, etc.) while Williams was at home playing quirky, bespectacled clerks, photographers and reporters.

Treen's a hoot in *Merton of the Movies* (1947) as a wisecracking studio casting office admin, and in *Red Hot Tires* (1935) she's not only the catch for once but her man is played by the great Roscoe Karns, father of *Wonderful Life* actor Todd Karns. Williams is in a scene-for-the ages in *The Thin Man* (1934), playing a drunken guest at a Christmas Eve party that's unlike anything we see at the Bailey house. You can also catch him in *The Pride of the Yankees* (1942).

DID YOU KNOW?: Two straw hats hang outside Peter's office. The one on the right looks suspiciously like the one Uncle Billy wears, and has trouble focusing on, several years later when he's overserved at Harry's party. If anyone would hold onto their straw hat that long, it would surely be Uncle Billy.

Anyway, in the 1910s and 1920s, straw hats were wildly popular as men's warm weather wear, but one had to mind strict social custom governing when it was acceptable to wear them. Cities would variously declare a Straw Hat Day—ranging from mid-April in the South to mid-May in the North—to kick off the straw hat season. By September 15, you were expected to revert to felt hats, and failing to do so came at the risk of someone smashing your fabulous boater hat. Yep, there was even a "straw hat riot" in Manhattan one year, with teenagers terrorizing unsuspecting straw hat-wearing pedestrians.

In this scene, we know it's a hot one because the office fan is blowing full blast. But we also know from the telegram that it's around May 3, so either Bedford Falls has an early "straw hat day" tradition or Uncle Billy better be on the watch for straw hat stompers.

HISTORY LESSON: The framed photo in Uncle Billy's office is of U.S. General John J. Pershing, who was the commander of U.S. forces in Europe during World War I. It makes sense that Uncle Billy would honor Pershing—this scene is just a few months removed from the end of World War I and Pershing was America's definitive World War I hero. Indeed, right after the war Pershing was promoted to the Army's highest rank, General of the Armies, and he remains the only one to hold that rank while alive. Pershing should have been able to parlay his war hero status into a presidency, but his stiff demeanor and seeming lack of commitment to the cause led to a fizzling effort.

CLOSER LOOK: George opens the door to his dad's office, and hanging on the wall inside the office is a photo of President Woodrow Wilson. He held office from 1913 to 1921, so Wilson fits in nicely for this 1919 scene. Actor Samuel Hinds, playing Peter Bailey, likely got a kick out of Wilson's image being on the set—Hinds played President Wilson in a 1933 film short. President Wilson is the first of five U.S. presidents whose likeness appears in the film—we will keep the running tally for you.

EXPLANATION REQUIRED: Peter Bailey wears a long-forgotten accessory in this scene—sleeve protectors. These were worn by store clerks, newspaper editors, book keepers and the like to keep their shirts clean in messy environments. Here, they kept ink off Peter's sleeves as he worked on the company books, preparing for his meeting with Potter.

And look for Uncle Billy making use of sleeve garters. Men typically did not tailor their shirt sleeve lengths, and garters kept the sleeves at their proper length and therefore free and clear of ink and other office grime. Though if Uncle Billy did have dirty cuffs it certainly would have fit the part.

CAST ANECDOTES: Jimmy Stewart contributed some authenticity of sorts to this scene. Look for three framed photos on Peter Bailey's desk. The one on the right is an actual photo of Stewart that he loaned to the scene. It shows George, er, Jimmy, age three, posing proudly on a tricycle. The same photo shows up on Christmas Eve in George and Mary's living room, resting on the mantel. (1:31:40) Later on, we'll point out a few more Stewart family photos that made it into the film.

CLOSER LOOK: Well we don't have to wait long for our second sighting of a U.S. president. As Peter Bailey stands up, a small portrait of George Washington comes into the frame, hanging on the wall, screen right.

EXPLANATION REQUIRED: Potter's helper is not a mere personal assistant. The film credits have him as "Potter's Bodyguard," which of course comes with the implication that Potter is in need of protection. Hilariously, the only bodyguarding we see from him during the film is when he pushes young George away from Potter ... but that's *after* George gets in a healthy shove.

CAST ANECDOTES: Throughout the film, actor Frank Hagney delivers a granite-faced scowl befitting a bodyguard, enhancing Potter's diabolic presence without ever uttering a word. Hagney actually was quite the outgoing fellow and his life story is full of fun surprises. For starters, he was Australian, born in Sydney in 1884. We hear faint hints of his Australian accent in some of his films, but he covered it well enough that moviegoers scarcely noticed. In his teens, he served in the Second Boer War (fought in South Africa), which means he was a war veteran six years before Jimmy Stewart was even born.

There's much more. Hagney was one of Australia's top sportsman, with an impressive professional resume as a boxer, cyclist and rower. Rowing was probably his best sport—in 1927, at age 43, he beat the world's sculling champion in a marathon race from Long Beach to Catalina Island. But his boxing escapades were beyond belief. Hagney was the personal sparring partner of world heavyweight champion Jack Johnson and travelled the world with Johnson as his go-to exhibition opponent. And in the 1910s he fought some big-name fighters, including Luis Angel Firpo, who went on to nearly beat world heavyweight champion Jack Dempsey.

Starting in 1919, Hagney leveraged his athletic and fighting skills into a Hollywood career. He was a cinch at stuntman jobs and in no time graduated to bit parts and larger roles as heavies, no-goods and, naturally, boxers. He became so well known for delivering a good fight that one film promoted him as "Fighting Frank Hagney." Plus, his boxing background tied in perfectly with Hollywood's soft spot for boxing storylines. During the silent era, he fought Jack Dempsey in *All's Swell on the Ocean* (1924) and Gene Tunney in *The Fighting Marine* (1926). In this last one, as Hagney told it, he barked at Tunney to not pull any punches on him during filming.

Unfortunately, both those films are among the "lost silents," but you can see Hagney in the ring with Wallace Beery in *The Champ* (1931), playing the heavyweight champion of Mexico. And for a fun Western-style brawl, he plays an awesome black hat who battles John Wayne in *Ride Him, Cowboy* (1932). Finally, look for him as a rough city cop arresting Joan Crawford's character in *Dancing Lady* (1933) and taking a punch in a street scuffle in *Kelly the Second* (1936).

EXPLANATION REQUIRED: Listen closely here for two lines of "bonus" dialogue just after Peter Bailey closes the door behind young George. Returning to the argument at hand, Potter asks, "Well, what's the answer?" Peter Bailey responds, "Mr. Potter, you just humiliated me in front of my son." Well, there's no doubt about that. If only we could hear Potter's retort—it must have been a real zinger.

FILM ANECDOTES: Prior to filming, the script called for the scene to continue on after young George got kicked out of his dad's office. In it George considers seeking help from Uncle Billy with his drugstore dilemma, but Uncle Billy is in his office on the phone desperately trying to fend off a demanding bank examiner. (Remember, just before George sneaks into his dad's office Uncle Billy gets a call from the bank examiner.) While on the phone Uncle Billy lights a cigar and carelessly throws the match into the wastebasket.

Meanwhile, George finds Eustace frantically preparing figures for the bank examiner and Tilly on the phone with her friend Martha explaining, "Potter's here, the bank examiner's coming. It's a day of judgment." As George starts to interrupt Tilly, Uncle Billy yells for help from his office. There's now a fire in the wastebasket and Tilly comes to the rescue, dousing the flames with a pot of coffee. Seeing this mayhem, George wisely decides he's better off solving this problem on his own.

Now this is one omitted scene that we would like to have seen. Plus, if it had been included, audiences would have known that Tilly and Eustace are George's cousins. The script, you see, called for George to refer to them as "Cousin Tilly" and "Cousin Eustace" when he asked them for help. This is a great example of how last-minute scene changes can have unexpected consequences.

George Returns to the Store

RANDOM THOUGHTS: When George returns from his dad's office, Mary is still at the counter working on her scoop of ice cream, even though Mr. Gower says that George left the store to deliver the capsules over an hour ago. Is this another film gaffe? That depends on whether or not you believe that Mr. Gower, in his drunken stupor, has lost track of time.

EXPLANATION REQUIRED: It's hard to follow Mr. Gower's drunken slur, so here's what he says upon George's return to the store:

> MR. GOWER (ON PHONE): "What?! Why that medicine should have been there an hour ago. Be over in five minutes, Mrs. Blaine."
>
> MR. GOWER (TO GEORGE): "Where's Mrs. Blaine's box of capsules? Didn't you hear what I said? What kind of tricks are you playing anyway? What, why didn't you deliver them right away? Don't you know that boy's very sick? You lazy loafer."

MUSIC NOTES: The score cues composed by Dimitri Tiomkin for *Wonderful Life* included two for the drugstore scenes, which Tiomkin titled "Death Telegram" and "Gower's Deliverance." However, director Frank Capra omitted these cues from the final version, electing instead to have the scenes run without music. This change, and a slew of others, led to a falling out between the two men. Before *Wonderful Life* Capra and Tiomkin had been best of friends, having collaborated on some of Capra's most successful films.

Tiomkin, who was accustomed to having his artistic judgment carry the day, believed Capra treated his score cues as if they were mere suggestions. Indeed, several of Tiomkin's cues were cut wholesale, while others were pared down, moved or toned down. Adding to Tiomkin's ire was Capra's use of cues from other films written by other composers (more on this later). In his autobiography, *Please Don't Hate Me*, Tiomkin described Capra's handling of the score as "an all around scissors job."

Despite Tiomkin's displeasure (he did not speak with Capra for quite some time, nor did the two work together again), in the end Capra's decisions proved sound. There is little doubt that the drugstore scenes, as with other scenes in which cues were omitted, work better without heavy, dramatic music. To see how the rest of Tiomkin's cues were treated be sure to check out the music section in the back of the guide.

FILM ANECDOTES: The name of Bedford Falls' resident druggist is a Capra touch. Columbia Pictures, Capra's employer during the 1930s, was for many years located on the corner of Sunset Boulevard and Gower Street. And RKO Radio Pictures, the studio that distributed *Wonderful Life*, was also located on Gower Street. And a favorite hangout of studio employees and extras looking for film work was a drugstore located on, you guessed it, Gower Street.

CAST ANECDOTES: The actor who plays young George, Bobbie Anderson, delivers a fine performance, particularly in the dramatic backroom scenes at Gower Drugs. But for sheer notoriety, he's at the wrong end of the picture—the actors playing George and Mary's children all get to participate in the high-profile Christmas Eve scenes at the end of the film. Just an unavoidable downside to taking on the "early years" role, we suppose.

Another standout film on Anderson's resume is *The Bishop's Wife*, which was a Best Picture nominee just one year after *Wonderful Life*. Somewhat improbably, that film is also a Christmas story that centers around a wingless angel (Cary Grant) sent down to earth to straighten things out. In his only scene, Anderson gets tagged in the face with a snowball thrown by none other than Karolyn Grimes, who plays his daughter Zuzu (technically speaking) in *Wonderful Life*.

CLOSER LOOK: Can't get enough of Gower Drugs? How about a few more details. There's a public phone by the back room. Phone calls are five cents, and there's a New Jersey phone directory by the phone (more on this later). There's an Underwood typewriter in the back room, presumably used to tap out prescriptions. And the store is open on Sundays—a sign says so. Okay, let's press on.

GEORGE PREPARES TO "SEE THE WORLD"

> "This business of nickels and dimes and spending all your life trying to figure out how to save three cents on a length of pipe... I'd go crazy. I want to do something big and something important."
>
> —GEORGE BAILEY

Still in flashback mode, we now go forward to June 1928 where we find George on the eve of an overseas excursion that he has been dreaming of since he was a young lad. George has apparently been working at the Building & Loan since graduating from high school. With his younger brother, Harry, now graduating, George has arranged for Harry to take over for him at the Building & Loan so that he can finally get a crack at college. But first, George intends to "see the world."

This rather extraordinary day in George's life starts off normally enough with George picking up a suitcase, a gift from Mr. Gower, at the luggage store. His new suitcase in hand, George makes his way through downtown Bedford Falls. Along the way George runs into several people we'll be seeing more of down the road, including his Uncle Billy, his cousins Eustace and Tilly, Bert the cop, Ernie the taxi driver, and the now decidedly grown-up Violet Bick. Bert, Ernie and George take a brief time out to admire Violet's, um, dress, before George heads home to prepare for his trip.

Later that evening, we find George at home, about to sit down for his last meal at the old Bailey boarding house before the big trip. Meanwhile, Harry is getting ready for his high school graduation dance. After George and Harry engage in some good-natured shenanigans with their parents and Annie, the family maid, George and his dad sit down for a heart-to-heart talk. Pop has some misgivings about Harry taking over for George, but George is adamant that he be allowed to pursue higher education.

As father and son discuss the Building & Loan's future, Harry heads out the door for the graduation dance. But before he goes he urges a reluctant George to drop by and join in on the festivities as there will be "lots of pretty girls." Let's hope George listens because one of those pretty girls might just be his future wife.

The Luggage Store

CLOSER LOOK: Waiting on George at the luggage store is Joe, and it turns out Joe's store is about more than just luggage. The name on the front door, "World Luggage and Sporting Goods Store," tells us so. The signage on the store's front window reads, "Boston Co. Suit Cases and Bags—Sporting Goods." Visible below that is, "New and Secondhand—Leather Goods." Sure enough, George does end up with a secondhand model.

On the sporting side of things, the window by the door advertises "Ammunition." Yep, Joe's store is the place to go for hunting ammo. On the counter is a cardboard, duck-themed display for "Winchester Ranger Shells." And there's another Winchester bird hunting display by the front window (screen right) that reads, "Winchester—Guns and Shells."

And here are a few other sporty things we spied in the store—a boat motor (down by the door), a pair of skis (crisscrossed in the window), juggling pins, a bowling bag (we think) and wooden dumbbells. Finally, the point-of-sale display hanging directly behind Joe has stumped us for years, owing to it being just out of focus. But we now know that it's a display for small leather "key containers," which is certainly something a travel-themed store might sell. If you can identify anything else in the store, let us know.

HISTORY LESSON: George tells Joe he needs room on his suitcase for labels from all of the places he will visit, and mentions three places by name: Italy, Baghdad and Samarkand. Whoa! This is no ordinary itinerary George has put together. Italy and Iraq are not exactly next door to each other. And Samarkand? It's a city in present-day Uzbekistan, located some 150 miles north of Afghanistan. Uzbekistan spent a good part of the twentieth century as a socialist republic of the Soviet Union, until it finally gained independence in 1991.

George surely was attracted to Samarkand by its rich culture and history, which has led writers and historians to dub it "the Rome of the East." Samarkand's cultural origin is diverse to say the least, grounded in a mixture of Iranian, Indian, Persian and Mongolian cultures. Its location on the Silk Road, the ancient trading route that linked China with Eastern and Western Europe, thickened the cultural mix. Samarkand had also passed through the hands of a rather eclectic list of conquerors, including Alexander the Great, Genghis Khan, the empire of Timur (Tamerlane declared Samarkand "the capital of the world"), the Khanate of Bukhara and the Russian Empire.

RANDOM THOUGHTS: Piecing together George's travel itinerary from his comments, he would have had his work cut out for him if was planning on being back for the start of school. After a 3,500-mile boat ride across the Atlantic (presumably to England), George would have traveled some 1,500 miles across Western Europe to two destinations that he mentions to Mary after the graduation dance, Rome and Athens. From there, it's another 1,500 miles or so across Turkey to Baghdad, the capital of Iraq. Then it's another 1,500 miles to Samarkand—via Tehran, Iran and Ashgabat, Turkmenistan, where he would probably have caught the Trans-Caspian Railroad.

Of course, once he got to Samarkand, he would have to get back. Assuming he took in a few other sites along the way, George had signed up to travel over 17,000 miles in a mere ninety days, all by boat, rail and dusty road. Incidentally, for Samarkand and other Central Asian destinations, George would have been well advised to have his travel papers in order. By 1928, the Soviet Union had already seized Samarkand and much of the surrounding region while creating the socialist republics of Uzbekistan and Turkmenistan.

CLOSER LOOK: The truck parked across street from the store is a "stake bed" delivery truck, likely a mid-1920s Ford model TT. Signage on the truck confirms that it belongs to a Bedford Falls furniture company. Look for two men slowly loading furniture onto the bed. Indeed, the downtown exterior set did include a furniture store right where this truck is parked; look for it in our downtown Bedford Falls map.

DID YOU KNOW?: George cracks that he's traveling to Europe by "cattle boat." George didn't have much choice but to get to Europe by boat—regular transatlantic airplane service did not begin until 1939—but a cattle boat would have made for some rough going. Cattle boats were, in fact, used for transporting livestock between North America and Europe. But they also served as a cheap way for humans (particularly immigrants) to get across the Atlantic. While the accommodations may have been luxurious from a cow's perspective, they were decidedly not so for the human cargo.

George Thanks Mr. Gower

CLOSER LOOK: The contraption that George uses to make his wish for "a million dollars" is an old-fashioned "jump spark" cigar lighter. This lighter was made by Hawkeye Manufacturing Company in Davenport, Iowa. Other companies made them over time, but this one's a Hawkeye. Capra used a similar, yet different, Hawkeye cigar lighter as a prop in *You Can't Take It With You.* These types of cigar lighters were commonplace in American drugstores in the early part of the twentieth century.

And while we're hanging out at the tobacco counter, here are some tobacco-related advertisements to look for as George and Mr. Gower exchange pleasantries: Sir Walter Raleigh Smoking Tobacco, Old Glory Rum Cured Cigarette Holders (10 cents), Beuscher's Missouri Hickory Pipes (25 cents), Cuesta-Rey cigars and Scotch Snuff.

RANDOM THOUGHTS: Well, George's wish for a million dollars may not have come through but he did pick up a taste for cigars along the way, perhaps from hanging around the drugstore's extensive tobacco counter. Recall that George enjoys a cigar in Potter's office as Potter offers him a job.

RANDOM THOUGHTS: George promised Mr. Gower that he wouldn't tell a soul about the poison capsules mishap, and given that Mr. Gower is still in business some nine years later, George appears to have been true to his word. But let's hope George got more than a secondhand suitcase out of the deal, like, say, lifetime dibs at the drugstore's soda fountain.

CLOSER LOOK: In the corner behind Mr. Gower is an early version of a drugstore jukebox. It's an old cabinet-style record player, with its lid up and a stack of 78 rpm records on top. This is a relatively new feature at Gower Drugs—it was not there in 1919.

FILM ANECDOTES: It feels to us like actor H.B. Warner got short-changed in this scene. For one, you really can't hear him even though you can hear Jimmy Stewart as clear as day. For another, he barely gets his line out before Stewart turns his attention to the cigar lighter. For the record, besides greeting George by name (hard to hear), Warner's one line is "Oh, forget it—hope you enjoy it."

But this is sort of how it goes for Warner the rest of the way. He is just a face in the crowd at George and Mary's wedding send-off. On Christmas Eve day with Ernie and George, we have no idea what he says. In Pottersville, it's a reprise of his drunken slur. And at the Christmas Eve gathering his one line at the collection basket is again hard to hear through all the merriment. That said, Mr. Gower's prayer at the beginning of the film ends up being the only real insight we have on what a clear-headed, full-throated Mr. Gower sounds like.

EXPLANATION REQUIRED: This 1928 Gower Drugs scene feels like an awful lot of trouble to go to for a mere fifteen seconds of footage. It's an elaborate scene, with dozens of child extras, several cars and even a "Bedford Falls Transportation" bus. Now, that's a lot of production time, effort and money for what amounts to a snippet.

Well, in fact, this scene was supposed to be more involved. First, just after the "cigar lighter" exchange, Mr. Gower and George were set to have a chat about George's travel and life plans (mostly for our benefit), with a long gag involving the "Nope, nope, nope, nope" line George had just uttered in the luggage shop scene. In the gag, George would respond to a few of Mr. Gower's questions with the same line, and after a while the kids in the store would mimic him, and then he would switch to, "Yep, Yep, Yep, Yep," as the nature of the question changed. All in all, it was a long journey for a small payoff.

More intriguingly, George was then to run into Potter at the drugstore entrance on his way out. The script describes Potter here as having a "vinegar face," which pretty much nails it for us. Vinegar is definitely Potter's resting face. Anyway, the two were to exchange barbs, with George cheerily bounding off, mood intact, to his travel adventures. One of the stills from the film shows George with his suitcase shaking hands with Potter at the front door. In this photo, actor Lionel Barrymore is "ready on the set," in full Potter costume and make up. This means the scene almost certainly got shot before ending up on the cutting room floor. Here again, we say omitting this scene was a good call. There was no great reason for Potter to be there, plus we already know he's a lout and the information we would have learned from George's talks with Potter and Mr. Gower was provided more efficiently elsewhere.

FILM ANECDOTES: So in this situation, the "Nope, nope, nope, nope" set up line at the luggage shop made it in to the film, but the line's second use, carrying the comedic punch, got cut. At the graduation dance, we'll clue you in to the opposite situation. In that scene, the set up line for a gag got cut, leaving the same line's second use with no context.

A Walk Through Downtown Bedford Falls

FILM ANECDOTES: The pigeons beneath the Building & Loan window were among the animals supplied by Hollywood animal trainer Curley Twiford. Curley and his brother had been supplying studios with trained animals since the 1930s, and for many years they were pretty much the go-to source in Hollywood for critters on the set. He had a flock of pigeons at his home in North Hollywood, a short drive from Encino Ranch. Note that in the wide shot from the street there are pigeons under the window as well, though not as many as in the tighter shot of the cousins and Uncle Billy. Twiford trained a wide variety of animals—cougars, foxes, coyotes, deer, eagles, rats, squirrels, owls, parrots—and was particularly adept with birds. He used to say the only animal he couldn't train was a chicken. There are many more Twiford-trained animals to come in this film, including his most prized one, a raven.

CLOSER LOOK: In the same scene, look for the street signs that appear beneath the window. (13:15) The signs tell us that the Building & Loan is located on the corner of Genesee Street and Jefferson Avenue. Genesee Street serves as the main road through downtown Bedford Falls. The Building & Loan offices are on the second floor (above Anderson's), with windows fronting on both Genesee Street and Jefferson Avenue.

EXPLANATION REQUIRED: We're still scratching our heads trying to figure out why Bedford Falls' main street is named Genesee Street. Whoever selected the street's name for the film undoubtedly knew that it had roots in New York, which is where Bedford Falls is located. *Genesee* is a Seneca Indian word meaning roughly "beautiful valley," and the Seneca Indians lived in what is now western New York, where the aptly named Genesee River runs. While we love the New York tie-in, it is still a little odd that Bedford Falls, which is itself a river town, would adopt the name of a different river from a different part of New York as the name for its main street.

HISTORY LESSON: As George greets his pals Bert the cop and Ernie the taxi driver, Bert is holding a newspaper with a headline reading SMITH WINS NOMINATION! (13:24) Some people assume that this headline is an inside joke referring to Jimmy Stewart's leading role in the film *Mr. Smith Goes to Washington,* a theory that seems even more plausible given that Frank Capra directed that film as well.

In fact, the headline refers to an actual event in American political history, albeit an obscure one. In late June 1928, the Democrats held their national convention in Houston, Texas, at which Alfred E. Smith won the Democratic Party's nomination for president. The headline references Smith's victory, which would have been of particular interest to Bedford Fallsians given that by 1928 he had served four terms as governor of New York.

Smith's nomination was historically noteworthy because he was the first person of Irish heritage to be nominated for president by a major political party. His Republican opponent, Herbert Hoover, launched a nasty little campaign, casting Smith as morally unfit for office given his support for the repeal of Prohibition (they dubbed him "Al-coholic Smith"). The tactics paid off as Hoover won in a landslide. But Smith seemed to have the last laugh as the Hoover administration was tagged with responsibility for the Great Depression, and Prohibition was repealed anyway in 1933.

CLOSER LOOK: A rather involved film gaffe occurs in the vignette when George, Bert and Ernie ogle Violet as she saunters down the street. Two separate shots show the guys slack-jawed by Ernie's taxi. Watch as the same woman—wearing a print dress and holding the brim of her hat with her right hand—walks past the taxi in both shots. (13:51)

But hold on a minute here. Is there more to this gaffe than first meets the eye? Let's back up a bit to when George first approaches Bert and Ernie. In the very first shot, look in the background for a familiar sight—a woman walking down the sidewalk in a print dress and holding the brim of her hat with her right hand. (13:25) Then, in the next shot of Ernie in the driver's seat of his cab, there she is again, holding that same hat! (13:32) This is getting weird.

And just when you think you've got your arms around this gaffe, the film cuts to Violet on the sidewalk, and guess who's walking a few paces behind her? You got it, the ubiquitous print-dress-wearing, hat-holding woman. (13:35) If you're keeping score at home, that's five walk-throughs by the same actor in the span of about thirty seconds. On this particular day the director must have been running a little short on extras.

CLOSER LOOK: Always willing to go, um, the extra mile, Ernie has not one but two taxi logos, and both are thoughtfully designed. In this scene, we get a nice view of both logos. One is diamond-shaped and reads, "Ernie's Night & Day Taxi Service." The other is in the form of a shield and reads, "Ernie's Taxi-Cab Service." Ernie is still making use of the diamond logo on Christmas Eve 1945. And while the shield logo is not visible in Bedford Falls 1945, it is visible on Ernie's taxi in 1945 Pottersville, so we're going to assume that his Bedford Falls 1945 taxi has it too.

CAST ANECDOTES: Bert and Ernie were played by character actors Ward Bond and Frank Faylen. Bond was at his best playing gruff characters with a soft side. Among his more than 250 film credits are two other American classics, *Gone with the Wind* (1939, as Yankee Captain Tom) and *The Maltese Falcon* (1941, as Police Sergeant Polhaus). What's more, he appeared in thirteen films nominated for Best Picture. Wow! He rode in several top Westerns, including *My Darling Clementine* (1946) and *Wagon Master* (1950), and his proficiency in playing cowpokes led to his landing the starring role in the 1950s television series *Wagon Train*.

Ward was also best pals with John Wayne and the two appeared in a slew of films together. In fact, they knew each other from their college football playing days at University of Southern California. Ward played tackle there for several years and was on the 1928 national championship team and the 1929 season

Rose Bowl-winning team. He actually broke into film while still playing at USC, when several USC players were recruited for roles in football-themed films. And while we're talking sports, we also like Bond in *Gentleman Jim* (1942), playing the mustachioed boxing legend John L. Sullivan, and Wayne's *Quiet Man* (1952), as the Irish priest who loves his fishing.

By the time Faylen took on the role of Ernie, he had already appeared as a taxi driver in no less than eight pictures, including *No Time for Comedy* (1940), starring Jimmy Stewart. His numerous portrayals of the trusty cabbie reportedly led a Los Angeles area taxi driver's union to make him an honorary member. Faylen, who came from a vaudeville family, formed a comedy team with Carol Hughes, with the two marrying in 1928. In 1934, they inched their way closer to film, appearing on stage at the Hollywood Music Box Theater. By 1936, they had converted their vaudeville stage talents into bustling cinematic careers. Both appeared in ten or so films that year, with one of Faylen's first-year credits being the Bogart film *Bullets or Ballots* (1936). Watch Faylen's facial expressions throughout *Wonderful Life*, and it's easy to see those vaudeville roots. Other notable Faylen film credits include *The Grapes of Wrath* (1940, also featuring Bond), *The Pride of the Yankees* (1942, as the Yankees' third-base coach, in which he shares a scene with Babe Ruth), *The Lost Weekend* (1945) and *Funny Girl* (1968, with Barbra Streisand).

CLOSER LOOK: Just as Violet drifts off from the taxi after her priceless "Why this old thing?!" line, we get a flash of something parked right in front of Ernie's cab. Freeze frame it and you'll see a beauty of a motorcycle, and it belongs to Bert the cop. This is one special ride—we have it pegged as a mid-1930s Harley-Davidson flathead and it's definitely police pursuit ready. It's really too bad that the production team couldn't have given the bike better placement. We've always thought of Bert as a traditional, walk-the-beat kind of cop, and it would have been great to see him riding in style through downtown Bedford Falls.

George at Home with the Family

MUSIC NOTES: Quick! Aside from the opening credits, when is the first time we hear Buffalo Gals in the film? The graduation dance? After the dance? Well, the song also shows up during this scene. Listen closely to George and Harry while they are upstairs (off screen) at the Bailey house getting ready for the evening—they can both be heard singing George and Mary's soon-to-be theme song. And maybe we are hearing things, but the tune that young George whistles in Gower Drugs after he arrives for work sounds like the song as well.

CLOSER LOOK: Did you pick up on the fact that the Baileys have a pet? It's a French sheepdog, and although he has no name in the film, his real-life name was Shag. This was, in fact, Shag's film debut. Shortly before filming began, Hollywood animal trainer Curley Twiford rescued him from a Los Angeles pound.

Shag appears in three scenes and each time he's hard to spot. In this scene, he can be found first lurking near Ma Bailey as she calls the boys down for dinner. (14:25) He then scoots past the dining room table, and starts barking as George and Harry throw their mother into Peter Bailey's lap.

Shag also shows up in an earlier scene, dashing in front of George and his pals as they head through downtown Bedford Falls. (5:08) Finally, Shag attends George and Mary's wedding send-off, bounding down the stairs just behind the newlyweds. (50:16)

FILM ANECDOTES: Shag barks so much in this scene that George turns around and tells Shag to "Shut up!" It's fun to think about whether that's George Bailey reprimanding Shag or rather an annoyed Jimmy Stewart coming out of character just for a moment in an effort to save the scene.

CAST ANECDOTES: Earlier we pointed out a photo of Jimmy Stewart, age three, slipped into the film for authenticity's sake. We promised to point out a few more Stewart family photos and here they are. First, just to the right of the opening to the dining room, on the top tier of a display stand, is a headshot of Jimmy in a suit and tie and sporting a period appropriate slicked hair style. This is Jimmy's senior year photo from his prep school, Mercersburg Academy. The photo dates to 1928, which happens to be the same year in which this scene is set. Fun stuff.

Now, let's move to the left of the dining room opening, and up on a wall shelf is a photo of little Jimmy and his mother, Elizabeth. Jimmy, around age two, is perched playfully on the arm of a chair with his mother by his side, positively beaming in the moment in a grand 1910s-style outfit. This photo is also on Peter Bailey's desk in 1919 (farthest left of the three photos); it's just super hard to make out given the frame's angle.

JUST WONDERING: We learn during George's dinner conversation with his dad that Peter Bailey appointed Potter to the Building & Loan's board of directors. What in the world was he thinking here? "Let's see...Potter, who has his own residential development business and clear aspirations to control the town, is a constant thorn in my side. So what should I do to get him off my back? I know! I'll give him a seat on my company's board of directors." Old man Bailey should hardly have been surprised when Potter later used his position to try to put the Building & Loan out of business. Potter may have had a small point in claiming that Peter Bailey was not business savvy.

FILM ANECDOTES: So does Harry have a special talent for balancing pies on his head? Well, film lore has it that actor Todd Karns was actually aided by a concave pie tin and a few strategically placed fasteners. This sounds likely, but there's no way to tell from watching the film. What is clear is that, with or without aid, Karns is definitely struggling to keep that pie on his head as he exchanges lines with Stewart. So we would not be surprised if a few pies were lost in capturing this scene.

CAST ANECDOTES: Serving up some well-timed one-liners in this scene is the Bailey's good-natured and sassy family housekeeper, Annie. Actress Lillian Randolph's voice and face would have been quite familiar to moviegoers back in 1946, as she had previously played Birdie Lee Calkins, the family housekeeper, in the wildly popular *The Great Gildersleeve* radio show (debuting in 1941) and film series (beginning in 1942). You can also catch her in the Cary Grant comedy *The Bachelor and the Bobby-Soxer* (1947), sharing some fun scenes with Shirley Temple and Myrna Loy. Later on we will explain why *The Bachelor and the Bobby-Soxer* is a must-see film for *Wonderful Life* fans.

EXPLANATION REQUIRED: It's a little tough to catch on the first go-around, but the question that George asks Harry as he walks through the dining room with his hands full of pies is "Got a match?" Thank goodness Harry doesn't fall for this old gag—dropping one of Annie's homemade pies surely would have earned him a broom swat or two.

JUST WONDERING: What will be Harry's alcoholic beverage of choice this evening? As Harry is leaving for the dance, his dad admonishes him not to drink any gin tonight. Harry briefly protests, but then gives up, no doubt because he's savvy enough to realize that his dad's rule has a loophole big enough to drive a beer truck through. Basically, Harry can drink any type of booze he pleases, just as long as it's not gin. Okay Pop!

CLOSER LOOK: You may have noticed that George inherits his parents' framed butterfly collection. Here, the framings hang in Mr. and Mrs. Bailey's dining room. In George and Mary's home, they are visible in the Christmas Eve scenes, to the right of the Christmas tree. But look also for two other pieces that George inherits—the grandfather clock in the entrance hall ends up in George and Mary's entrance hall, and the display stand we just mentioned in the dining room ends up in George and Mary's living room. Look for the grandfather clock as Harry heads out the door with the pies.

CAST ANECDOTES: Playing George's honest, hardworking father and doting mother are Samuel Hinds and Beulah Bondi. Both are perfect fits for their roles. Hinds could convey the wise old soul with the best of them, which makes sense considering he had Harvard schooling and a law degree from New York University. In fact, Hinds had a most improbable road to film. He had been practicing law in Pasadena for several decades before Depression-era financial troubles led him to take a flyer on a career in film acting. He was in his fifties when he made the move. He had been appearing in local theater productions through the years, and this experience, combined with his professional background and modest-yet-dignified personality, made him a natural for roles as lawyers, judges, mayors, executives and kindly fathers.

He also had the inside track on the role of Peter Bailey, having previously nailed the role of the patriarch in Capra's *You Can't Take It With You*. To see Hinds in a less genteel role, watch *Destry Rides Again* (1939), a hoot of a Western starring Jimmy Stewart in which Hinds plays a delightfully crooked mayor. And we like him in *Test Pilot* (1938) as a U.S. general, sharing some nice scenes with Lionel Barrymore.

Bondi had a more traditional transition to film than Hinds, arriving from Broadway to recreate a role on film in *Street Scene* (1931). But her making it to Broadway was in itself improbable as she grew up in the Midwest with no early ambitions for a career in theater. When she did get serious about theater, she soon recognized she could pull off older roles and thrived playing kind-hearted matronly types. To be sure, she was equally skilled at playing the mean ones. So it was her good fortune that *Wonderful Life* made use of a plot device that allowed her to play both types in the same film.

Bondi was a natural for the role of Ma Bailey as she had already played Jimmy Stewart's mother in *Of Human Hearts* (1938, nominated for Best Supporting Actress), *Vivacious Lady* (1938) and *Mr. Smith Goes to Washington* (1939). They were also in *The Gorgeous Hussy* (1936), though with no scenes together. If you want to see more of Bondi's devilish side, her portrayal of a wicked aunt in *Shepard of the Hills* (1941) is a great choice. One part she missed out on was Ma Joad in *The Grapes of Wrath*. She lobbied hard for it and aced her screen tests, only to have the producer pass her over for being, somehow, too good of a fit. It's really too bad—not only did she look the part with her gaunt features, but her knack for realism and avoiding oversentimentality would have served the role well.

THE HIGH SCHOOL GRADUATION DANCE

"What is it you want, Mary? What do you want? You want the moon? Just say the word and I'll throw a lasso around it and pull it down. Hey, that's a pretty good idea, Mary. I'll give you the moon, Mary."

—GEORGE BAILEY

We now come to a gem of a scene—the high school graduation dance. Remember, it's Harry Bailey and Mary Hatch's graduation, both of whom are four years George's junior. Although George and a few of his pals (namely Sam Wainwright and Marty Hatch) are crashing the dance, no one seems to mind. Anyway, Mr. Partridge reminds us that the new retractable gym floor built atop the pool was George's idea, so that seems like reason enough for him to be there.

George soon finds himself dancing with the resplendent Mary Hatch, and it's pretty obvious that she is just as enamored with George now as when she was a little girl hanging around the soda fountain at Gower Drugs. But the dance comes at a price—George, it seems, has "stolen" his dance with Mary from another boy, who soon seeks revenge by activating the retractable gym floor. The teenage rascal's plan works to perfection, and with a throng of amused dancegoers looking on, George and Mary "Charleston" ever closer to the edge of the parting gym floor before taking a most unexpected plunge.

George and Mary walk home from the dance under the light of a full moon, having traded in their wet clothes for a robe and an ill-fitting football uniform. By now these two are in full flirtation mode. They share a song. They exchange wishes by throwing rocks at the old Granville house. George, feeling quite amorous, promises to "lasso the moon" for Mary, and then shares some deep metaphysical thoughts about moons being swallowed and moonbeams shooting from fingers and toes and such.

But there seems to be more smoke than fire here; at least that's what a grumpy neighbor thinks who has been privy to their coquetry and is convinced that

George will never get around to the real task at hand—planting one on Mary. Before George can prove the neighbor wrong, the clumsy lout steps on Mary's robe and forces her to take cover in a nearby bush, sans clothing.

As George contemplates how to best capitalize on his good fortune, the evening takes a tragic turn. (Get used to the emotional roller coaster—we'll be seeing this pattern of juxtaposed emotional highs and lows several more times before this one's over.) Harry and Uncle Billy arrive on the scene with news that George's father has suffered a stroke. With that, George and Mary's magical evening together comes to an end.

The Graduation Dance

FILM ANECDOTES: The beginning of this scene features an impressive long take involving George, Harry, Sam, Violet and Mr. Partridge. For a full sixty-five seconds, uncut, the group exchanges lively and perfectly-time banter. But this take almost had to be scrapped when Harry Holman, playing Mr. Partridge, struggled to get Harry's name out of his mouth—it comes out sounding like "Harrah." Yep, that's right, an actor named Harry got tripped up by his own name.

CLOSER LOOK: Did you catch Sam flipping George's tie? This old jokester move typifies how Sam treats George. They are life-long friends but George is on the receiving end of constant razzing. George takes several seconds to calmly tuck his tie back into his jacket. He's so used to Sam's hijinks that he just moves on, seemingly unaffected.

CLOSER LOOK: Notice how much older George looks compared to the other kids at the dance. While Donna Reed was a still plausible twenty-five years old at the time the scene was filmed, Jimmy Stewart was thirty-eight, a full sixteen years older than the character he was playing.

MUSIC NOTES: The first tune heard playing at the dance is a catchy little number called "Collegiate," which was among the top hits of 1925. As with "The Charleston," the song had an accompanying dance that was all the rage among the raccoon coat-wearing crowd. Filled with cheeky lines about those heady college campus days of the Roaring Twenties (*C'lle-giate. C'llegiate. Yes! We are col-le-giate./ No-thing inter-med-jate. Noooo Ma'am./ Trou-sers, bag-gy. And our clothes look raggy*), the song will have you reaching for your skimmer hat and ukulele in no time.

EXPLANATION REQUIRED: During this scene, Marty Hatch asks George whether he remembers his younger sister Mary. This prompts Sam Wainwright to jokingly chime in, "Mamma wants you, Marty! Mamma wants you!" The group has a knowing laugh at Sam's imitation. But if the line leaves you wondering whether you missed something, there's a good reason.

The film's opening sledding scene originally included a young Mary nagging her brother to come home just before the accident, yelling, "Mamma wants you, Marty! Mamma wants you!" However, after some last-minute script changes young Mary was cut from the scene.

Unfortunately, the graduation dance scenes—including the one with Sam mimicking young Mary—were shot several months before the sledding scene. Thus, cutting Mary's part from the sledding scene left Sam's line dangling without any context. Another great example of why it's not such a good idea to make major script changes on the fly.

DID YOU KNOW?: Mary, Violet and the rest of the girls at the dance make use of dance cards. Violet flashes her card as she talks with George (19:57), while Mary's card can be seen on her wrist as she dances "The Charleston" (21:44). Back in the 1920s, dance cards were commonplace at high school dances and provided a fun way for dancegoers to keep track of their dance partners for the evening.

Here's how they worked. The dance card (or booklet) listed the evening's dance program, and had a space next to each dance for entering one's dance partners. Boys solicited dances from the girls, and the girls either accepted or declined. Once a girl said yes and entered a boy in her card she was not supposed to back out of the deal.

Here, Violet and Mary have a lot to learn about dance card etiquette. First, Violet announces to George, Marty and Sam that she has a "third of a dance" left. While this is a clever way to increase your exposure to the boys, penciling in more than one dance partner for a single song is plain old bad form. Violet then asks George, "What am I bid?" This is an auctioneer's term that means "How much will you pay for this item?" Auctioning off dances to the highest bidder? Also bad form.

As for Mary, she commits a dance card faux pas by allowing George to cut in on her scheduled dance partner. But surely Mary can be forgiven for this behavior since she is, after all, simply seeking to dance with her destiny.

CAST ANECDOTES: If you can believe it, the freckle-faced teen who corners Mary on the dance floor is none other than Carl "Alfalfa" Switzer of *Our Gang/Little Rascals* fame. Born on August 7, 1927, in Paris, Illinois, Switzer enjoyed huge success as a child actor, making dozens of *Our Gang* comedy shorts between 1935 and 1940. In the 1950s the shorts were repackaged for television as *The Little Rascals*, but neither Switzer nor any of the other *Our Gang* members shared in the financial gains brought about through syndication.

The gangly Switzer was eighteen when he appeared in *Wonderful Life*. While his career in feature films consisted largely of bit parts and small supporting roles, he did appear in some pretty high-profile films, including: *The High and Mighty* (1954, with John Wayne), *Going My Way* (1944, with Bing Crosby), *Pat and Mike* (1952, with Spencer Tracy and Katherine Hepburn) and *The Defiant Ones* (1958, with Tony Curtis and Sidney Poitier). To make ends meet, Switzer tended bar and, of all things, guided bear hunts. On January 21, 1959, at the age of thirty-one, Switzer was shot dead by an acquaintance after a drunken Switzer confronted him over a fifty-dollar debt. The man somehow walked based on a rather dubious story that he had acted in self-defense after Switzer came at him with a knife.

The Big Charleston Contest

EXPLANATION REQUIRED: In announcing "The Charleston" contest, Harry states, "Oyez, oyez, oyez! The big Charleston contest!" Oyez basically means "hear ye" and is typically used by an officer of the court to call a courtroom to order, as in "Oyez, oyez, oyez! The court is now in session!"

CLOSER LOOK: The band playing at the dance is Bedford High's very own—you can just make out the high school's name on the face of the band's drum set. (21:29)

FILM ANECDOTES: In the gym-wide view of Harry announcing "The Charleston" contest, we wondered whether the main actors were actually in the shot. Indeed they are. Todd Karns is on stage, beneath the basketball hoop. Reed and Stewart are on the dance floor straight out from the drum set. Some thirty feet to their right, Grahame and Albertson are paired up and ready to dance. And Harry Holman, playing Mr. Partridge, is by the "eats" table (where the scene started) with Hal Landon (Marty), bottom right in the shot.

CLOSER LOOK: During the contest, look for the boy whose tuxedo bib unexpectedly rolls up on him while he's dancing. (22:00)

EXPLANATION REQUIRED: As Sam and Violet set their sights on winning the loving cup, the school's principal, Mr. Partridge, taps Violet on the shoulder. At first blush it appears that he's acting as a judge and eliminating the couple from the contest. But recall that Harry announces that couples *not* tapped by the judges are to remain on the floor. And rather than clearing the floor, Violet and Sam keep dancing.

So what gives here? We think that Mr. Partridge is playing the role of chaperone and is good-naturedly letting Violet know that she's showing a little too much leg as she swivels. Look for Mr. Partridge gesturing to Violet's hemline, just before she pauses to give Mr. Partridge an apologetic hug.

JUST WONDERING: With Violet and Sam hitting it off so well on the dance floor, don't you think it's a shame that they don't end up together? We think they would have been a perfect match: Sam was destined to make a fortune, and Violet, with her extravagant tastes, would have been a natural at spending that fortune.

CLOSER LOOK: Notice anything different about Violet's appearance compared to the other girls at the dance? How about the fact that Violet is pretty much the only girl wearing a black dress? Here, director Frank Capra appears to have resorted to some subliminal messaging to convey the notion that Violet is a "bad girl." As if that was really necessary.

EXPLANATION REQUIRED: As George and Mary dance "The Charleston," a brooding Freddie is approached by another boy, Mickey, who has seen George cut in on Freddie's dance with Mary. Mickey asks Freddie, "What's the matter,

Othello? Jealous?" For those not up on their Shakespeare, this is a reference to the play *Othello*. The story, as you might suspect, is one of jealousy. Othello is duped into believing that his wife has been unfaithful to him. In a jealous rage, Othello kills her, and at the same time seeks to do away with her suspected lover. Thankfully, life does not imitate art at the graduation dance, and Freddie is content with paying back George and Mary through a harmless prank.

MUSIC NOTES: While George and Mary's song may be "Buffalo Gals," it's actually "The Charleston" that seals their fate. How could they not end up together after performing such an unforgettable aquatic rendition of the dance? Derived from an African American folk dance, "The Charleston" swept the country in the mid-1920s and remained hugely popular for the rest of the decade. The original version of the dance was considered so wild in nature that some ballrooms either banned it or displayed signs admonishing dancers to "Please Charleston Quietly." Obviously, no such sign was posted in the Bedford Falls High School gym.

FILM ANECDOTES: If a retractable gym floor seems a bit implausible to you, think again. This scene was filmed at Beverly Hills High School, which in 1940 installed a gym floor above its pool as a space-saving measure. Called the "Swim-Gym," the facility remains fully functional today. In the film, a basketball backboard is located behind the band (21:17), and you can just make out the center court markings of the basketball court as the floor begins to spread (23:02). With its full-arched roof and skylights, the Swim-Gym has the look and feel of an old airplane hangar. Happily, all these decades after filming the place hasn't changed much—even the courtside "well" in which Freddie and Mickey conspire to open the floor, is still there. The one surprise, though, is its size. Though the Swim-Gym looks positively cavernous in the film, it's actually pretty cozy, with just enough room for six or so rows of bench seats around the perimeter of the court/pool.

FILM ANECDOTES: The shooting instructions for the scene called for an eight-piece orchestra, thirty boys and thirty girls as dancing extras, twenty boys and twenty girls as non-dancing extras, twenty adult extras, six bit boys, six bit girls and six life guards. Capra actually paid a bonus of $50 to any teen willing to jump into the pool. That's an extra $700 in today's dollars. No wonder so many took the plunge.

CLOSER LOOK: The pool scene is best described as organized chaos, making the hiring of six lifeguards seem like a good call. There's not much room to land and everyone is basically jumping on top of each other. There is some method to the madness, though. As extras jump in, most get out of harm's way by swimming underneath the gym floor. The head-first dives that some of the male extras perform would seem to be a bad idea as the depth marker on the far side of the pool indicates that the pool is only five feet where the floor splits. (23:37)

FILM ANECDOTES: Leaving nothing to chance, Capra assigned champion swimmer Harold "Stubby" Kruger to head lifeguard duties for the Swim-Gym scene. Kruger was definitely the right person for the job. He made the 1920 and 1924 U.S. Olympic swim teams and swam in the 1920 Olympics, headlined a wildly entertaining swimming/diving comedy show and spent years as a Hollywood stuntman and film extra, including a role as a lifeguard in another 1946 RKO film, *Till the End of Time.*

CAST ANECDOTES: Among the dancers in this scene is Arden Ruth Black, who happens to be the daughter of the film's assistant director, Arthur Black. We think she's in the mix, dancing behind, and to the left of, George and Mary during "The Charleston," including when George does the staple "Charleston" knocky knees move. Capra engaged a Los Angeles music and theater workshop run by Gladys and Maurie Rubens to supply thirty young students, and Black was one of those students. This was a big win for the workshop, which relied heavily on film placements of their students in their marketing.

CLOSER LOOK: Look for Freddie and Mickey actually jumping twice, first in a medium shot (23:41), and then again a few seconds later in a long shot of the very same action (23:49). This doubling up on scene footage is understandable given that the scene was undoubtedly a "one taker." Look also for Stewart and Reed's stunt doubles as they try to swim out of the way with extras diving in from all sides. (23:35) Stewart's double is particularly noticeable as he does not appear to have much hair on his head.

JUST WONDERING: Say, where did Sam and Violet sneak off to? We just saw them mid-contest with Mr. Partridge yet, just a few seconds later, they are nowhere to be found during George and Mary's plunge. At least Grahame and Albertson avoided the risk of being pushed in by an over-zealous extra.

FILM ANECDOTES: In the final shot, look for the two members of the graduation committee farthest to the right, with the woman imploring kids to stop jumping. These two are a couple, and apparently old friends of the Baileys. Four years later they are guests at Harry's "welcome home" party. In that scene, look for them off to the right as the Baileys and their guests pose for the photo.

RANDOM THOUGHTS: Earlier we flagged *The Bachelor and the Bobby-Soxer* as a must-see film for *Wonderful Life* fans, and here's why. Not only do you get to see Lillian Randolph (Annie), Charles Halton (Mr. Carter) and Gary Owen (Bill Poster), but the film contains truly unprecedented insight into what the Swim-Gym looked like just a few months after *Wonderful Life* was filmed there. You see, there's an extended scene of a high school basketball game, and it's filmed entirely in the Swim-Gym. The perspective in the film is nearly identical to the wide shot of Harry announcing "The Charleston" contest, only it's a much wider shot and contains way more detail. For example, the Swim-Gym's scoreboard is covered up in *Wonderful Life* by a large curtain running along the top of the bleachers, and it's hard to get a sense for the dimension of the basketball court with all the dance commotion. Now if only that film had also featured a swim meet scene. Okay, we have one more reason for you watch *The Bachelor and the Bobby-Soxer*, and trust us, it tops them all. But it will have to wait until the bank run scene.

Walking Mary Home

CLOSER LOOK: The name "B. C. Berkley" appears on a mailbox that George and Mary walk past in this scene. (24:50) We were hoping to stumble upon a story to go along with the use of this name, but so far we've got nothing. If you figure this one out, by all means let us know.

CLOSER LOOK: As George and Mary flirt their way down the sidewalk, keep an eye and ear out for a single line of dubbed dialogue. Mary playfully tries to coax George into saying, rather more directly, that she's the prettiest girl in town. George replies, "I don't know, maybe I will say it." But on film it's clear that George is not saying it at all. Instead, the first time his lips move is when he says the next line, "How old are you, anyway."

RANDOM THOUGHTS: George doesn't think much of the old Granville house, declaring that he wouldn't even live in it if he were a ghost. But we respectfully disagree. In addition to its ruinous condition, the house's architectural style is perfect for a haunted house.

The style is known as Second Empire, an ornate French style that was quite popular in America in the 1870s. The telltale feature of this style is the mansard roof—basically a two-sloped roof, with a steep lower slope and a near-horizontal upper slope (picture the house in *Psycho*). (25:47) Our theory on why houses with mansard roofs are so creepy is that they create the impression that something untoward is happening up in the attic. Hey, whatever did happen to the Granvilles, anyway?

RANDOM THOUGHTS: George and Mary take turns making wishes by throwing rocks at the Granville house windows. Now the cardinal rule of wish-making is that you're not supposed to tell anyone what you just wished for; else the wish won't come true, right? Wise to this, Mary refuses to tell George her wish, revealing it only on their wedding night after it had come true. George, on the other hand, just can't help himself and blurts out his wish mere seconds after making it. And just like that, George's fate is sealed: instead of a life filled with adventures in Italy and Greece, George will be keeping the Granville ghosts company for decades to come.

CLOSER LOOK: Another newspaper headline appears during this scene, but this one is a challenge to read. As George and Mary flirt, a grumpy neighbor watches them with disdain from his porch, annoyed that they have interrupted his reading of the newspaper. In the first shot of the neighbor, the headline of his newspaper reads REPUBLICAN CHIEFS HAIL MAINE AS SIGN OF HOOVER VICTORY. (26:03) In those days, Maine was widely viewed in American politics as the bellwether state for election outcomes. The oft-stated axiom was, "As Maine goes, so goes the nation." The headline therefore fits somewhat plausibly with actual events taking place in the 1928 presidential campaign, which pitted Herbert Hoover against Alfred E. Smith.

FILM ANECDOTES: These scenes were actually filmed outdoors and late into the night on the Encino Ranch backlot. One big clue that this is not a soundstage is that you can actually see Reed and Stewart's breath a couple of times during the scene. (24:13; 26:58). It turns out that the film crew ran into a rather cold night in the San Fernando Valley, which means that Reed sure must have appreciated the script fortuitously calling for her to wear a cozy oversized bathrobe.

CLOSER LOOK: At the top of our list of random and obscure scene details is the fact that for some reason the grumpy neighbor is wearing not one, but two undershirts. Who knows, maybe this second layer is attributable to the chilly night on the set.

CLOSER LOOK: Our grumpy neighbor is also the source of a couple of film gaffes. Recall that earlier that same day George runs into Bert, who is holding a newspaper with the headline SMITH WINS NOMINATION! Unless the neighbor is reading the evening edition, he should have a paper with the same headline as Bert's. And any doubt as to whether this is a true gaffe is removed in the next scene when George addresses the Building & Loan's board of directors. Although that scene is set a full three months after the night of the graduation dance, Tilly Bailey is shown holding a newspaper with the very same REPUBLICAN CHIEFS HAIL...headline. (34:24)

The other gaffe appears during the third shot of the neighbor when the top of one of the pages appears to read, "Los Angeles," as in, a Los Angeles newspaper. We originally thought this was an actual Los Angeles newspaper that accidentally made it into the film when, say, the actor playing the grumpy neighbor (Dick Elliott) got tired of reading a fake newspaper and decided to catch up on some real news. But on closer inspection, the font does not match the *Los Angeles Times* or, as far as we can tell, any other local paper from that time.

FILM ANECDOTES: Film lore has is it that Donna Reed, an Iowa farm girl, had a pretty good arm and actually broke the window of the Granville house with her throw. Well, there's no doubt she has an impressive throwing motion and this is one story that Reed herself confirmed through the years.

DID YOU KNOW?: This scene has a few horticultural references worth mentioning. First, the tall, slender, flowered stalks along the fence line are hollyhocks. Later on, look for Ruth Dakin Bailey brandishing a hollyhock stalk as the Bailey clan poses for a picture on Mrs. Bailey's front porch. (37:47)

Second, after losing her robe, Mary hides in the middle of a hydrangea bush. Director Frank Capra later insisted that the hydrangea bush was real but we've never bought it. Not only does the bush look fake, but it also sounds fake. And when Mary gives the bush a good shake, a flowered clump falls to the ground—not what you'd expect with a real one.

But you don't have to take our word for it. Earlier we mentioned film crew member George Zermano's insights on the downtown trees. Well, he also confirmed that the hollyhocks and hydrangeas are artificial and that he actually had a hand in making both.

JUST WONDERING: What exactly is the mischievous "deal" that George has in mind when he negotiates with Mary for the return of her robe? Wherever your imagination takes you, rest assured that the deal was not going to be, "I'll give you back your robe if you promise to marry me."

CAST ANECDOTES: For both Donna Reed and Jimmy Stewart, getting from small-town America to Tinseltown was no small trick. Upon graduating from high school in 1938, Reed was all but headed for college in the Midwest when her aunt offered her a place to stay in Los Angeles. Reed seized the opportunity and was initially intent on pursuing a career in radio broadcasting. Before long, Reed landed in the drama department at Los Angeles City College. Although she had done some acting in her high school days, she hadn't yet established herself as a standout in her stage classes.

Then in December 1940 she caught a huge break. At the college's "Queen's Ball" she was voted most beautiful coed, and the next day the *Los Angeles Times* carried the news along with a fetching photo of her. Studio executives took notice, realizing that her fresh, wholesome features would transfer nicely onto the silver screen. Within a few months Reed inked a modest deal with MGM, and by the end of 1941 she had already appeared in four films, the most prominent of which was *Shadow of the Thin Man*, the fourth installment in the popular *Thin Man* series.

When Stewart graduated from prep school in 1928, he had no ambitions of becoming an actor. Instead, he enrolled at Princeton University and pursued a degree in, of all things, architecture—wouldn't George Bailey have been jealous! While Stewart was set on a career as a builder, the dearth of construction during the Great Depression forced him to reconsider.

Now, Stewart had learned to play the accordion at an early age—his father acquired it at the hardware store as a sort of in-kind payment for goods, and gave it to Jimmy. At Princeton, Stewart cashed in on his father's gift. His accordion skills landed him a spot in a renowned performing arts group headed by some of his Princeton mates. Stewart soon found himself acting in Broadway plays, and after a string of well-received theatrical performances, MGM took notice and called Stewart in for a screen test. By the summer of 1935, Stewart had a contract with MGM and was cast in the role of a young go-getting reporter in a film called *The Murder Man*, starring Spencer Tracy.

GEORGE'S PLAN TO "SEE THE WORLD" GETS DERAILED

"This town needs this measly one-horse institution if only to have some place where people can come without crawling to Potter."

—GEORGE BAILEY

In the next sequence, twice George finds himself on the brink of escaping the town and business he loves to hate, only to have circumstances cruelly conspire to keep him put. First we learn that George's father has, in fact, passed away after suffering a stroke on the night of the graduation dance. Foregoing the obligatory deathbed scene, the film skips ahead three months to a meeting of the Building & Loan's board of directors. At the meeting the board pays its respects to Peter Bailey and his work, and then sets out to appoint his successor.

But Potter, himself a board member, has his own agenda and presents a surprise motion to the board to dissolve the Building & Loan. This sets off some fireworks in the room, with Uncle Billy nearly jumping across the table to get at Potter after one of his more venomous remarks. (George and Uncle Billy better get used to Potter's antics, though, as things are only going to get worse.) George counters with an impassioned speech on why Bedford Falls needs the Building & Loan. The board responds by rejecting Potter's motion, but there's a hitch. George must agree to assume his father's position as head of the Building & Loan, else the board will vote with Potter and liquidate the business.

We now skip ahead nearly four years to June 1932 for a watershed day in George's life. The day kicks off with George and Uncle Billy at the train station awaiting Harry's return from college. George, now around twenty-six, has begrudgingly spent the last four years running the Building & Loan.

After his father's death, George gave his college tuition money to Harry with the understanding that upon graduating Harry would return to Bedford Falls and relieve George of his duties at the Building & Loan. With Harry's impending return, George is convinced that his days in the backwaters of Bedford Falls are numbered. But just seconds after arriving Harry drops a couple of bombshells. Not only has he secretly married, but he's also all but decided to take a job offered to him by his new bride's father. The consequences of Harry's actions are painfully evident to George: he won't be going to college, he won't be "seeing the world" any time soon, and he won't be ridding himself of this albatross of a family business.

Later that night, Mrs. Bailey hosts a party to celebrate both Harry's return from college and his new marriage. Not surprisingly, for George the occasion is bittersweet as it sinks in that he will remain cooped up in Bedford Falls for the foreseeable future. Sensing George's disappointment with the state of affairs, his mother tries at least to get his love life back on track by encouraging George to call on his one-time dance partner Mary Hatch, who has just returned from college.

But George is reluctant to do so since he knows that his old pal Sam Wainwright has been courting Mary. Instead, George wanders downtown, where he runs into the ever-sultry Violet Bick. Violet sees this chance encounter as the perfect opportunity to finally snag the man who has eluded her all these years. But when she learns that George's idea of a good time is walking through the grass in his bare feet, the far less adventurous Violet sends George scurrying back off into the night, alone again.

George Addresses the Building & Loan Board

CLOSER LOOK: At the board meeting George wears a black armband on the left sleeve of both his suit and his overcoat in memory of his father. A board member confirms that George's dad died a full three months ago, so it seems a little odd that George is still wearing an armband. But given the purpose of the board meeting—to appoint Peter Bailey's successor—and the fact that this may well be the first board meeting since Peter Bailey's death, we say it's more than appropriate.

JUST WONDERING: Okay, this is the second time that Potter is shown in the offices of the Building & Loan, so now we have to ask: How has the wheelchair-bound Potter been getting up to the second floor of the Building & Loan all these years? Unless there's an elevator we don't know about or Potter is able to negotiate stairs with assistance, then the only way Potter is getting up those stairs is by a "fireman's carry" courtesy of his bodyguard.

FILM ANECDOTES: Having a wheelchair be part of Potter's character profile worked well, but there was also a more practical aspect to it. Lionel Barrymore, who plays Potter, had been using a wheelchair since the late 1930s as a result of breaking the same hip twice—the second time on the set of the 1937 film *Saratoga*—and worsening arthritis. Interestingly, even in *Navy Blue and Gold*, filmed shortly before *Saratoga*, Barrymore is shown throughout walking with the aid of two canes. That film and *Captains Courageous* (1937), were two of his last pre-wheelchair era films. Going forward, the studio helped him find roles that could be shaped to accommodate a wheelchair. While he could still get around on crutches for a time, he increasingly preferred the ease of the wheelchair. For example, even in the more casual setting of the *Wonderful Life* post-production cast picnic he attended in a wheelchair.

CAST ANECDOTES: Barrymore's family was, in his words, "of the theater," though he tried his best to escape that inherited path. His true passion was art. He studied painting and etching in Paris for years and pursued both art forms through the decades. He eventually succumbed the reality that he could actually earn a living on stage. Yet even with his stage successes, he did not hesitate to take on film as an early adopter. And you may be surprised to learn that he directed several pictures, and even has an Academy Award Best Director nomination to his credit for *Madame X* (1930). Directing was, as told by him, another attempt to escape acting. Thankfully for us, he did not succeed.

His brother John and sister Ethyl were also accomplished stage and film actors, but he was the first to break into film. If you want to see them all together on film, *Rasputin and the Empress* (1932) is the one. And, yes, Lionel is related to actress Drew Barrymore: Lionel's brother John is Drew Barrymore's grandfather, which makes Lionel her great uncle.

Barrymore won his only Academy Award for his performance in *A Free Soul* (1931), which he cited as his favorite film role. Other film highlights include *The Grand Hotel* (1932), *Camille* (1936), Capra's *You Can't Take It With You* (1938) and his ever-popular *Dr. Kildare* series as the wise-but-ornery and wheelchair-bound Dr. Gillespie. He was also an accomplished radio actor, best known for his annual portrayal of the Potteresque Scrooge in *A Christmas Carol.*

EXPLANATION REQUIRED: When Dr. Campbell turns the discussion to naming Peter Bailey's successor, look for George subtly tapping Uncle Billy on the shoulder, as if to signal their intention that Uncle Billy will take things over. And did you catch Uncle Billy's heated response to Potter's motion to dissolve the

Building & Loan? It comes a little too fast for most to take in, so here it is: "Potter, you dirty, contemptible! I'll ring his neck so help me! George, did you hear what that buzzard....?!" We love seeing Uncle Billy all fired up.

EXPLANATION REQUIRED: Dr. Campbell does a nice job steering the board meeting and ensuring the future of the Building & Loan. But he also played a key role in the previous scene. On graduation night, Uncle Billy and Harry find George to tell him that Peter Bailey has had a stroke. George asks about a doctor and Uncle Billy replies, "Yes, Campbell's there now."

CLOSER LOOK: When Ernie pops his head into the office to see if George wants him to keep waiting for him, there's a sign for a doctor's office on the third floor. This is the same doctor's office referenced on the stairs leading up to the Building & Loan during the 1919 scenes.

RANDOM THOUGHTS: The scatterbrained Uncle Billy claims that he is fifty-five in this scene, but Tilly reminds him that he's actually fifty-six. Since this scene is set in 1928, that would make Uncle Billy a rather youthful-looking seventy-three at the end of the film.

CAST ANECDOTES: Speaking of age, Lionel Barrymore's birthday is April 28. Filming started in April 1946, and when Barrymore's sixty-eighth birthday came around the cast and crew decided to throw him a little party. Photos of the event show Capra, Stewart and Thomas Mitchell hamming it up with Barrymore in front of an over-sized birthday cake. The production materials reveal that, while no filming took place on the 28th, filming on the previous days covered 1928 Building & Loan scenes. And it's easy to tell from the photos that the birthday party took place amid Building & Loan scene filming—Barrymore is still in Potter's fancy wheelchair and Stewart is wearing the suit with the black armband we just pointed out.

CLOSER LOOK: The sign above the conference room door is tough to read, but a hard study revealed the following inspirational quote: "In the Courage of Convictions Lies Valor."

RANDOM THOUGHTS: In this meeting, George mentions that Peter and Billy Bailey started the business twenty-five years ago, which means the business opened its doors in 1903. That's before George was born.

George and Uncle Billy Greet Harry at the Station

CLOSER LOOK: This scene begins with George and Uncle Billy talking before Harry's train arrives. The first audible line is George saying, "There are plenty of jobs for a man who likes to travel." But the two clearly exchange a few lines before this one. Unfortunately, these lines are obscured by Clarence and Joseph's voiceover. Fear not, though. We have reconstructed this "lost" dialogue with a little help from the script as it stood prior to filming. Referring to his desire for Harry to relieve him at the Building & Loan, George says, "He's going to take my job, and I'm gonna bolt like that," as he smacks his hands together. A more pragmatic Uncle Billy replies, "Have you heard of the Depression? Where you gonna find another job in these times?"

CLOSER LOOK: On the platform, awaiting the train's arrival, is a vendor selling peanuts and popcorn. The vendor's cart boasts the "Best Popcorn in Town" and "Hot Peanuts and Popcorn." Uncle Billy fancies the peanuts—he's eating a bag of them before the train arrives. Later on, George samples the popcorn—he and Ruth have a piece or two during their sidebar. As told by *Wonderful Life* actor Virginia Patton, the vendor and cart looked so convincing that at one point a neighborhood onlooker, to the amusement of the cast and crew, unwittingly tried to pay the vendor five cents for a bag of peanuts.

FILM ANECDOTES: You may be thinking that this station scene was just a standard studio backlot shoot. But take a good look at that train. It's really big! Sure enough, this scene was filmed on location at the now-defunct Lamanda Park railroad depot in Pasadena, California. Lamanda Park was a stop on the Santa Fe Railway line that ran between Los Angeles and San Bernadino. Until 1953 the depot stood at the intersection of what is now San Gabriel Boulevard and Walnut Street. Today, there's scarcely a trace of the old line in the area.

In the film you can see several coach cars and a baggage car, but for some reason Capra chose not to show the real attraction—the vintage 1921 steam engine that was pulling whole thing. In fairness, Capra had to keep the shots for this scene fairly tight due to the presence of some palm trees on the depot grounds—palm trees simply would not do for a scene that is supposed to take place in New York, right? From what you can see of the depot, it appears largely as it stood, just with a few props mixed in. The Western Union sign visible at the beginning of the scene is authentic and original to the depot.

FILM ANECDOTES: Well, we are excited to say that you no longer have to take our word for what the broader set looked like. And it's all thanks to an intrepid young teenager named Stan Kistler, who decided to skip school on a Wednesday in May 1946 to investigate the filming activity at the depot. Kistler grew up in Pasadena, just a few blocks from the Lamanda Park depot, and had always loved locomotives. In fact, he hung around the depot so much that he was friends with all the regular train engineers.

His engineer friends tipped him off to the *Wonderful Life* film shoot. In truth, he was keen on photographing the locomotive that was being used for the scene. And he did just that, framing up engine No. 3736 standing patiently in the depot as filming transpired. In so doing, he fortuitously captured the broader surroundings of the set that escaped Capra's lens.

Check out Kistler's photo in the guidebook's Photos section. Note the aforementioned palm tree in the upper right corner. And of the two Bedford Falls signs visible, the smaller one is in the film while the larger one, which incorporates a Santa Fe logo, is not—that's how tight Capra shot the scene. The "No Parking/Bus Stop" sign is an unused prop, and one of the bikes in the foreground is Kistler's. Finally, we are always fascinated to learn the colors of objects in this film, and Kistler confirmed, of all things, the 1946 paint scheme for the depot: dark yellow with dark green trim.

FILM ANECDOTES: It's a good thing the weather cooperated on shooting day—there was no back-up day for this on-location shot. The production materials alerted: "Weather permitting. If weather is bad company will shoot cover set." In other words, had it rained that day we would now be looking at soundstage footage, which would have been a visual letdown.

RANDOM THOUGHTS: Harry's sensibilities are a little off in this scene. While he gave us hints of his carefree style on graduation night (planning to take his mom's china without permission), the stunt he pulls at the station is one for the ages. Not only does Harry go back on his word to take over for George at the Building & Loan, he fails to muster up an apology for his older brother. Instead, he awkwardly blames his wife for speaking out of turn. And after lamely excusing himself to fetch his bags, Harry will not be heard from again on the subject. Come on, Harry, get with it! You wouldn't even be alive if it wasn't for George.

RANDOM THOUGHTS: Well, thankfully, if anyone is capable of straightening Harry out, it's his new wife. From this scene alone it's clear that this girl has a lot of moxie. First, with an air of casual confidence, Ruth corrects Harry on her new name. Then she good-naturedly mocks George's stiff greeting with an equally stiff and affected, "How do you do?" Only then does George realize that a kiss—not a handshake—is in order for his new sister-in-law.

CAST ANECDOTES: The gorgeous Virginia Patton gives a refined performance as Ruth Dakin Bailey, yet we come away with the feeling that she should have had a few more scenes. Just shy of twenty-one when her scenes were filmed, Patton has a front-and-center moment at the train station and in-the-scene time at Harry's "welcome home" party, and that's it. We don't even get to see her at George and Mary's wedding send-off or on Christmas Eve. Well, later on we will clue you in to why Ruth Dakin Bailey didn't make it to the Christmas Eve gathering.

This film was a big break for Patton and she took great pride in being Capra's first direct signing for the film. Before that signing, she had appeared in a handful of films, though largely uncredited. And if there was any doubt as to the faith Capra had in her abilities, Patton landed an always-coveted spot in the film's opening credits.

Earlier in 1946, Patton played an Oregon pioneer bride in *Canyon Passage*, a Technicolor Western about life in Oregon in the mid-1800s. That film actually premiered in mid-July, right in the middle of filming for *Wonderful Life*. The premiere took place in downtown Portland, Oregon, and was a good old-fashioned Hollywood junket, with a grand parade and celebrities flying in for the occasion. This must have felt like old home week for Patton, who grew up in Portland and whose great-grandmother was, coincidentally enough, a true Oregon pioneer bride. The year after *Wonderful Life*, she appeared in the lead role in *The Burning Cross* (1947). But film wasn't a long-term priority for Patton, and a few pictures later she retired with confidence from cinema to start a family in Michigan (not, as we had secretly hoped, in Buffalo.)

EXPLANATION REQUIRED: With George in a daze after talking with Harry, Uncle Billy introduces Ruth (off-screen) to some family friends. Here's our reconstruction of the exchange:

> UNCLE BILLY: "...bride to be. This is the new Mrs. Bailey. My nephew's wife, from Buffalo. These are all old friends of the Baileys."
>
> RUTH BAILEY: "Oh really?! Oh, what are their names? Let's see, now... Oh, of course, I've heard him speak of you. Oh!"
>
> UNCLE BILLY: "...Ohhh, just got in here now. We're taking her home, and I want to tell you that we're gonna give the biggest party this town ever saw."
>
> RUTH BAILEY: "Oh! Oh, that sounds wonderful!"

Ruth's back-and-forth with Uncle Billy appears to have been layered in separately—Patton is eating popcorn when she's supposed to be delivering this last line.

RANDOM THOUGHTS: Note that Harry's bride is wearing white gloves as she daintily munches on her popcorn while talking with George. Our crack research reveals that proper glove etiquette calls for their removal before handling food. In fact, Virginia Patton had that very same thought on the set (as well as some trepidation over her having to pull off eating on screen), but the scene nevertheless went forward with a gloved Ruth happily snacking away.

CLOSER LOOK: Okay, so you know this scene features George, Harry, Ruth and Uncle Billy. But what you almost surely don't know is that there's another familiar character lurking in this scene. As George approaches Ruth to quiz her on Harry's job offer, we get an ever-so-brief glimpse of a mugging Ernie. (37:16) A split second later Harry and Uncle Billy walk past George in the foreground and Harry hands Ernie (off-screen) the newlyweds' luggage. Ernie then carries the luggage out to the parking lot (visible in background). If Ernie is here to pick up Harry and Ruth, we're stumped as to why—that's what George and Uncle Billy came to do.

Harry's "Welcome Home" Party

CLOSER LOOK: This scene opens with the Bailey family and other guests posing for a photo on Ma Bailey's front porch. The photographer is George's cousin, Eustace Bailey. Look for him skirting past everyone, camera in hand, just after he takes the picture. (37:57) Photography must be Cousin Eustace's thing—he can also be seen taking photos at George and Mary's wedding send-off.

FILM ANECDOTES: Legend has it that the off-screen sound of Uncle Billy crashing into what sound like garbage cans was unscripted. As the story goes, a stage hand inadvertently knocked over some props at the end of the shot, prompting Thomas Mitchell to ad-lib, "I'm all right. I'm allllllll right!" Well ... the script as it stood just prior to filming already called for Uncle Billy to crash into garbage cans. Now, an earlier version did not include the "I'm all right" line, so who knows, maybe a mishap did occur, inspiring Thomas Mitchell to improvise that line. But whatever the case, any unscripted clanking likely would have resulted in the scene being reshot with proper sound effects.

CLOSER LOOK: Virginia Patton's screen time does not end with the party photo. Starting with Uncle Billy's crash landing, Ruth is visible inside the house for a full minute, with a lovely medium shot of Ruth, Harry and Ma Bailey thrown in for good measure. While inside, Ruth has a private word with Ma Bailey before Harry joins them. And after Ma comes outside to talk with George, Ruth and Harry dance for several seconds in the entrance hall before drifting off into the living room.

FILM ANECDOTES: Remember, like Gower Drugs, Ma Bailey's house is an exterior set on the Encino Ranch backlot that also served as a convincing interior set. You can see a good part of the living room on the night of the graduation dance as George and Harry carry their mom into the dining room.

RANDOM THOUGHTS: In case you haven't yet figured out that George isn't busting out of Bedford Falls anytime soon, the sound of a train whistle as George steps outside for a smoke serves as a not-so-subtle reminder that the train has once again "left the station" without him.

CLOSER LOOK: After hearing the train whistle, a sullen George pulls out the same three travel brochures that he was perusing earlier at the station. For one of the brochures all we can read is the heading "Europe." However, we are afforded a nice close-up of the other two. (39:16) The brochure on the left reads: "South America/ New York to Brazil–Uruguay–Argentina/Schedule and Passenger Rates." This particular brochure was distributed by the Munson Steamship Lines, which was an actual line based in New York City. When George pulls out the same brochure at the train station (35:29), the name Munson appears at the bottom. On the front and back cover is a colorful illustration of the Harbor of Rio de Janeiro. The brochure on the right reads: "Travel with the Foremost Student Tours/College Travel Club." This was an actual travel club that operated during the 1930s.

RANDOM THOUGHTS: So we now know that George has in his hands actual travel brochures, but, curiously, he's reading international job postings from these brochures. Construction workers needed in Venezuela's oil fields, engineers needed in the Yukon. Well, no surprise, these brochures have no such postings, only travel packages available for purchase.

MUSIC NOTES: As George and his mother share a moment on the front walkway, party guests dance inside the house to a wonderfully wistful tune called "Avalon." The song, which is about the romantic harbor town of Avalon on California's Catalina Island, was among the top hits of 1920 and a favorite of Benny Goodman's through the years. It was written by Al Jolson and Vincent Rose, though the two lost a lawsuit alleging that they lifted the melody from the Italian opera *Tosca*. The song appears in equally unheralded fashion in another American film classic, *Casablanca*. At the time Ilsa asks Sam to "play it," meaning "As Time Goes By," Sam is playing "Avalon."

George and Violet Downtown

FILM ANECDOTES: It's not possible to figure this out from watching the film, but the final script reveals that Violet is supposed to be closing up her beauty shop for the evening when she spies George across the street. In fact, she's shown here closing up the American Florists flower shop, which we can tell from the striped awnings and floral arrangements in the windows.

Now, earlier we mentioned our discovery that, in 1945 Bedford Falls, there is actually a small beauty studio next door to the American Florists. While Violet could easily have been shown locking up the studio, we can only guess that the production team decided that the flower shop's façade made for a better shot.

Look for the key to the shop in Violet's right hand as she turns around and sees George. (41:18) The script confirms that the two men around her are salesmen who make regular sales calls on the beauty shop and are now angling for a date. A bizarre early version of this scene had George exchanging blows with one of them after the guy refused to stop hounding Violet.

CAST ANECDOTES: For the role of Violet, Capra was looking for what he described as a "good bad girl," and he sure found it in Gloria Grahame. This film was Grahame's first big break in Hollywood, where her sultry features made her a natural in the role of the temptress. Grahame went on to star in a slew of top-flight films, including *Crossfire* (1947, Academy Award nomination for Best Supporting Actress), *In a Lonely Place* (1950, cast opposite Humphrey Bogart), *The Bad and the Beautiful* (1952, Academy Award for Best Supporting Actress) and *The Big Heat* (1953). She's amazing in all of them, but, honestly, we can't get enough of her performance in the comedy *Merton of the Movies* (1947). There, she plays a diva actress who tries to seduce a naïve, greenhorn actor and all at once channels Violet Bick and Scarlett O'Hara into a super funny and entertaining character.

Though her film career was a success, her personal life was a bit of a mess. For one, she had serious hang-ups with her facial features, so much so that she had several cosmetic surgeries in an attempt to "fix" the appearance of her lips. The surgeries left her upper lip paralyzed, which only served to further fuel her insecurities.

Moreover, her love life was odd indeed. In the wake of one failed marriage, she married director Nicholas Ray in 1948. He was reputed to have a rather abusive personality, and they had a major falling out during the filming of *In a Lonely Place*, for which Ray was the director. She then had an affair with Ray's stepson (who was a teenager) and later married him. The effect of this scandal on her career was not altogether positive.

GEORGE CALLS ON MARY

"He says it's the chance of a lifetime."

—MARY HATCH

After his rather humiliating run-in with Violet, a brooding George soon finds himself in front of Mary's house, not entirely sure of his intentions. Mary, having been tipped off by Mrs. Bailey that George may come a-calling, is not about to let this golden opportunity slip through her hands. Donning a fetching party dress, Mary deftly exploits their dalliance on the night of the graduation dance by playing "Buffalo Gals" on the phonograph and presenting George with a caricature of him "lassoing" the moon. But her thoughtfulness appears to be lost on George, who mopes about and is, generally speaking, a complete pill. The visit quickly unravels on account of George's surly demeanor and George heads out the door in a huff.

Just seconds later a crestfallen Mary receives a phone call from George's old pal Sam Wainwright, who has been courting Mary from New York City. Mary sees that George has returned to fetch his hat and begins speaking flirtatiously with Sam in the hopes of making George jealous. Her scheme works and a curious George dawdles just long enough that he is within earshot when Sam asks Mary to put him on the phone. Sam, oblivious to the heat being generated at the Hatch household, jokingly accuses George of trying to steal his girl—an accusation that George vehemently denies.

As Sam gives them both the lowdown on his new business venture, George and Mary realize that they are cheek to cheek on the phone. Their physical proximity is too much for either of them to bear, and George soon finds himself blurting out a heartfelt, if unconventional, profession of his love. Mrs. Hatch, who has done her level best all evening to prevent these two from hooking up, will have to get used to George, because by the end of the night there's not much doubt that these two are gonna get hitched.

Mary Hatch's House

CLOSER LOOK: The mailbox outside Mary's house reads, "Mrs. J. W. Hatch." Curiously, we're never told the whereabouts or fate of Mr. Hatch. (42:36) However, given that he's not mentioned on the mailbox, and that he's a no-show to his own daughter's wedding, we can safely assume that, wherever he is, he's not coming back. Another unanswered question regarding the Hatch family is whether Mary has any other siblings besides Marty. Might Mary have a sister? One can only dream.

MUSIC NOTES: We've heard snippets of "Buffalo Gals" before now, but this scene offers a longer listen. "Buffalo Gals" is an old minstrel song that was composed back in 1844 by Cool White (aka John Hodges), who performed in a minstrel group called the Virginia Serenaders. Variations of the song have arisen through the years, and performers sometime swapped out "Buffalo" for the name of the town in which they were performing the song. Ironically, while the song seems innocent enough, it's actually about Buffalo, New York, prostitutes being courted by gents in the rough-and-tumble days that came with the completion of the Erie Canal.

The following lyrics can be heard on the record that Mary plays for George—feel free to sing along:

As I was lumb'rin down the street
Down the street, down the street,
A handsome gal I chanced to meet
Oh! She was fair to view

I asked her if she'd have some fun
Have some fun, have some fun
Her feet covered up the whole sidewalk
As she stood close by me

Buffalo gals, can't you come out tonight
Can't you come out tonight, can't you come out tonight
Buffalo gals, can't you come out tonight
And dance by the light of the moon

This song shows up from time to time in Westerns, such as *My Darling Clementine* (1946), in which it's playing in the bar on a tinny piano.

CLOSER LOOK: Use freeze-frame to read the record label for "Buffalo Gals" as it plays on the old Victrola phonograph. The label attributes the song to Arthur Black and His Orchestra and shows Velvet Tone as the recording label. Velvet Tone was an actual "budget" label produced by Columbia Records from the late 1920s to the early 1930s. But the discography for Velvet Tone does not include any recordings by a band named Arthur Black and His Orchestra, or of "Buffalo Gals," by anyone. Nor is the design of the label itself consistent with that of actual Velvet Tone labels.

So what's the story here? Well it appears that we are all victims of an inside joke. The film's assistant director, you see, was one Arthur Black.

FILM ANECDOTES: Capra felt that a top-shelf technical crew was essential to the success of his films, and Arthur Black was one of Capra's go-to ace crew members. Black was an assistant director on several of Capra's best films, including *Mr. Smith Goes to Washington*, *Meet John Doe*, *Lost Horizon* and *You Can't Take It With You.*

In his autobiography, Capra explained how invaluable Art Black was to him:

> Without [Art] around I was … a basket case…. An assistant director's enemy is the clock. His prime function is to anticipate and magically produce on the set the myriad of details it takes to keep the director shooting without delay. At this, Art Black, an uneducated, gravelly voiced Irishman had no peers. But his chief asset was his constant line of unique chatter—mostly ad-lib malaprops—that disarmed, amused, and revivified the most exhausted actors and crews.

And we found an old quote of Art Black's, from a film he worked on in the 1930s, that provides keen insight into what it was like to work under his direction. Picture Black barking out these orders in his Irish brogue:

> Put away those newspapers, folks, and hide the dark glasses! Who sat that lady on the aisle?! Will the gentleman please change places with her. Stop that hammering up there! Who cares if it's only two more nails?! Stop it! Remember, folks in the boxes, you are being paid to watch the stage and not the camera crane. And you up there on the stage. This is a <u>gay</u> scene. You're giving a toast to Ms. Moore. She's having a good time and you must be having one, too. You're drinking <u>the same</u>! All right, folks, this is the picture! We're ready, Mr. Griffith!

Fun stuff, and it's easy to picture the no-nonsense but lovable Black shouting similarly pointed and scattershot directions at all the *Wonderful Life* extras on the chaotic downtown Bedford Falls set.

EXPLANATION REQUIRED: When Mrs. Hatch asks Mary what George wants, Mary declares, "He's making violent love to me, mother!" Blush no more when you hear this line. In the old days "making love" basically meant "courting" or "flirting."

CLOSER LOOK: It's clear from this scene that Mrs. Hatch is not a big fan of George—and the feeling is apparently mutual. Check out the scowls the two of them exchange as George grabs the phone. In fact, Mrs. Hatch is so distraught over George's presence that she calls her own daughter an "idiot" for putting George on the phone. And when she heads back up the stairs, she utters a panicked, "Oh, dear!" We're not entirely sure why Mrs. Hatch is down on George, but we have a pretty good idea that it's about money: Sam has it, and George doesn't.

JUST WONDERING: What in the world was Sam thinking when he placed this phone call to Mary? Sam has been courting Mary for some time, yet he phones her from his swanky office in New York City with a mink-shawl-wearing gal draped all over him. Huh?! This would be the definition of a cad. If only Mrs. Hatch had been able to see the full picture here.

CLOSER LOOK: Look for the lighted sign outside Sam's office window that reads, "Hotel Piccadilly." (47:39) This was an actual hotel in New York City back in the 1930s, located at 227 West 45th Street. The hotel's address tells us that Sam's office is located in tony Times Square. Also visible from Sam's office window is a sign for Chevrolet; directly beneath it scrolls an ad that reads, "Genuine Fisher No Draft Ventilation."

The name *Fisher* refers to the Fisher Body Company, which became a division of General Motors in 1926. The term "no draft ventilation" refers to a feature introduced on all GM cars in 1933, which consisted of triangular side windows that pivoted to create controlled cabin air flow. This technology was no substitute for air conditioning (which was not introduced in automobiles until the late 1930s), but was certainly better than just rolling down the windows.

Unfortunately, while GM first introduced "no draft ventilation" in January 1933, this scene is set in June 1932. So unless this is an advertisement for next year's models, we have here a most obscure continuity gaffe.

EXPLANATION REQUIRED: When the film shows George and Mary on the phone listening to Sam explain that he wants to make plastics from soybeans, listen for the voice of Sam's business partner on the phone as he jokingly corrects Sam that he means "chili beans," not soybeans.

DID YOU KNOW?: Is Sam really going to get rich making plastics from soybeans? At first blush it may sound like a crackpot idea, but actually the concept is scientifically sound. The likely inspiration for this plot device was Henry Ford, who in the early 1930s developed a strange affinity for the humble soybean. Ford devoted considerable financial resources toward developing various uses for the commodity, including soy-based plastics. Eventually Ford incorporated various parts made of soybean meal into his automobiles, and even developed a prototype plastic car body in 1941 molded from soybeans. Still, fast forwarding to the war years, Sam was never going to be able to produce from soybeans a clear plastic suitable for airplane hoods.

RANDOM THOUGHTS: Sam boasts that the idea of making plastics from soybeans is the best thing since "radio." Radio was invented at the turn of the century. Here are a few things invented between then and the early 1930s (the time of Sam's remark)—you be the judge on how Sam's invention stacks up: the airplane, color photography, instant coffee, the bra, stainless steel, air conditioning, liquid-fueled rockets, television, penicillin, the jet engine, and, of course, sliced bread.

FILM ANECDOTES: Film lore has it that Capra shot this film largely in chronological order, which sure sounds like something Capra do in the spirit of promoting continuity and more immersive acting. Well, we checked the production materials and can confirm that for the years depicted—1919, 1928, 1932, 1934 and 1945—Capra did his level best to film the years chronologically. This made practical sense given the need to have sets evolve over time. Swapping set designs back and forth for downtown Bedford Falls, for example, would have been a logistical nightmare, not to mention the added expense.

Of course, there were a few notable exceptions. The high school graduation dance was one of the first scenes shot. And the sledding scene was filmed all the way at the end. As we mentioned earlier, both scenes had continuity glitches attributable to the out-of-sequence shooting. Finally, while the Christmas Eve gathering scene was filmed around other 1945 scenes, Capra did not wait until the end of production to film the scene. And that made sense. There was no point in waiting to film George's extended detour through Martini's and the tollhouse and Pottersville, for example, just for the sake of filming 1945 in literal film sequence. With respect to the Bailey house Christmas Eve scenes, really the only one filmed after the Christmas Eve gathering was George and Zuzu in Zuzu's room.

FILM ANECDOTES: More film lore surrounds George and Mary's torrid exchange while on the phone. As the story goes, this being Stewart's first film since returning from the war, he was feeling a bit off his romancing game—so much so that he kept delaying filming of the scene. But the first take was so electric that Capra gave the order to "print it" despite the fact that the actors had omitted several lines of dialogue.

While it may have happened that way, we suspect otherwise. First, it turns out that no dialogue was dropped. The dialogue in the scene, as shot, is nearly identical to the dialogue in the script as it stood prior to filming. Second, given Capra's reputation for shooting multiple takes, it's unlikely that Capra could have resisted filming a few more takes as insurance. Consistent with our theory, the production materials show that several days of filming went into capturing the scenes at the Hatch house.

Note that Stewart fails to lay a kiss of any length on Reed. In 1930, the film industry began self-regulating (read: censoring) film content by means of an absurdly restrictive set of guidelines known as the Motion Picture Production Code. Among other things, the code prohibited "excessive and lustful kissing," which in practice apparently translated into no kiss being allowed to last more than a few seconds. Interestingly, George and Mary have a much longer kiss on their wedding day in the back of Ernie's cab then they do here.

RANDOM THOUGHTS: Before moving on, let's review George's actions during the last few hours. First he tells his mother that he's going to find a girl to "do some passionate necking with." Then he finds himself standing on a street corner in downtown Bedford Falls ogling girls as they pass by. Then he tries to pick up Violet and take her to "the Falls," surely Bedford Falls' version of lovers' lane. Then, just minutes later, we find him over at Mary's house professing his love for her. Now that is some turn of events.

GEORGE AND MARY'S WEDDING DAY

"Welcome home, Mr. Bailey."
—MARY BAILEY

Brace yourself for yet another whirlwind day in George's life. After we get stiffed on an invitation to the wedding ceremony, we pick up with George and Mary leaving their reception. Bound for a fabulous two-week honeymoon vacation, it looks as if George is finally going to bust out of Bedford Falls. But everything comes to a screeching halt on the ride to the train station when Ernie spots a crowd gathering in front of the bank and quickly deduces that a bank run is in progress.

Over Mary's protestations George heads back to the Building & Loan, where he is greeted by a throng of panicked shareholders. He tries to reason with them, but they're having none of it. They want their money and they want it now. Complicating matters is the fact that Potter, ever the opportunist, is scheming to put the Building & Loan out of business by offering to buy out its shareholders at a steep discount. When the shareholders get wind of Potter's offer and start heading out the door, Mary saves the day by offering up their honeymoon kitty to pay the shareholders off. This enables the Building & Loan to close its doors for the day still solvent, albeit by the slimmest of margins.

Thankfully, not even a bank run can ruin George and Mary's wedding day. As George is busy placating the shareholders, Mary slips out the door, and with a little help from Bert and Ernie, creates a makeshift bridal suite for their wedding night. Somehow Mary has managed to acquire the old Granville house, which, despite its ramshackle condition, provides a thoroughly romantic setting for their first night together as husband and wife.

The Wedding Send-Off

RANDOM THOUGHTS: It's not altogether clear here that Violet is over George. She looks a bit emotional during the send-off, first calling out, "Goodbye George, have a wonderful time," and then looking on wistfully while blowing a kiss and appearing to say, "I'll miss you."

CLOSER LOOK: Three brands of rice can be found during the send-off: MJB, Iris Brand and Water Maid. All three are actual brands and were around in the 1930s, though Iris was a private label brand specific to southern California. The Water Maid box is hard to spot—it's screen right in the shot just before George and Mary kiss.

CLOSER LOOK: Don't forget to look for George's dog in this scene. As mentioned, this is one of the three scenes the dog appears in and he's easy to miss at the very beginning of the scene. Just train your eyes behind George, Mary and Mrs. Hatch as they come down the stairs, and you'll see him, happily wagging his tail.

DID YOU KNOW?: George does not wear a wedding band during the film. Double ring ceremonies were not in vogue in America until World War II, when this largely European tradition caught on with American servicemen.

CLOSER LOOK: The list of attendees at George and Mary's wedding reception is a strange one indeed. No Uncle Billy (we're told later that he was trying to hold down the fort at the bank). No Harry Bailey. No Marty Hatch. No Sam Wainwright. And of all of George's friends around town, only Mr. Gower gets the nod. Ernie is there for the send-off, but if his taxi driver's uniform is any indication, he's strictly hired help.

As for those who are in attendance, how did Violet make the cut? Mary never liked Violet and thought all along that she was trying to steal George away from her. Indeed, her suspicions were well founded as George was just one climb up Mt. Bedford away from taking his relationship with Violet to another level. Still, in a small town like Bedford Falls, a friend is a friend, and George sees to it that Violet gets an invite.

CLOSER LOOK: Did you notice who catches Mary's bouquet? Yep, it's Violet! (50:17) Unfortunately, Violet never enjoys the benefits that are supposed to befall one who catches a bride's bouquet. Some twelve years later Violet still had not married.

DID YOU KNOW?: George wasn't kidding when he tells Ernie that he and Mary are planning to "shoot the works" on their honeymoon. George and Mary set out on their trip with $2,000 in cash. In today's dollars, George and Mary's kitty is worth around $40,000. Now that would have been some trip.

RANDOM THOUGHTS: Ernie passes along a bottle of champagne to George and Mary, compliments of Bert. It's certainly a nice gesture on Bert's part, but hold on a second here. This is June 1932, which means that Prohibition is still in effect. So what in the world is Bert doing gifting alcohol during Prohibition? Quick! Somebody call the police! Oh yeah, that would be Bert.

HISTORY LESSON: The 18th Amendment to the U.S. Constitution made it illegal from January 1920 to December 1933 to manufacture or sell any drink containing more than 0.5 percent alcohol. Prohibition proponents, mostly descendants of early American settlers, believed that alcohol abuse among newer immigrants was tearing the moral fabric of American society. World War I then set the stage for Prohibition when Americans in large part bought into the notion that abstinence from alcohol was a patriotic way to further the war effort.

Intended to decrease lawlessness, Prohibition had the opposite effect. Bars were replaced by an even greater number of illegal speakeasies, average Americans were forced to break the law just to have a recreational beer, and the newly created bootlegging industry served as the foundation for the kudzu-like growth of gangster activity in America. While Republicans held fast in their support of Prohibition throughout the Hoover administration, after Democrat Franklin Delano Roosevelt defeated Hoover in 1932, Prohibition's days were numbered.

The Bank Run

CLOSER LOOK: Just as George starts running back to the Building & Loan, there's a blur-of-a-sign behind him. Turns out it's a building advertisement for automobile maker Willys-Overland and features an old Willys touring car. (53:10) The ad is on the side of the building across the street from the Bedford Falls bank. Willys-Overland's was one of the companies that manufactured the iconic World War II U.S. military jeep, one of which we will see on Christmas Eve day in 1945 Bedford Falls.

CLOSER LOOK: Although we've seen the Building & Loan's offices once before back in 1919, this scene offers the first good look at the office layout. Take a look at the floor diagram that we've created for the location of various office details and events. Note that the interior design is surprisingly consistent with the building's exterior and even incorporates the building's flattened corner into the design of George's office. (13:19)

CAST ANECDOTES: Right when we get inside the Building & Loan, look for a shareholder off to the right, with glasses and a light-colored raincoat, staring down George as he invites everyone to pile in. While this shareholder does not speak during the scene, we do hear from him, only much later. On Christmas Eve, he's in George's living room and merrily shouts, "Here you are George, Merry Christmas!" This is just one of many more surprises we have for you concerning George's Christmas Eve guests.

FILM ANECDOTES: The office mascot at the Building & Loan is a raven. The raven actually has a name—Jimmy the Raven. Listen for Jimmy Stewart muttering "Look out, Jimmy" as he hurdles the office counter during the bank run. This is technically not Jimmy's first scene—in 1919, he's in Uncle Billy's office, though visible only for a second. We will see Jimmy again on Christmas Eve, which means he's well beyond twenty-six years old by film's end. This is actually plausible as these birds can live upwards of forty years in captivity.

In fact, Jimmy was about twelve when *Wonderful Life* was filmed. Animal trainer Curley Twiford, as he told it, found him in the desert as a baby, and nursed him back to health. Through the years, he was unquestionably Twiford's favorite animal, his pride and joy. Jimmy was super smart, knew dozens of words and tricks (dealing cards, combing hair, typing, opening zippers, picking flowers, fetching and offering up cigarettes, turning magazine pages, you get the picture), actually commanded stand-ins for his scenes, and over the years made Twiford a lot of money in film.

THE BAILEY BROTHERS BUILDING AND LOAN ASSOCIATION

1. Location on Genesee Street of street-level entrance to Building & Loan.
2. Window from which Uncle Billy, Tilly, and Eustace yell to George after George picks up his suitcase.
3. Where George jumps the counter during the bank run.
4. Tilly and Eustace's shared desk.
5. Eustace's adding machine.
6. Tilly's phone operator equipment.
7. Location of Peter Bailey's portrait at the time of the bank run.
8. Location of the loving cup from "The Charleston" contest (resting on a file cabinet).
9. Where George pleads with shareholders not to sell their shares to Potter.
10. Where George talks on the phone with Harry on Christmas Eve.
11. Entrance to the conference room where George meets with the bank examiner.
12. Where Violet wipes lipstick off George's cheek and wishes him "Merry Christmas."

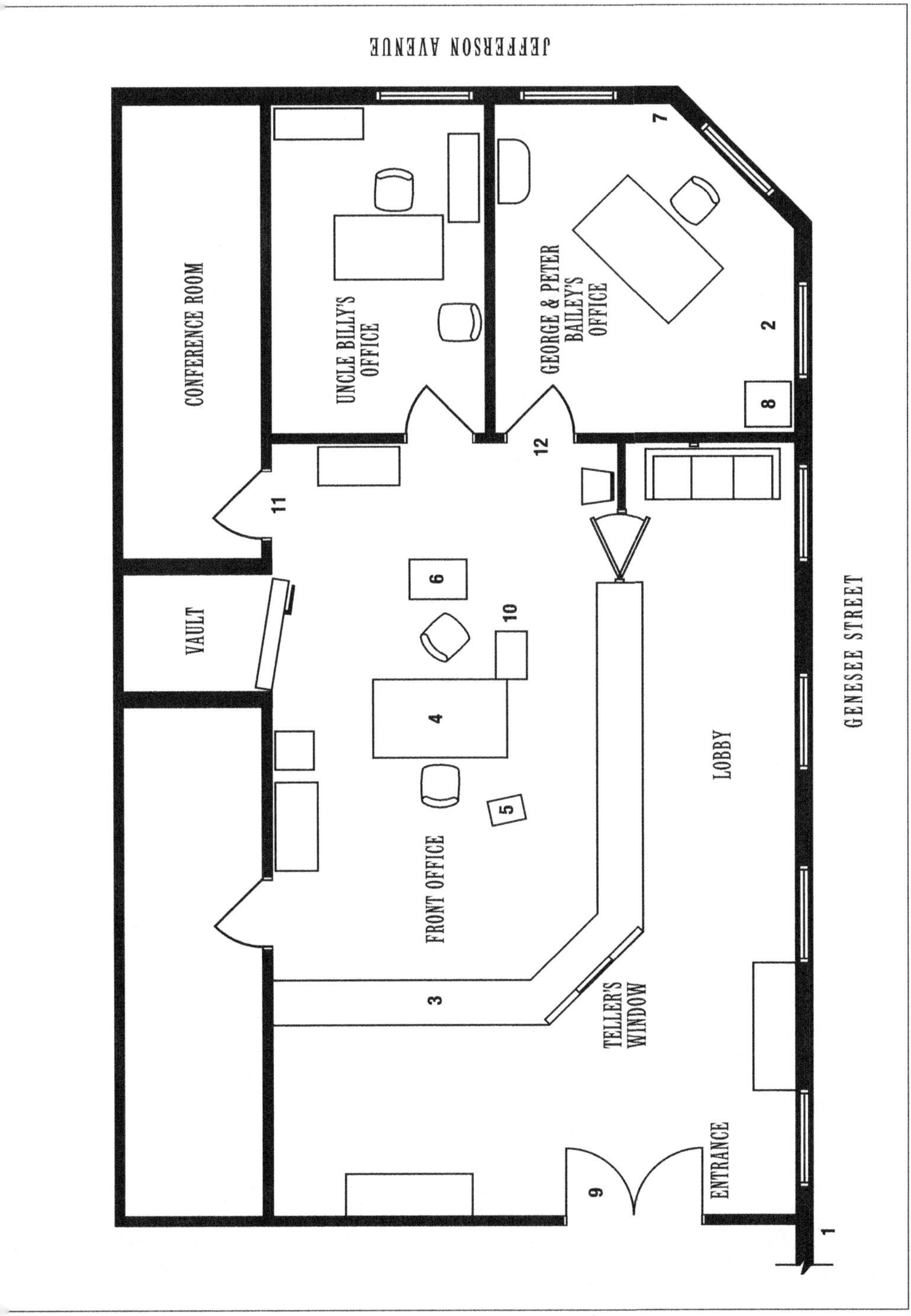
JEFFERSON AVENUE
CONFERENCE ROOM
UNCLE BILLY'S OFFICE
GEORGE & PETER BAILEY'S OFFICE
7
2
8
12
11
VAULT
6
10
4
5
FRONT OFFICE
3
TELLER'S WINDOW
LOBBY
GENESEE STREET
ENTRANCE
9
1

CAST ANECDOTES: Frank Capra was a big fan of Jimmy the Raven's talents and had previously featured him Capra's *You Can't Take It With You.* Impressively, Jimmy also appeared in *The Wizard of Oz*, sharing a scene with Dorothy and the Scarecrow, in which he plucks some straw from the Scarecrow. Including Jimmy in the film was another great casting call by Capra as the bird contributes nicely to the quirky, family-owned feel of the Building & Loan. When Jimmy Stewart appeared with Jimmy the Raven in *You Can't Take It With You*, Stewart quipped on the set, "When they call Jimmy we both answer." He added that Jimmy the Raven was the smartest one on the set: "They don't have to make as many re-takes for him as for the rest of us."

HISTORY LESSON: As George walks back to his office, a newspaper sits on Tilly's desk with the headline SENATE DEFEATS BONUS. (53:12) This headline refers to a most bizarre and unfortunate event in American history. For more than a decade, American veterans of World War I lobbied vociferously for additional monetary compensation for their military service. In May 1932, tens of thousands of Depression-battered veterans made camp on the outskirts of Washington, D.C., and formed protests demanding passage of a long-pursued "veteran's bonus" bill.

The bill made it through the House of Representatives, but on June 17, 1932, the Senate voted it down. Incensed, the so-called Bonus Army refused to leave the city. This prompted President Hoover to call in the real Army, which proceeded to use guns, bayonets, Army tanks, and even the cavalry to remove its own war veterans from the nation's capital. Incredibly, three of America's most celebrated war heroes—MacArthur, Eisenhower, and Patton—orchestrated the veterans' military ouster.

FILM ANECDOTES: Capra's use of the SENATE DEFEATS BONUS headline likely stems from the fact that he himself was a veteran of World War I. We give Capra full credit for using another reality-based headline, but unfortunately the timing of the event does not quite coincide with the setting for the scene. The Senate's vote on the bonus bill took place in June 1932, whereas the bank run scene is set in October 1932.

CLOSER LOOK: If you're wondering who Potter's historical role model is, look no further than the bust of Napoleon in Potter's office. (53:53) Thankfully, while Napoleon had his sights set on conquering the world, Potter would settle for Bedford Falls. Potter should know, though, that Napoleon's run did not end so well. After the British finally got their hands on him, he spent the rest of his life imprisoned on a craggy island in the middle of the South Atlantic. Anyway, Napoleon's bust (there are actually two) can be seen several different times in Potter's office at the bank. The bust is one of several ornamental pieces that migrated from Potter's home office to his new digs after he took over the bank.

RANDOM THOUGHTS: Uncle Billy sort of implies that he missed the wedding because of the bank run. But George has seen this act before and thinks his scatterbrained uncle just plain forgot, telling him that he can take the string off his finger now. But let's give poor Uncle Billy the benefit of the doubt. Maybe he was at the office before the wedding and really did forget when he got sidetracked by the emerging trouble.

Anyway, what's more odd, Uncle Billy forgetting George and Mary's wedding or the fact that no one from the wedding bothered to track Uncle Billy down? And don't forget that he missed the wedding and the reception. There are only so many places that a man can be in Bedford Falls, and a phone call to the most obvious one—the Building & Loan—would have solved the mystery. Whatever the case, Uncle Billy has got to come up with a better way to remember things—the strings just ain't working.

CLOSER LOOK: Two portraits hang in George's office. One is of his father, beneath which appears the following inspirational quote: "All you can take with you is that which you've given away." (54:48) If you think about it, it's really a variation of the title of one of Capra's top films, *You Can't Take It With You.*

The other is of America's thirty-first president, Herbert Hoover. Look for it by the window closest to the door. (53:42) Hoover was still in office in October 1932 when this scene was set, but not for long. By that time he was not exactly a popular guy, as millions of poverty-stricken Americans held him accountable for failing to pull the country out of its economic death spiral. And just one month later Franklin Delano Roosevelt scored a landslide victory over Hoover in the 1932 presidential election. This Hoover portrait gives us three U.S. president sightings so far in the film.

CLOSER LOOK: Look for a framed photo of Ma Bailey on George's desk. This same photograph shows up later in the film, first in Uncle Billy's study and then twice in George and Mary's living room—in a frame resting on the piano and pinned to the wall in George's work corner.

CLOSER LOOK: There's a photo on the wall that looks to be of a football team, with fourteen men, including a well-dressed manager. The uniform styles are consistent with those from the early 1900s. Now, we know Harry played football, Sam told us so at the dance. But what about George, was he a gridiron gladiator? Signs point to no, with George saying to Mary, "I guess I'm not quite the football type." Interestingly, Jimmy Stewart did play some football in prep school at Mercersburg Academy, so if the script had called for him to take the field he would have been well prepared for it.

CAST ANECDOTES: If you are dying to see Stewart playing football, you're in luck. In *Navy Blue and Gold* (1937) he suits up for the Navy Midshipmen football team. This is another super film for *Wonderful Life* fans to see because *Wonderful Life* actors abound, and all with entertaining roles. Lionel Barrymore plays a mentor of sorts to Stewart's character and his roommates, Samuel Hinds plays the father of the girl who is sweet on Stewart's character, and Frank Albertson plays an upperclassman who puts the roommate of Stewart's character through the ringer during an impromptu room inspection, with Stewart's character holding back laughs throughout.

JUST WONDERING: Ever wonder whether George and Mary won "The Charleston" contest? Given their performance, you would think they would have been a shoo-in to take home the hardware. Well, the bank run sequence provides evidence that they were, in fact, victorious. In the scene where George and Uncle Billy confer in George's office, a loving cup-style trophy sits on a cabinet by the window closest to the door. Look for it as George stands at the window just before getting on the phone with Potter. (53:42) It's definitely the same trophy and you can even see part of the phrase "Charleston Contest" engraved on it. Now, where is that prop today?

RANDOM THOUGHTS: Okay, here's our final installment of "Reasons to Watch *The Bachelor and the Bobby-Soxer*," and this one's a doozy. In the film, Cary Grant wins a trophy for his athletic performance at a picnic. If you have done your homework here and examined the loving cup from "The Charleston" contest, then the trophy handed to Grant in *The Bachelor and the Bobby-Soxer* should look very familiar.

But this prop is not merely similar in looks. It is the exact same trophy from *Wonderful Life*. How do we know? Grant moves his hand and for a split second you can see, clear as day, half of what's engraved on the cup. The engraving reads, in full, "Charleston Contest–1928–Bedford Falls High School." That's right, both films were RKO pictures, and RKO's prop department recycled "The Charleston" contest loving cup here. So what do we take from all of this? Cary Grant is the last known person to have had his hands on that loving cup.

HISTORY LESSON: The Bedford Falls bank run was, of course, a by-product of the Great Depression, the most severe and prolonged economic downturn America has ever endured. Beginning in 1929, banks were failing left and right as bad investments in the stock market and overly risky loans came home to roost. Nervous bank customers decided en masse that maybe their mattresses weren't such a bad place to store their money after all. But because banks were required to keep on hand only a fraction of deposited funds at any given time, they did not have enough cash to repay all their depositors at once. George's explanation of this concept to the shareholders falls on deaf ears.

Between 1929 and March 1933 some 9,000 banks went bust. Only after President Roosevelt took office in March 1933 did things start to turn around. Roosevelt's first order of business was to shut down the entire national banking system and declare a two-week "bank holiday." Meanwhile, Roosevelt went to work, largely through a series of his legendary fireside chats, trying to convince a skittish public that the banking system was indeed trustworthy. Depositors slowly returned, and, with the institution of a federal deposit insurance system in the summer of 1933, the bank run problem was largely put to rest.

FILM ANECDOTES: Capra already had experience framing up a bank run scene. In *American Madness* (1932), he captured, through some dark humor, the rumor-spun build up to a bank run followed by the frenzied convergence.

CLOSER LOOK: We spotted an attention to detail by the film's production team that may well top all the rest. Some twenty minutes ago George and Mary were showered with rice during their wedding sendoff. Well, after George takes his hat off in his office, white specks are visible in his hair in several shots, particularly when he's on the phone with Potter. Yep, that's rice in his hair. Now, how cool is that—this scene was filmed in a different location on a different day, and someone had the foresight to say, "Hey, George should have rice in his hair."

RANDOM THOUGHTS: Look for the home models here and in other Building & Loan scenes. It appears George has been building them through the years. On Christmas Eve, his work area in the living room includes a few work-in-progress models.

CLOSER LOOK: Well, quite a crowd has gathered at the Building & Loan, with everyone looking for their money. While most go nameless, George mentions several shareholders by name. Here's the list:

- Charlie—He's in the back of the crowd and asks if Potter is going to guarantee Building & Loan shares; when George says no, Charlie shouts back, "Then I'll take mine now!"
- Mrs. Macklin and the Kennedys—George mentions them but it's not clear who he's pointing to.
- Joe—He's wearing a rain slicker and rain hat. He doesn't talk but George addresses him twice.
- Randall—He shows up mid-scene to tell everyone that Potter is paying fifty cents on the dollar for Building & Loan shares.
- Tom—He's first in line and insists on getting paid in full—$242.
- Ed—He gets paid right after Tom; he has $300 on deposit but only asks for $20.
- Mrs. Thompson—She's in line after Ed, and only takes $20 on account of it being George's own money. Early on she asks Tom if he's going to take Potter's deal and then cries that her husband has been out of work for a year and she needs the money.
- Mrs. Davis—She asks for $17.50.

RANDOM THOUGHTS: We always presumed that Mary hung around as George doled out their honeymoon kitty, at least for a little while. But just a few seconds after Mary hands over the money, Mary and Ernie can been found slipping out of the Building & Loan, circling around the crowd and past the windows as George says to Tom, "Your account's still here. That's a loan."

In fact, a few seconds earlier, in a shot of George starting to help Tom (taken from behind George), you can see Mary and Ernie in the foreground, with Mary whispering something to Ernie before they start to dash off. Wow, if Mary figured out their Plan B—converting the Granville house into a makeshift honeymoon suite—in fifteen seconds, then cheers to her.

FILM ANECDOTES: Another storied tale from the film relates to the sequence where George distributes the get-me-by funds to Building & Loan shareholders.

As this one goes, Capra secretly instructed the actress playing Mrs. Davis, Ellen Corby, to request an even smaller amount ($17.50) than called for in the script, with the intention of surprising Jimmy Stewart. It worked, leading Stewart to plant an impromptu kiss on Corby. This is a story that actually can be confirmed, not only through the preproduction script (it called for Corby to ask for more than twice the amount and did not include the kiss from Stewart) but also through Corby's recollection. And if anyone ought to know, it's Corby!

RANDOM THOUGHTS: And now it's time to correct our own gaffe. We originally tried to figure out the date of George and Mary's wedding, based on the scene's October 1932 setting, through an office clock. What we thought was a calendar hand is in fact a "seconds" hand, so there's no way to know what day in October they wed on. We can say that it was probably not a weekend wedding. Office clocks inform us that the bank run dramatics occur around 2:45 P.M. and the Building & Loan closes at 6 P.M., which do not sound like Saturday banking hours. In fact, on Christmas Eve (albeit some thirteen years later) the entrance door shows the office closing at 1 P.M. on Saturdays. (1:20:52)

Still, there are some curious things going on with the office walk clocks. The one in George's office is a calendar clock made by the New Haven Clock Company, except it's missing the third hand for the calendar. These clocks typically had a window at the bottom for a decorative insert or the name of an establishment; George's has a woodsy motif. Anyway, a few hours later, the Bailey clan counts down to 6:00 P.M. using the front office wall clock, and the film cuts to a shot of the clock's face. Well, it's the exact same clock face that's back in George's office, only the prop team has added a third hand to track the seconds. Later, on Christmas Eve, we finally do see the front office wall clock (at the end of Violet's visit), and it's a completely different clock.

RANDOM THOUGHTS: It appears that the characters in *Wonderful Life* were typical Americans when it came to skirting the law during Prohibition. First Harry plans to drink gin on graduation night. Then Bert the cop gives George and Mary a bottle of champagne on their wedding day. And now in this scene, George, Uncle Billy, Eustace and Tilly break out a bottle of bootlegged firewater to celebrate the Building & Loan surviving the bank run.

MUSIC NOTES: While celebrating their having saved the Building & Loan, George, Uncle Billy, Eustace, and Tilly parade around the office humming "Stars and Stripes Forever" by John Philip Sousa.

The Bridal Suite

JUST WONDERING: Just how and when did Mary come to acquire the old Granville house? It could be that she secretly bought the house before the wedding with the intention of surprising George when they returned from their honeymoon. But an earlier script had her buying the house during the bank run.

If that was the case, here's how things might have transpired. As George pays off shareholders, Mary slips out, heads for town hall, and purchases the abandoned house by paying the back taxes with her own savings and, perhaps, a cash refund from their honeymoon train tickets. She then enlists the help of Bert and Ernie and bedecks the house with makeshift wedding night accoutrements. All of this would have to have taken place in just over three hours.

CLOSER LOOK: Bert, Ernie and a handyman hang several posters around the house in an effort to create a little ambience. One poster appearing at the bottom of the stairs (by the entrance to their makeshift bedroom) shows a child in a nightgown holding an old candle lamp. (1:01:36) On the child's shoulder is, of all things, a car tire, and beneath the child a slogan reads, "Time to Retire—Get a Fisk." This clever product slogan was part of a popular advertising campaign launched by the Fisk Rubber Company, which back in 1928 was a major American car tire manufacturer. Fisk was bought out in the late 1930s by the company that eventually became Uniroyal.

Three more posters hang in the "dining room." Two of them read, "Winter in Florida—Gulf Tours" and "No Other Vacations Like These in U.S.A." The third one shows an ocean liner and reads, "Cruise the South Seas—Luxurious Travel on the Dollar Line." (1:02:08) The Dollar Line was a popular cruise ship line that serviced the South Seas out of San Francisco from 1924 to 1938. Unable to weather the economic "perfect storm" known as the Great Depression, the line was eventually taken over by the U.S. government and renamed the American President Lines. Most of the liners were lost during World War II after being commandeered by the government for the war effort.

CLOSER LOOK: In the bedroom of the honeymoon suite (which ends up being the dining room once the house gets fixed up), Mary has carefully laid out her nightgown and a pair of pajamas for George. (1:01:39) We say, forget the nightgown, Mary looks stunning even in the kitchen apron that she's wearing. In the dining room (which becomes the living room post rehab), Mary is roasting chickens in the fireplace. To power the spit, Mary ingeniously connects it to a hand-crank phonograph, using a large spool as an interface. For dessert, they're having wedding cake, of course, which serves as the centerpiece on the dining room table. Check out the bride and groom figurines on the cake. (1:02:12) And don't overlook Bert's champagne wedding gift chilling on the table.

CLOSER LOOK: Above the fireplace is a framed piece of needlework that reads, "The Lord Will Provide." (1:02:43)

MUSIC NOTES: To set a romantic mood, Mary plays a dreamy, hypnotic Hawaiian tune called "Song of the Islands." The verse heard in *Wonderful Life* is a little tough to make out, so here's some help:

> *Islands of Hawaii*
> *Where skies of blue are calling me*
> *Where balmy air and golden moonlight*
> *Caress the waving palms of Waikiki*

The song was written by Charles E. King, a popular Hawaiian music composer in his day. Originally written in 1915, the song experienced a revival of sorts in 1929 when it was used in the film *Melody Lane.* Unfortunately, there is no known surviving copy of this film, but you can hear the song in *Navy Blues* (1941, one verse) and *Cheaper by the Dozen* (1950, played beachside on a ukulele) and, naturally, *Song of the Islands* (1942, during credits only), a musical comedy starring Betty Grable and the ever-present Thomas Mitchell (Uncle Billy).

MUSIC NOTES: The "bridal suite" scene ends with Bert and Ernie putting on a little vaudeville routine, serenading the newlyweds with a fine rendition of "I Love You Truly." The duo goes off script a bit here in singing, *Life with its shadows, life with its tears.* It's supposed to be, *Life with its sorrow, life with its tear.*

JUST WONDERING: When Mary whispers to George what she had wished for years ago when they threw rocks at the Granville house, do you think George hears a word of it? It's the same ear that George lost his hearing in during the sledding mishap.

RANDOM THOUGHTS: This was a charming night to be sure, but as for the rest of the honeymoon, they missed out on some things. According to George, they were going to stay in the "highest hotels," drink the "oldest champagne," eat the "richest caviar" and hear the "hottest music." Instead, they will stay on the ground floor of an abandoned house, drink Bert the cop's bootlegged sparkling wine, eat spaghetti dinners at Martini's and hear yesterday's hits on Martini's jukebox.

CAST ANECDOTES: The romantic lives of Jimmy Stewart and Donna Reed bore little resemblance to those of George and Mary Bailey. Stewart played the role of the Hollywood bachelor, and was romantically linked through the years to quite a few leading ladies, including Margaret Sullavan, Ginger Rogers, Marlene Dietrich, and Olivia de Havilland. He managed to remain single until 1949, when at the age of forty-one he exchanged vows with Gloria McLean, who was ten years his junior.

Reed went to the altar three times, the first time at the young age of twenty-one. In 1942, just as she was making a name for herself, and with a myriad of suitors vying for her attention, Reed quietly married her regular makeup artist, a rather unassuming man named Bill Tuttle. The marriage ended as mysteriously and quietly as it began, with Reed traveling to Juarez, Mexico, in 1945 to obtain an expedited divorce. On the way back from Mexico she got bumped from her flight. This seeming bit of bad luck soon proved otherwise when her scheduled flight crashed while trying to land at the Burbank, California, airport, killing all twenty-four aboard.

Just a few months later, Reed remarried, this time to her agent and confidant, Tony Owen. They had four children together and divorced in 1971. In 1974, Reed married a retired Army colonel named Grover Asmus who, once smitten, launched a full-scale campaign for her hand.

MOVING DAY FOR THE MARTINIS

> "You wouldn't mind living in the nicest house in town, buying your wife a lot of fine clothes, a couple of business trips to New York a year, maybe once in a while Europe? You wouldn't mind that, would you, George?"
>
> —HENRY F. POTTER

The Building & Loan's goal through the years has been to make homeownership a reality for Bedford Fallsians of modest means. And there is perhaps no better example of the Building & Loan's achievements on that front than the Martini family. For years the Martinis had no choice but to rent from Bedford Falls' resident slumlord, Henry F. Potter. But on this momentous day in June 1934, we find the Martinis finally moving into a home of their own, located in a bucolic development known as Bailey Park. Thanks to that "measly one-horse institution," no more will the Martinis have to "live like pigs" in Potter's Field.

Reflecting their commitment to the Building & Loan's shareholders, George and Mary gladly pitch in to help the Martinis move across town. As George and Mary oversee the christening ceremony for the Martinis' new home, the entrepreneurial Sam Wainwright stops by for an impromptu visit. Though Sam is a childhood friend, George is unnerved by his presence, undoubtedly because Sam serves as a walking reminder of how George never made it out of Bedford Falls.

Meanwhile, across town, Potter is hatching yet another plan to sink the Building & Loan. Potter's rent collector has advised him that the Bailey Park development is cutting into his real estate profits. So Potter decides to offer George a job, knowing full well that the Building & Loan's days would be numbered without George at the helm. Potter dangles an impressive employment package: a salary that is nearly 900 percent higher than George's current draw, and the prospect of regular business junkets to New York and beyond. This all sounds swell to George, until he gets a bad vibe from a handshake with the old codger and, in an instant, wises up to Potter's deceitful plan.

George returns home late that night feeling as glum as ever about the purgatory he knows as Bedford Falls. As rough as this day has been, George needs some good news, and lo and behold Mary has some: George, it seems, has "lassoed a stork." Mary is pregnant!

The Martinis Move Out of Potter's Field

CLOSER LOOK: Can you spot the various animals that make cameos as the Martinis pack up their belongings and head for Bailey Park? Some are more obvious than others. First, there is the Martinis' goat, which hitches a ride with George and Mary. Check out a concerned Donna Reed taking firm hold of the goat's horns after realizing that they pose a serious health threat to the little girls in the back seat. (1:04:26)

Two other pets also get a lift from the Baileys. Keep your eye on the third Martini daughter as she climbs into the backseat—she has two puppies tucked under her arms. (1:04:20) Also appearing in the scene are two adult dogs, some rabbits (right side of the cage on Mr. Martini's truck), some chickens (left side of the cage) and what looks to be a rather sad-looking turkey, which can be found in the box George carries out of the Martinis' house. (1:03:52) We also know from a film still that there was a donkey was on the set, but, poor little guy, he didn't make the cut.

FILM ANECDOTES: Actually, the reactions of Stewart and Reed to the goat's antics are priceless. Stewart flashes a look of helpless panic, while Reed sees the peril and reaches over as cool as can be and wrangles that goat like only a farm girl could. Completely different in-the-moment reactions, and both are so talented that they manage to save the scene and make it even more authentic.

DID YOU KNOW?: And while we're talking about goats, do you know what the word for *goat* is in Italian? It's *capra*! No wonder director Frank Capra wrote a goat into this scene.

FILM ANECDOTES: A near-final film script had the Martini's with four children, all girls. But if all their kids hitch a ride from George and Mary, which is the stated plan, then they have five girls. Four pile in the back seat while Mary holds a baby. They were all surely instructed to not look at the camera, but kids will be kids, and two of them can't resist sneaking a peek.

RANDOM THOUGHTS: Okay, we all get the not-so-subtle payoff on Potter's name here. With a *potter's field* being a common burying ground for the poor and the unidentified, Potter's Field is figuratively a cemetery. But what about Bailey, is there anything to that name? Well, we doubt it was intentional but a *bailey* is an architectural design element for a castle; basically a walled enclosure within the castle grounds. That works for us given George Bailey's architectural aspirations and life's work building residential castles. Anyway, we do like the sound of Bailey Park. Conjures up visions of a 1930s baseball stadium, which is miles better than a cemetery.

FILM ANECDOTES: This Potter's Field scene was among the many filmed at the RKO Encino Ranch backlot. The set was actually just a few yards away from where the Bedford Falls bank was located on the set, down the side street that's called Washington Avenue in the film. Of course, only on a studio backlot would the slums be on the same block as the bank. The side street was lined with shacks and a few stores (you can see "Grocery Store" signage in the scene fade out) as it transitioned into the backlot's Western set.

JUST WONDERING: The Martinis seem like a great family, but how are their pets—particularly the goat—going to go over in the suburban environs of Bailey Park?

HISTORY LESSON: The fact that the Martinis can afford a new house is particularly impressive given that by 1934 America was deep into the throes of the Great Depression. While many folks believe that the stock market crash of October 1929 was the cause of the Great Depression, in truth it was simply the first tangible symptom of an already sick economy. Throughout the 1920s, economic instability in America grew undetected as industrial and agricultural production far outpaced consumer consumption. Complicating matters was the fact that the European economy was still struggling mightily to right itself in the aftermath of World War I. The economic house of cards eventually collapsed with the 1929 stock market crash.

After that, things really got ugly. From 1929 to 1933 the unemployment rate rose from around 3 percent to a staggering 25 percent, which translates to more than 13 million people unable to find work. And those numbers don't account for the millions more who were forced to take pay cuts and reduced hours. At one point, home foreclosures were averaging 1,000 per day. After taking office in 1933, President Roosevelt tried every trick in the book to jumpstart the economy, but nothing seemed to work. In 1939, more than a decade after the crash, unemployment was still in excess of 17 percent.

The Martini Castle in Bailey Park

FILM ANECDOTES: If the scraggly hills of Bailey Park do not exactly remind you of upstate New York, it's because this is an on-location scene, filmed in the foothills outside Los Angeles. Capra hit on the idea of having an actual suburban housing development serve as Bailey Park. By mid-1946, the post-war, G.I. Bill-driven housing boom was in full swing, so he had lots of options and he eventually chose a subdivision in La Cañada Flintridge, California, next door to Pasadena.

Today, anyone standing at the spot of the Bailey Park entrance film location would hardly recognize it as such. But the basic road and housing configuration is unchanged, it's just that the trees planted in 1946 all grew up to the point where it's hard to see the foothills or even very far up the ascending street. But nearly all the houses from this 1946 subdivision are still there.

RANDOM THOUGHTS: When George enters Bailey Park, he immediately take a wrong turn. In this La Cañada Flintridge subdivision, the house selected for use as the Martini Castle is actually straight ahead, twelve or so houses up on the left. No matter, it's easy for George to circle the block.

DID YOU KNOW?: We can tell from this Bailey Park entrance shot that the Martini house was part of an early phase of this La Cañada Flintridge development. The lots farther up the hill from the Martini house remain undeveloped, and some of the houses around the Martini house are not yet finished. In the opening shot of the Martini house the houses down the street are still in various stages of construction. But that "under construction" visual is exactly what Capra sought for the storyline of George Bailey building dreams.

The Martini Castle is a classic cape cod-style house, which was by far the most popular home style in the post-war housing boom era. The efficient 1,750 square foot layout featured 2 bedrooms a den and a "rumpus room." And not long after this scene was filmed, the house was vacant and available for the very reasonable price of $19,750, which is around $220,000 in today's dollars.

FILM ANECDOTES: The Bailey Park scenes were filmed on two separate days in June 1946. The second day of filming focused on shots of Bailey Park entrance. The entrance scene ended up being a montage shot, but William Edmunds and Argentina Brunetti (Mr. and Mrs. Martini), the moving truck driver and the goat were all on the set that day, so who knows what else the film crew had in mind. Interestingly, Capra cast a well-known actor for the truck driver role, Chris-Pin Martin; he had played the Cisco Kid's sidekick, Gordito, in several films. But either the character's screen time got cut or never built out, leaving audiences with no hint that it's Martin sitting on the back of the truck. In most circles he remains uncredited for *Wonderful Life*.

DID YOU KNOW?: The Martini Castle is still there today, and the exterior looks remarkably similar to how it looked in 1946. The inside has been rehabbed and expanded a few times, but the original core layout is there. In the film you can see the handles of some built-in cabinets down the hallway, and sure enough, those handles are still there. Really, Capra could not have picked a more pleasant home and neighborhood to serve as the Martini Castle and Bailey Park.

DID YOU KNOW?: George and Mary's blessing for the Martinis goes like this:

> *Bread! That this house may never know hunger.*
> *Salt! That life may always have flavor.*
> *And wine! That joy and prosperity may reign forever.*

This blessing is something of a cross between a Polish wedding tradition of presenting newlyweds with bread, salt and wine, and a Russian housewarming tradition of bringing bread and salt to new homeowners.

FILM ANECDOTES: Look for the Martinis making the sign of the cross during the christening ceremony. (1:05:11) RKO's in-house lawyers advised director Frank Capra to omit this religious reference on the grounds that British censors were doing the same. Other stuff flagged by the legal wonks as unacceptable under the stifling provisions of the Motion Picture Production Code included: "My answer is nuts to you!"; "I hate this dang place"; "I wish to God I'd never been born"; "pulling the chain"; "impotent"; "jerk"; and "lousy." Lest there be any doubt about the code's impact, none of this made it into the film.

RANDOM THOUGHTS: It's probably a good thing that Sam and his wife have a chauffeur and limousine as they have at least 1,000 miles to cover on their trip to Florida. Next time how about splurging on a couple of first-class train tickets?

CLOSER LOOK: The automobiles owned by George and Sam pretty much sum up their respective financial well-being. In contrast to George's clunker of a car, the well-to-do Sam shows up at the Martini Castle in one of the finest automobiles of its time, a Duesenberg town car. (1:04:58) Founded by two German-American brothers, Duesenberg Motors opened up shop in Indianapolis in 1920. Just a year later, they took the racing world by storm by building the first American-made racecar to win the International Grand Prix at Le Mans. Duesenberg cars went on to win the Indianapolis 500 in 1924, 1925 and 1927.

The company's stated goal was to make the finest luxury automobiles in the world, and, with the car that appears in *Wonderful Life*, they absolutely succeeded. This particular car was manufactured around 1930 and retailed for some $16,000; that's $260,000 in today's dollars. That's more than the Martini Castle!

It was owned early on by actress Dolores Del Rio before being acquired by Pacific Auto Rental, which specialized in renting cars to movie studios, hence its appearance in *Wonderful Life*. For the past several decades, the car has been in the private General William Lyon automobile collection, one of the finest collections in the world; it is a multi-million dollar car. The Murphy-style town car body was one of only a handful ever made and, as you can see in the film, it featured an open-air driver's cabin with an enclosed passenger cabin. While the open-air design may not have been very practical for, say, Sam's 1,000-mile plus road trip to Florida, it made for an unmistakable show of status.

If George and Mary had gone along for the ride, they would have been in the jump seats, which folded out to face back toward Sam and Jane. Just before the door closes, look for Sam grabbing onto what resembles a grab bar in front of him. It's actually a robe bar, designed to hold a folded lap robe for use by chilly passengers.

CAST ANECDOTES: The actor playing Sam Wainwright, Frank Albertson, plays a far less likable millionaire in another film classic, *Psycho* (1960). His oilman character gets his money stolen by eventual Bates Motel guest/victim Marion Crane. And be sure to track him down in *Alice Adams* (1935), playing Katherine Hepburn's character's shifty brother, who due to his vices, doesn't have two nickels to rub together.

CLOSER LOOK: George seems to have developed a genuine disdain for his poor little car, perhaps because it's a constant reminder of his modest lifestyle. After Sam pulls away, a frustrated George gives the driver-side door a mean-spirited kick. The door does get its revenge later in the film, though. After George meets with Potter on Christmas Eve, the door will not open, forcing George to climb into the driver's seat. (1:35:20) Then, an hour or so later, George crashes into a tree, and the door inexplicably refuses to close. (1:37:41)

FILM ANECDOTES: Well, if we're going to talk about Sam's Duesenberg, we have to give the backstory on George's car. As the production materials confirm, it's a 1919 Dodge Touring car with a canopy top. And the great news is, this is another *Wonderful Life* car that still exists. Compared to the palatial interior of the Duesenberg, this Dodge is like a shoebox. The driver's compartment is one tight fit, especially for someone of Stewart's height. You can sense how cramped things were for him when he climbs into the car on Christmas Eve. Interestingly, the car's front bumper has seen extensive repairs, and all signs point to this damage being attributable to the *Wonderful Life* Christmas Eve car crash scene in which the stuntman crashed the car into the "tree" a little too hard.

Potter Summons George to a Meeting

EXPLANATION REQUIRED: The film offers no explanation of how George gets word way out in Bailey Park that Potter wants to see him. That's because the segue between the two scenes got cut. Before filming, the script called for the quirky Eustace to ride up on his bicycle, just after Sam drove off, with urgent news that Potter wanted to meet with George. George was to then have trouble starting his car, prompting Eustace to jokingly offer up his bicycle. We can tell you that actor Charles Williams, who played Eustace, was among the actors scheduled to be on the set that day, which means they almost certainly filmed the gag. Yet another cut scene that we sure wish would have survived.

CLOSER LOOK: Potter's desk is covered with intriguing items, most notably a creepy skull-and-chain metal casting. Yikes, at least it's not staring George down! Nearby is a lighter and a well-worn wax seal desk set, complete with a candle-based burner for heating the wax, a wax spoon resting over the burner and a stamp handle. The stamp head likely has Potter's personal monogram engraved on it, the perfect finishing touch on a sharped-tongued Potter nastygram.

Dominating the desk is a wildly ornate inkwell desk set. Note the two glass inserts for ink, the bell for calling servants and the horn-and-brass candle holders. Near Potter's left arm is a rocking ink blotter (used to absorb excess ink) and a mallet, which pairs with the bell on the desk set. To Potter's right is a cigar box and small inkwell that looks to be porcelain with an oriental style design. There's also a globe lamp with a dragon motif.

Look for a few desk items moving slightly during the scene, most notably the skull and lighter, which change places in different shot angles. These desk items, together with other collectibles in the room, combine to convey not just that Potter is rich, but that, unlike George, he has travelled the world. They also scream that Potter is hilariously behind the times—who exactly is penning ink-dipped letters with wax seals in 1934? Finally, Potter brought quite a few of these items over from his house—look for several of them on the desk in his study during the bank run scene.

FILM ANECDOTES: Potter refers to Building & Loan shareholders as a bunch of "garlic eaters," a thinly veiled, disparaging reference to their Italian heritage. While RKO's legal department flagged this term as offensive dialogue, the film's director, Frank Capra, a first-generation Italian immigrant himself, saw fit to keep it in.

DID YOU KNOW?: By the time he made *Wonderful Life*, Capra was a major force in Hollywood, having already racked up five Academy Award nominations for Best Picture and five more for Best Director. Of these he won for Best Director three times (*It Happened One Night, Mr. Deeds Goes to Town*, and *You Can't Take It With You*) and for Best Picture once (*You Can't Take It With You*). His films from the 1930s—and specifically the revenue generated by those films—were responsible for elevating Columbia Pictures from a B-movie house to a major film studio. By 1938, Capra's popularity had reached such heights that he graced the cover of *Time* magazine.

Wonderful Life actually marked the beginning of the decline of Capra's directing career. It was his first picture after a four-year hiatus from directing feature films brought about by World War II. Though he succeeded in recapturing the Capra magic of years past, the film felt more like a failure when it underachieved both at the box office and the Academy Awards. After *Wonderful Life*, Capra directed a series of uninspired films and seemed to lose track of the formula that had made his earlier films so enduring. Indeed, even a remake of one of his own pictures—*Pocketful of Miracles* remaking *Lady for a Day*—missed the mark. His many successes notwithstanding, Capra had a reputation for developing overly-sentimental storylines, which ultimately led some to refer to his work as "Capra-corn." (For the record, while most meant "corny," one of the first critics to use that term actually used it to describe Capra's film "magic.") No matter, Capra leaned into the term through the years and viewed it as a testament to his honest, common man portrayals.

JUST WONDERING: Just what does the F stand for in Henry F. Potter? We are never told, but given his snake-like, venomous character we like to think it's short for fer-de-lance.

RANDOM THOUGHTS: George tells Potter that he's making $45 per week, which equals $2,340 annually. $2,340 in 1934 is equal to around $47,000 today. In contrast, the $20,000 annual salary that Potter offers George converts to a whopping $400,000 in today's dollars. Throw in a couple of business trips to New York and Europe, and who could blame George for thinking, however briefly, that his ship really had come in?

CLOSER LOOK: Look for the portrait of Potter (or perhaps it's one of his ancestors) on the wall by the office door. (1:07:53) A similar portrait appears in two other places during the film: Potter's study, when Potter talks on the telephone with George during the bank run (53:53), and the lobby of the Bedford Falls bank, when Uncle Billy loses the deposit (1:20:18). Whether in portrait or in person, Potter is dressed pretty much the same throughout the film.

FILM ANECDOTES: For Lionel Barrymore, one small downside of playing Potter was that he had to spend a lot of time in the make-up chair. To give Potter a more fiendish appearance, Capra hit on the idea of Potter having an over-sized head. Capra's vision of Potter certainly channeled Scrooge, but for this aspect Capra said he drew inspiration from, of all things, the high-domed forehead of the pitchfork-holding farmer in *American Gothic*. To achieve the desired effect, his make-up team created a form-fitted, spongy, rubber cap, which added an inch in both height and diameter to Barrymore's head. Well, the make-up team definitely delivered for Capra—the side-by-side comparison of Barrymore's modest features to Potter's imposing mug is striking.

RANDOM THOUGHTS: This sequence contains one of the better insults directed at Potter. After George figures out that Potter has it in for the Building & Loan, he calls Potter a "scurvy little spider." Other disparaging remarks directed at Potter include an "old money-grubbing buzzard" (George); a "warped, frustrated old man" (George); "a hard-skulled character" (Peter Bailey); and "…a sick man. Frustrated and sick. Sick in his mind, sick in his soul, if he has one." (Peter Bailey).

Mary's on the Nest

RANDOM THOUGHTS: When George arrives home from his meeting with Potter, Mary is already in bed and a clock on the nightstand reads 12:25 A.M. (1:14:26) Hmmm. Do you think George might have stopped by Martini's for a couple of pops to take the edge off?

CLOSER LOOK: As George enters the bedroom, we get a glimpse of the second floor hallway railing outside their door, confirming that their bedroom is located at the right end of the second floor hallway, which we later learn is just down from Zuzu's room. (1:11:51) (In truth, there's really no other choice as there are only two doors off the upstairs hallway.)

We can also see the wallpaper in the hallway. Well, believe it or not, there's a problem with the timing of this wallpaper's appearance. The pattern matches the pattern of the wallpaper Mary hangs in the entrance hall during the Bailey family montage. Only problem is, she's hanging that paper after their second child, Janie, is born, which means this pre-children scene should have had a different wallpaper pattern, or, we suppose, none at all.

CLOSER LOOK: The bedframe in this scene, with its spindled metal headboard, is the same one seen in their "bridal suite" scene a few years earlier, when their temporary bedroom was located in what eventually became their dining room.

THE WAR YEARS

"Hold on...hold on...hold on now. Don't you know there's a war on?"

—GEORGE BAILEY

It's been pretty slow going so far getting back to present-day 1945, but we're about to cover eleven years in less than two minutes by switching to montage mode. First we learn about life for George and Mary in the mid- to late 1930s. While George has had his hands full keeping the Building & Loan afloat and fending off Potter, Mary has been busy fixing up the house and looking after their first two children.

Next we learn about life in Bedford Falls during World War II. George and Mary have two more babies during the war years, and we see how George and Mary and their friends and family contribute to the war effort. George's brother and friends all make heroic and high-profile contributions "over there." But George is deemed unfit for military service on account of his bad ear. He is therefore left fighting "the battle of Bedford Falls," assuming a number of war-related responsibilities that, although important, nevertheless leave him unfulfilled. Poor George. Not even a war, it seems, can spring him from Bedford Falls!

The "Bailey Family" Montage

CLOSER LOOK: Some interesting graffiti shows up during the Bailey family montage. George is shown by the staircase after returning home from another hard day's work. Behind him, on the portion of the wall that has no wallpaper, appears the word *spooks.* (1:15:00) On the same wall, farther to the right, the name *Potter* is scrawled above a drawing. (1:14:59) It seems that spooks was scrawled years ago by vandals while the house sat abandoned. We know this because on George and Mary's honeymoon night, the same graffiti can be seen protruding from behind the "Get a Fisk" poster, with an arrow pointing upstairs; in other words, "this way to the ghosts." (1:01:36) (By the way, during the bridal suite scene, *spooks* also appears on the wall behind George, screen left, as he surveys the accommodations.) As for the *Potter* graffiti, it was either scrawled by the same vandals or by a very frustrated George Bailey.

CLOSER LOOK: We used stains on the wall as references to confirm a small continuity gaffe. The section of wallpaper that Mary hangs by the stairs is not present in the very next shot when George has his first of three run-ins with the newel post cap. (1:14:55)

RANDOM THOUGHTS: Another interesting thing about Mary's wallpapering is that the pattern changes by the time we get to 1945. It's certainly plausible that George and Mary would change out their wallpaper that quickly, but we love that the set designers actually went to the trouble of applying new wallpaper in the spirit of showing the household evolving.

CAST ANECDOTES: The film features several younger versions of characters (George, Sam, Marty, Ernie, Mary, Violet), and this montage puts a fun twist on that narrative technique. Here we learn that the toddler standing in the crib is "Baby Pete," and that Mary is holding "Baby Janie." But seconds before that we see newborn Pete, who we will call "Newborn Pete." So technically, three actors play Pete in the film.

Well, we don't know who plays Newborn Pete, but we've got Baby Pete narrowed down to one of two people—Donald Collins or his brother Ronald. You see, Donald and Ronald were cast as identical twins, a common casting strategy that gave the production crew some flexibility in case one became less agreeable or sleepy. And, go figure, the Collins' boys have never been able to sort out which one of them actually appears in the film. Cheers to them both—through a team effort they nailed their scene, displaying the calm curiosity for Baby Janie that the director demanded of them.

CLOSER LOOK: Look for a toy on the floor, just to Mary's left. It's a good-sized wobble toy or roly poly. And hiding behind Baby Janie's blanket is a toy horse, likely a modified pull toy. While the wobbling clown and horse only appear in this montage, we know the Bailey child actors played with them on the set. Carol Coombs' mom took a photo of Carol and the other Bailey family actors, and in that photo Jimmy Hawkins is holding the roly poly and Karolyn Grimes has the horse.

The "War Years" Montage

DID YOU KNOW?: Kicking off the war montage is a sign that reads, "Checking Station—Recruit Reception Center—Casuals Report at Side Door." Upon being drafted (or volunteering), selectees were instructed to report to one of several "reception centers" scattered around the country. The next clip shows selectees marching at an actual reception center. (1:15:11) It's hard to pin down the military base that this clip was filmed at, but the Army reception center for Marty, Bert and Ernie would likely have been Camp Upton in Long Island, New York.

Upon arrival, selectees would first be shuttled to the aforementioned "checking station" (basically a large warehouse) for roll call, a physical examination and assignment to a company and barrack. The selectees shown marching in the montage have probably just left the checking station and are headed to their new barracks—they're still in civilian clothes and still carrying their personal travel bags.

After an IQ test and some military lectures on this and that, they would have been put through interviews aimed at determining their military assignment and issued uniforms. They would then have had a few days of downtime awaiting orders to ship out to a training camp.

HISTORY LESSON: How exactly did Harry, Marty, Bert and Ernie become eligible for military service in the first place? In September 1940, more than a year before America entered World War II, they all would have been subject to a federal draft law known as the Selective Training and Service Act. The act originally required all men between the ages of twenty-one and thirty-six to register. During the war, registration was gradually expanded to all men between eighteen and sixty-five. Of the more than 16 million who entered the military during World War II, 10 million did so courtesy of the act.

MUSIC NOTES: The song accompanying the beginning of the war years montage is a popular World War II number, "This Is the Army, Mr. Jones." The song was written by Irving Berlin for the 1942 musical play *This Is the Army,* which was later made into a film. The basic tongue-in-cheek message from this soldier's lament: Hey, bub, this is the Army, not the Waldorf Hotel—no private rooms, no housemaids, and you sure as heck ain't getting breakfast in bed.

DID YOU KNOW?: Mrs. Bailey and Mrs. Hatch contribute to the war effort by sewing for the Red Cross. As volunteers for the Red Cross, Mrs. Bailey and Mrs. Hatch had plenty of company. In 1945, over 7 million Americans were registered as Red Cross volunteers. Mrs. Bailey and Mrs. Hatch most likely were members of the Production Corps of the Red Cross' Volunteer Special Services, which was responsible for, among other things, repairing millions of pieces of clothing during the war.

CLOSER LOOK: Keep an eye out for two Red Cross posters behind Mrs. Hatch. They are tough to make out, but here are the details. Both posters are authentic. The one on the left features a female Red Cross worker tending to a young man in a wheelchair and reads, "YOUR RED CROSS must carry on! Give." The other one features a young woman tending to a bedridden patient. The top reads, "Now—more than ever—you need a HOME NURSING COURSE. Call Your RED CROSS." After 1941, as nurses and doctors pivoted from general hospital duties to war-related support, the pressure for home care capabilities spiked, with the Red Cross reporting that over 500,000 women completed the home care training course by the end of 1942 alone.

DID YOU KNOW? Despite having to care for her growing family, Mary found time to run Bedford Falls' USO chapter. The United Services Organization was formed back in 1941 by six or so organizations (including the Salvation Army, the YMCA, and the YWCA), with the goal of providing social services to military personnel and their families. In the montage she is shown serving coffee and doughnuts (with powdered milk available for any takers) to travel-weary servicemen at the Bedford Falls train station, a typical USO service.

FILM ANECDOTES: Conspicuously absent from the montage is Violet Bick. In fact, the script as it stood prior to filming did account for Violet's goings-on during the war years. Violet was to be shown in a park wearing a military uniform and surrounded by eight or so sailors, with the voice-over explaining that she "joined the WAVES until they found her kind of morale building would sink the Navy." The WAVES was a Navy women's volunteer reserve corps, short for Women Accepted for Volunteer Emergency Services. Fortunately, someone on the production team recognized that the bit crossed the line on taste.

We believe the WAVES montage did get filmed and, to add to the disappointment of losing the footage, it was an on-location shoot. Filming took place in Holmby Park, a sliver-of-a park tucked into the tony Los Angeles neighborhood of Holmby Hills. Then and now, Holmby Park features a throwback pitch-and-putt golf course, lawn bowling greens and a meandering water feature. Jane Wyman lived a few houses down and frequented the park in the late 1940s; the Playboy Mansion is nearby. It's a shame the footage didn't survive—it would be fun to see a uniformed Gloria Grahame with her sailor entourage and to match the scene to the park's current environs. As a consolation prize, you can see Grahame in military uniform in *It Happened in Brooklyn* (1947), and we must say she looks pretty spiffy.

HISTORY LESSON: During Sam Wainwright's segment of the war years montage, check out the female factory workers carrying airplane hoods on their heads—the one girl is cracking up pretty good. (1:15:25) In stark contrast to the Great Depression era, where women were urged to give up their jobs to men, the onset of

World War II pressed millions of women into the workforce to fill vacancies left by male draftees.

From 1940 to 1945, the percentage of females in the national workforce rose from 25 percent to 36 percent, with many women performing jobs that had traditionally been held only by men. Indeed, the need for women factory workers led to the creation of an iconic female figure dubbed "Rosie the Riveter." The workforce contribution of American women was crucial to the war cause as it enabled America to maintain wartime productivity. But at war's end, existing social mores led most women to relinquish their jobs to returning servicemen.

DID YOU KNOW?: Potter is shown reviewing draft registration papers and assigning draft classifications. For all three draftees he declares, "1A," which means that the person is fit for general military service. The implication here is that Potter doesn't let anyone off the hook, and this 1A bit likely got a chuckle out of audiences back in 1946.

Later on we learn George received a 4F draft classification due to his bad ear. 4F was a service deferral classification and meant that the person was physically, mentally or morally unfit for service. While George surely was hoping for 1A status (if for no other reason than to finally escape from the town he loves to hate), this is the one time where Potter actually does him a favor by correctly designating him as 4F, thus keeping him out of harm's way.

DID YOU KNOW?: As head of the local draft board overseeing Bedford Falls, Potter wielded considerable power. The World War II draft system included the formation of over 6,000 local draft boards, which were responsible for, among other things, registering men and determining their eligibility. While decisions of local boards were subject to review by a network of appeal boards, as a practical matter the ultimate military fate of a potential draftee was decided by the likes of Potter.

CLOSER LOOK: Mr. Gower and Uncle Billy, we are told, do their part by selling war bonds. While that may well have been the case, in the accompanying footage Mr. Gower is shown stumping with Mr. Martini and another guy who, to your eye, doesn't look much like Uncle Billy. (1:15:38) In any event, check out the platform the men use—it's an Army tank, parked right outside the county courthouse. The hatch that's open on the front left is for the driver. Mr. Martini is standing inside one of the turret hatches. Fear not! In case of a German invasion, Bedford Falls is prepared for battle!

This particular tank is a Sherman M4, the U.S.'s go-to tank during World War II. The U.S. cranked out an astounding number of M4s—more than 50,000—for use by all Allied forces. While it's fair to say the German tanks outclassed the Sherman, the Allies got by on strategy and sheer tank numbers.

FILM ANECDOTES: Of all the big-ticket vehicles Capra baked into the film, the Sherman M4 definitely takes the cake. It's not like he could call up a Hollywood rental outfit and have one delivered to the set the next day. In fact, Capra had to work directly with the Department of War to source the tank. Film correspondence reveals that the production team finally got a line on one just a few weeks before filming was scheduled to end, scrambling to get it delivered from out-of-state to RKO's Encino Ranch. An extraordinary amount of effort for a few seconds of film, and pure Capra.

CLOSER LOOK: A poster hanging from the tank's gun features the face of a battle-weary, bandaged soldier, with a decimated battlefield in the background. At the top, the poster reads, "Doing all you can do, brother?" A call to action at the bottom reads, "Buy War Bonds." The poster is authentic and was widely-distributed as part of the U.S. Treasury's war bond campaign. There is also a banner on the side of the tank (partially obscured) that includes the war-time slogan, "It's up to you."

HISTORY LESSON: War bonds were a critical source of government financing during World War II. With the national deficit rising sharply during the war, the government obtained half of the necessary funding for the war from war bonds. (The rest came mainly from increases in corporate and personal income taxes.) Through the War Finance Committee, which was in charge of the sale of bonds, the government raised nearly $200 billion.

Buying a war bond was a somewhat involved process. First you bought war bond stamps in various denominations (10 cents, 25 cents, 50 cents, etc.). Then you pasted the stamps into booklets until you had $18.75 worth of stamps. Then you traded in a full booklet for your war bond, which in ten years would be worth $25.

No American, it seems, was exempt from purchasing war bonds. Some 80 million people participated in the program. And in classrooms across the country, it was a weekly ritual for school children to purchase stamps with any small change they could get their hands on and paste them into their booklets.

RANDOM THOUGHTS: All these years after World War II, more than $16 billion worth of war bonds from that war remain unclaimed. They have all reached maturity and are no longer earning interest. So when you're looking for that Honus Wagner Sweet Caporal baseball card in your grandfather's attic, it wouldn't hurt to also keep an eye out for long-forgotten war bonds.

DID YOU KNOW?: While serving in North Africa, Bert the cop earned the Silver Star. Awarded for gallantry in action performed with marked distinction, the Silver Star was, at the time of Bert's service, America's fourth highest military honor (after the Medal of Honor, the Distinguished Service Cross and the Distinguished Service Medal). The fact that Bert was wounded in North Africa means that he also would have received the Purple Heart.

HISTORY LESSON: While the North Africa campaign of World War II is not as well known as the Western Europe and Pacific campaigns, it played a crucial role in shifting momentum in favor of the Allies and ultimately paved the way to Allied victory. The Allies sought control of North Africa to open up a strategically desirable "second front" in Western Europe via the Mediterranean Sea. For the Axis powers the gem was Egypt, which offered oil fields and the Suez Canal—a key strategic shortcut to the Far East.

In the summer of 1942, things were looking pretty grim for the Allies when Axis forces pounded the British in Libya and forged eastward, deep into Egypt. But the British hung tough, and by October had turned the tables, forcing the enemy into a full retreat back through Libya. One month later, the Americans got into the mix, coordinating with the British three huge land invasions to the west of Axis forces, one in Morocco (near Casablanca) and two in Algeria (at Oran and Algiers).

Converging now from the east and west, the Allies cornered Axis forces in Tunisia, and by May 1943 had ousted them from North Africa. And with that, the Allies turned their attention to opening up the aforementioned "second front," a process that kicked off in July 1943 with the invasion of Sicily.

HISTORY LESSON: The only thing we learn about Ernie's war experience is that he parachuted into France. If he did so on D-Day (June 6, 1944) he would have been a member of either the 101st or the 82nd U.S. Airborne Division. Over 13,000 paratroopers from these two divisions participated in the drop, which was complicated by low visibility, heavy German antiaircraft artillery, flooded landing zones, and gear that weighed nearly as much as the paratroopers themselves. Casualties were high—some 2,500 between the two divisions on D-Day alone—so Ernie could have used a guardian angel of his own to get through this mission unscathed.

HISTORY LESSON: As for Marty Hatch, we learn that he fought in Western Europe and helped capture "Remagen Bridge." In so doing, Marty participated in one of the more storied battles of World War II. The bridge was strategically significant as it spanned the Rhine River. In the spring of 1945, the Rhine had become a natural barrier between advancing Allied troops and retreating German troops. As the Germans moved east across the Rhine, they systematically destroyed bridges to inhibit Allied pursuit.

However, on March 7, 1945, an American armored division discovered to its amazement a railway bridge in Remagen, Germany, still standing. Although the division was supposed to remain on the west side of the Rhine, the opportunity proved too great to pass up, and the division seized the bridge and secured the area immediately east of it. For ten days, the Americans held the bridge intact, enabling troops and heavy equipment to cross the Rhine. By the time the bridge collapsed, the Americans had constructed backup pontoon bridges and established significant footholds east of the Rhine.

Capturing the bridge was a huge strategic coup in that it enabled Allied forces to quickly surround and capture several hundred thousand German troops and, in consequence, shortened the war. For that reason, General Eisenhower declared the bridge to be "worth its weight in gold."

FILM ANECDOTES: The background footage used for Marty's vignette is actual Army footage taken during the bridge's capture. We've viewed it, and it's super cool to watch proud U.S. soldiers, just like Marty, enjoying their success. Now, look for a small white sign posted on the bridge tower, just to Marty's right. That sign is not original to the bridge—it had just been posted by U.S. soldiers and reads, "CROSS THE RHINE WITH DRY FEET COURTESY OF 9TH ARM'D DIV." Good stuff from Marty and his mates.

CLOSER LOOK: Marty apparently led a charmed life during the war. Check out the back of his helmet—it appears to have been struck by a bullet. (1:15:49)

RANDOM THOUGHTS: While Harry's downing of fifteen enemy planes is impressive by any standard, his numbers are well short of those posted by the real-life flying aces of World War II. The record for downed enemy planes during World War II was set by Richard Bong of Poplar, Wisconsin, who took out forty during the Pacific Campaign before being discharged in 1944. After surviving hundreds of combat missions, Bong was killed in a routine test flight just months after returning home.

CLOSER LOOK: As Harry heads out the door on his next mission, a flight board next to him announces a temperature of 83 degrees and a dew point of 73. The forecast reads, "increasing cloudiness and [showers] expected in the afternoon." (1:15:55) Below that is "point option" information, which tells the pilots where the carrier is expected to be when they return from their mission. Well, that sounds important. Okay, Harry. Good luck, be careful out there and don't forget the point option!

FILM ANECDOTES: You may have already guessed that the footage accompanying Harry's montage segment is real World War II footage. But what you surely didn't know is that the footage was borrowed from another film, *The Fighting Lady* (1944). The film is a Navy wartime documentary about life aboard an American aircraft carrier as it battled its way through the Pacific theater from July 1943 to June 1944. Shot entirely in color, the film is chockablock with amazing footage of American bombing raids, dogfights with Japanese Zeros and surprise Japanese air attacks. Most of the film's footage came from the USS *Yorktown*, including all four clips that appear in *Wonderful Life*.

The first of the four clips shows Harry (through the wonders of a process shot) heading out onto the flight deck with his fellow *Yorktown* pilots. The next clip, filmed from the nose of a *Yorktown* plane (perhaps Harry's), shows a Japanese fighter plane being shot down during a battle known as the Great Marianas Turkey Shoot. The Americans downed well over 300 Japanese planes during the battle, so Harry surely got a few of his fifteen here.

The last two clips are from a surprise attack on the *Yorktown* by a swarm of Japanese torpedo planes, which means that Harry and his fellow pilots would have been stuck on the flight deck for this action. The first shows a torpedo plane being relentlessly strafed by *Yorktown* fire. The second shows a *Yorktown* crewman cheering as an enemy plane heads into the drink in flames.

HISTORY LESSON: Following Harry's exploits, the montage shows George serving as a war ration administrator for the Office of Price Administration (OPA); signage in the window tells us so. Other signs explain that he's overseeing rationing for tires and gasoline. And look for the ration books clutched by a few of the folks pressing in on George.

The OPA was a federal agency established in 1941 for the purpose of preventing inflation during the war. The OPA created ceiling prices for various commodities and also had the power to ration scarce commodities such as sugar, gasoline, tires and coffee. Gas rationing was a particular source of anxiety as those stuck with a lower-tier ration book had to get by on just a few gallons of gas per week.

FILM ANECDOTES: Across the street from the OPA is Bedford Falls' barber shop—you can see the shop's signage through the front window of the OPA as George attempts to bring order to the rationing process. From this we know that the OPA is a wartime tenant of the space occupied by Anderson's. The Building & Loan is above Anderson's, so George has a short commute to his wartime job

HISTORY LESSON: Next George is shown performing another thankless wartime job—that of the air-raid warden. Concern over enemy bombing raids, and the general need for federal, state and local coordination on wartime emergencies, led to the creation of the Office of Civilian Defense (OCD). George would have volunteered for the position and responsibilities included coordinating and implementing town-wide blackouts in an effort to prevent enemy planes from finding their targets. Typically, every neighborhood had its own air-raid warden, who was responsible for patrolling the neighborhood during blackout drills to ensure compliance.

Visible on George's standard issue air-raid warden armband and helmet is the actual OCD insignia for an air-raid warden. George is shown bringing a "light violation" to the attention of a slightly perturbed neighbor. (1:16:18) Any light visible from the street, even the faintest glow from a radio, would invite a knock on the door from a fastidious warden. To alleviate the inconvenience, many folks installed blackout curtains in a designated room; otherwise you had to ride things out in the dark until you received the "all clear" signal.

CLOSER LOOK: The montage contains stock footage of what a banner identifies as an "Official Rubber Collection Depot." This particular rubber collection depot was in Washington, D.C.—at the very beginning of the clip you can see the U.S. Capitol in the background on the left. (1:16:31) Also on the banner is the slogan, "Get in the Scrap." This slogan was created by the Office of Emergency Management to encourage wartime donation of metals, paper, rags and rubber.

Another popular conservation program called for Americans to plant "Victory Gardens" as a means of decreasing the demand for certain food staples. While some programs had more direct relevance to the war than others, as a whole the programs were a huge success as morale boosters, giving Americans at home a sense of contributing to the war effort.

HISTORY LESSON: Joseph explains that, like everyone else, George "wept and prayed" on "VE-Day" and "VJ-Day." VE-Day stands for "Victory in Europe," which took place on May 8, 1945, the day after the Germans officially surrendered. VJ-Day stands for "Victory over Japan." President Truman announced Japan's surrender on August 14, 1945, U.S. time, but the U.S. has historically recognized VJ-Day as September 2, 1945. That's the date Japan signed the surrender agreement on the USS *Missouri*. President Truman also declared that day to be VJ-Day in a national radio address.

HISTORY LESSON: The last piece of the montage shows a church calendar calling for "special prayers" on Sunday, August 19, 1945, "as requested by President Truman." (1:16:39) Sure enough, our research revealed that on August 16, 1945, Truman issued a proclamation that designated August 19 (the first Sunday after Japan's unofficial surrender) as "a day of prayer" and called upon Americans "to dedicate this day of prayer to the memory of those who have given their lives to make possible our victory."

RANDOM THOUGHTS: As Joseph continues to explain who did what during the war, the head angel, Franklin, suddenly interjects, "Joseph now show him what happened today." Well, this is a pleasant surprise. We thought Franklin had excused himself from the meeting right after getting Joseph and Clarence together, leaving them to figure things out. But apparently he's been a silent participant in Joseph and Clarence's meeting throughout.

CAST ANECDOTES: Just like George and Mary Bailey, Jimmy Stewart and Donna Reed both made substantial contributions to the war effort. Among Hollywood actors, Stewart led the charge to volunteer for military service. After World War II broke out in September 1939, Stewart actually began taking flying lessons with the aim of becoming an Army pilot. By March 1941, he had joined the Army Air Corps as a private, and by 1943 he was stationed in Norfolk, England, as a combat pilot with the 445th Bombardment Group.

Stewart's military achievements as a flyboy are impressive indeed. With some twenty combat missions to his credit, Stewart served as squadron commander, was twice awarded the Distinguished Flying Cross, and by war's end held the rank of colonel. And, to top it off, several years after the war, Stewart was promoted to brigadier general (that's a one-star general) in the Air Force Reserve.

Reed did her part by touring stateside military camps with other performers, providing much-welcomed entertainment for the troops. These tours would have been organized by the USO, the same organization that Mary Bailey worked for during the war. Reed also spent considerable time selling war bonds, where her smarts, charm and beauty made her a natural pitch person.

CHRISTMAS EVE 1945

"You just can't keep those Baileys down, now can you, Mr. Potter?"

—UNCLE BILLY

We made it! We're finally back to Christmas Eve 1945. And the day actually starts off quite well for George. The town is bedecked with Christmas decorations and abuzz with news that its very own war hero, Harry Bailey, is coming home for a grand celebration. Harry's accomplishments have George brimming with pride, and George brags about him to anyone who will listen.

So Harry's coming home and it's Christmas Eve—what could possibly throw such a joyous day into turmoil? Enter Uncle Billy. All he has to do is walk over to the Bedford Falls Trust and Savings Bank, fill out a deposit slip and head for the teller's window and all will be right in the world. But Uncle Billy can't help himself—he has to stick it to that "old buzzard" Potter in the bank lobby. While doing so, Uncle Billy accidentally slips the deposit money into Potter's newspaper and hands the entire bundle back to Potter.

Moments later Potter discovers Uncle Billy's blunder and instantly realizes that losing this money would spell doom for the Building & Loan. Having been handed a golden opportunity to finally put the Building & Loan out of business, Potter has nary a thought of returning the money.

Back at the Building & Loan the bank examiner is anxious to review the company's books, while a case of the "holiday blues" has Violet seeking help from George so she can skip town and get a fresh start. When the scatterbrained Uncle Billy returns from his bank errand, it's apparent that he's in more of a fog than usual. Before long Uncle Billy is forced to come clean—he has lost the deposit money. It takes George about a half a second to figure out that if they don't find the money today, they will be in a serious pickle with the authorities. With that, he and Uncle Billy set out to retrace Uncle Billy's every last step.

George Spreads News of Harry's Return

FILM ANECDOTES: The scene opens up with a nice establishing shot of downtown Bedford falls, and more specifically the corner on which the Bedford Falls Trust and Savings Bank is located. Now, take a hard look at the bank's front door and, surprise, you will see George and Uncle Billy coming out the bank's entrance and walking down the sidewalk. Wow, what is going on here? Well, here's another instance of the production team making use of excess footage that actually captures action from a later scene. You see, this footage is from the start of George and Uncle Billy's search for the $8,000. And in a few minutes we will see more footage from the same shoot, showing George and Uncle Billy a little farther down the sidewalk and, then, crossing the street.

CLOSER LOOK: Also by the front door is Potter's horse-drawn carriage. We'll get a better look at the carriage once Uncle Billy gets to the bank. His continued use of the carriage as his main mode of transportation post-World War II perfectly captures what stubborn old bird he is.

EXPLANATION REQUIRED: The "present day" in the film seems obvious as Christmas Eve 1945, largely because the day is devoted to Harry's war accomplishments. But the film never says as much, and for some reason the film's shooting schedule repeatedly refers to the Christmas Eve scenes as being set in December 1946. So technically it's possible that Harry received the Medal of Honor a year and three months after the war ended in September 1945. While the local newspaper should have cleared things up, no date appears on the front page. (1:16:55) Fortunately, the film playing at the theater next to Gower Drugs, *The Bells of St. Mary's*, provides the answer as it was released in 1945.

RANDOM THOUGHTS: By the way, *The Bells of St. Mary's* is itself a film worth checking out. The film features Bing Crosby as a good-natured priest charged with turning around a run-down parochial school. It's the sequel to *Going My Way* (Best Picture in 1944) and stacked up quite well with the original, earning nominations for Best Picture, Best Actor (Crosby), Best Director and Best Actress (Ingrid Bergman), though it lost in all four categories.

CAST ANECDOTES: If you need further incentive to check out *The Bells of St. Mary's*, how about the fact that the actor who plays Clarence, Henry Travers, is featured in it. Plus, you get to see him playing a curmudgeon, in contrast to his typical role as the affable gent. Travers' most acclaimed film was *Mrs. Miniver* (1942), a war propaganda film designed to invoke sympathy for the British war cause among isolationist-minded Americans. Interestingly, Travers played the leading role in the stage version of *You Can't Take It With You*, which *Wonderful Life's* director Frank Capra later adapted for film. But Capra cast Lionel Barrymore for the part played by Travers. Perhaps this earlier casting oversight was weighing on Capra's mind when he decided to cast Travers in the plum role of Clarence.

CLOSER LOOK: No word on what the "Second Great Feature" is advertised on the theater's marquee, but the side of the marquee indicates that moviegoers will also be treated to a newsreel from RKO-Pathe and a cartoon short starring Donald Duck. (1:16:52) These listings are also legible when George runs past the theater at the end of the film. (2:03:05)

RKO-Pathe was one of the major newsreel companies in the 1930s and 1940s that supplied American movie theaters with news shorts covering topical events. These newsreels were an important means of communicating news in the pre-television era, and were especially popular during World War II as Americans clamored for updates on the war. As for Donald Duck, he had been around since June 1934. His cartoon shorts were a staple at theaters in the 1940s, particularly during the war.

FILM ANECDOTES: Liberty Films engaged RKO Radio Pictures to distribute *Wonderful Life*, so it makes perfect sense that the production team incorporated into the marquee a reference to RKO's newsreel arm. Same goes for the Donald Duck short—at the time RKO was the sole distributer of Disney cartoons. And what about *The Bells of St. Mary's*, is that an RKO film? You bet. There was zero chance that another studio's film would find its way onto that marquee.

RANDOM THOUGHTS: Forgive us for being picky, but we must take issue with the wording of the portion of the newspaper headline announcing Harry's latest military exploit that reads, LOCAL BOY WINS CONGRESSIONAL MEDAL OF HONOR. (1:16:55) First, military personnel well know that the Medal of Honor is earned, not "won." Second, the medal's official name is the Medal of Honor, sans "Congressional." Finally, as long as we're flyspecking, Harry is hardly a "boy" as he would be around thirty-four in this scene.

DID YOU KNOW?: Make no mistake—Harry's receipt of the Medal of Honor is a huge deal. Awarded for "conspicuous gallantry and intrepidity at risk of life above and beyond the call of duty," the Medal of Honor is America's highest military decoration. It was first awarded in 1863 during the Civil War, and since then just over 3,500 military personnel have received the award.

Out of approximately 440 military personnel receiving Medals of Honor during World War II, only two were Navy pilots like Harry Bailey—David McCampbell and Butch O'Hare. Of these two men, O'Hare's accomplishments most closely resembled Harry's saving of a transport full of soldiers. In 1942, O'Hare received the Medal of Honor for singlehandedly saving the USS *Lexington* by downing five Japanese planes in one skirmish. O'Hare returned home to receive the medal, but then headed back to the Pacific theater, where he was killed in combat in 1943. O'Hare's heroics prompted the city of Chicago to rename its airport, then known as Orchard Field, in his honor.

CLOSER LOOK: Here are the other headlines appearing on the newspaper's front page:

- PRESIDENT DECORATES HARRY BAILEY
- PRESIDENT DECORATES OUR OWN HARRY
- NATIONAL HERO
- CITY TO CELEBRATE HERO'S HOMECOMING
- COMMANDER HARRY BAILEY, FAMOUS NAVY AIR ACE, BORN AND RAISED IN BEDFORD FALLS, WAS DECORATED YESTERDAY WITH THE NATION'S HIGHEST HONOR

FILM ANECDOTES: A photograph on the front page portrays Harry receiving the Medal of Honor from President Harry S. Truman, who more than once declared, "I would rather have that medal than be president." RKO's legal advisors were sufficiently worried about having someone impersonating the president in the photograph that they actually recommended obtaining permission from the White House to do so. With that, we are now up to four U.S. president sightings in the film.

CLOSER LOOK: Impressively, the Medal of Honor is accurately depicted in the photograph, shown attached to a ribbon and worn around Harry's neck. It's the only American military award worn around the neck.

JUST WONDERING: On the newspaper's front page, look for the film crew's playful use of shadows, featuring George and his pipe and Ernie and his taxi cap. Now, were those shadows cast by the actors or the work of shadow doubles?

CLOSER LOOK: Bedford Falls' newspaper is *The Bedford Falls Sentinel.* It costs five cents and boasts that it is the COUNTY'S LEADING NEWSPAPER. The weather forecast appears in the upper right corner of the front page, and calls for SNOW TONIGHT. Sure enough, it's not snowing during the day when George and Uncle Billy search for the bank deposit, but by evening the predicted snowstorm has arrived.

FILM ANECDOTES: While the forecast on Christmas Eve in Bedford Falls called for snow, temperatures were actually in the mid-eighties on the set. These snow scenes were shot on the Encino Ranch on a mid-June day, and temperatures topped out at 86 degrees that day in nearby Van Nuys. Stewart certainly looks cold, but he had to be more than a little uncomfortable wearing a winter overcoat and scarf.

DID YOU KNOW?: By the end of the war Harry had reached the rank of commander, which meant that Harry was fully qualified to serve as the commanding officer on a warship.

CAST ANECDOTES: The actor who plays Harry Bailey, Todd Karns, appears as a Navy man in another film classic, *The Caine Mutiny* (1954). In a somewhat reminiscent storyline, his character, a helmsman aboard the USS *Caine*, saves the lives of every man on that ship by deciding not to follow the navigational orders of Lieutenant Commander Queeg (Humphrey Bogart) during a raging typhoon. One of Karns' first films was *The Courtship of Andy Hardy* (1942), in which an upstart Donna Reed also appears.

FILM ANECDOTES: Christmas Eve starts with Ernie at his call box, which all these years later is still located right across the street from Gower Drugs. But something has changed. That is definitely not the taxi we've seen Ernie driving in previous years.

Well, it certainly make sense to have Ernie in an updated ride by the time we reach 1945. Seventeen plus years would be a long time to maintain a taxi, particularly in snowy New York. But while he upgraded in size, he didn't upgrade in years by all that much. Ernie went from a 1930 GMC taxi (yep, not quite old enough for the 1928 downtown scene with George, Bert and Ernie) to a 1936 DeSoto Airstream sedan. The DeSoto was a seven-passenger behemoth that was a better fit for New York City than Bedford Falls. Here, Ernie sprung for the deluxe model.

This Airstream has two cool features. First, its unique rooftop call light—a series of three sunbursts—tracks to a real taxi outfit, the Sunshine Taxi Cab Company. Sunshine managed a fleet of these cars in nearby New York City. And the fact that it's a Sunshine cab means that it comes with a sliding sunroof over the backseat passengers. Sure enough, later on in the film, when Ernie drops off George at 320 Sycamore in Pottersville you can see the edges of the sunroof. The sunroof may not be a hit with passengers in Bedford Falls, but it definitely was with those gazing at the skyscrapers of Manhattan.

CLOSER LOOK: We pointed out earlier that Gower Drugs has a delivery bike. In this scene, you can see a bike stand on the sidewalk outside the store as George and Ernie revel in Harry's accomplishments. (1:15:46)

Uncle Billy Heads to the Bank

FILM ANECDOTES: There's a celebration in the works for Harry, and parked outside the courthouse is an ideal car for the occasion—it's a late 1930s Cadillac convertible sedan. This car is a monster, with a noticeably long wheelbase, and really is a car in search of a parade. The car is all set for Harry's return, with American flag bunting draped on the front and off the sides. But we know that snow is on the way, so someone will need to put the top up on this beauty.

RANDOM THOUGHTS: While black-and-white will always be our preferred format for watching the film (that was Capra's artistic intent, right?), the downtown scenes on Christmas Eve day are pretty wild to watch in the colorized format. With the festivities for Harry occurring over Christmas, downtown Bedford Falls looks like Christmas meets the Fourth of July. That's because there is American flag bunting and other patriotic-themed decorations hung throughout downtown, layered on top of the elaborate holiday-themed decorations. It's really quite a fun visual.

FILM ANECDOTES: And while we are talking about Christmas decorations, Capra borrowed some of the downtown Bedford Falls Christmas decorations from the city of Glendale, California. These would have been Glendale's decorations for the 1945 holiday season. Indeed, one photo of the city's decorations that year matches the decorations on the streetlamp behind George, Ernie and Mr. Gower in this scene. This makes perfect sense. Why go to the huge trouble of creating all those props and on such a massive scale when a city like Glendale would have decorations ready-made and be more than happy to loan them out.

EXPLANATION REQUIRED: Uncle Billy salutes the occupants of a vehicle that passes in front of him because they're driving a military jeep. The same jeep appears in the very first shot of downtown Bedford Falls on Christmas Eve, passing in front of Potter's bank. Willys-Overland and Ford both made jeeps and worked off the same blueprints, and the differences are so subtle that it's hard to say whether this one's a Willys MB or a Ford GPW. Unlike the Sherman tank, it would have been easy for Capra to rent this military jeep—over 640,000 were made during the war and plenty stayed home-side. In this shot, you can see the military star on the hood, and a smaller one on the right back panel. (1:17:24) The jeep should have military identification markings on the side of the hood, but they've either been removed or covered up by fake snow.

JUST WONDERING: Is it really a good idea, or even necessary, for the Building & Loan to maintain an account at Potter's bank? The Building & Loan is essentially a savings and loan, which means that it is a bank itself and should have no need to deal with Potter. At the very least, how about finding another bank, perhaps in a nearby town? By depositing money at Potter's bank, the Building & Loan is allowing its direct competitor to make money off the backs of Building & Loan shareholders.

George Arrives at the Building & Loan

CLOSER LOOK: Another tough day for the prop team makes for a few more film gaffes during the Building & Loan office scenes on Christmas Eve. First, George walks into the office with a Christmas wreath on his arm and sets it down on a chair to take a call from his brother Harry. (1:17:38) However, when the film cuts to George talking on the phone the wreath magically appears back on his arm. (1:17:42)

Next, as George walks with the bank examiner to another office, the film cuts again and George's pipe suddenly switches from his left hand to his right. (1:18:51) Finally, a few scenes later when George meets with Violet in his office, his pipe suddenly disappears from his mouth in between shots. (1:21:46)

RANDOM THOUGHTS: This scene opens with George completing what we like to call the smoking trifecta. At Harry's "welcome home" party, he has a contemplative cigarette in front of the house. In Potter's office he accepts and puffs away on a cigar. And here George shows up with a pipe in his mouth, albeit unlit. But this is actually not the first time we find George chomping on a pipe. During the war montage, as he gruffly carries out his rationing duties at the OPA, he does so with pipe in mouth.

Uncle Billy at the Bank

CLOSER LOOK: Watch Uncle Billy thumb the bills as he prepares to fill out a deposit slip. (1:19:08) Slow motion shows that the wad is comprised mostly of five dollar bills, and perhaps a few tens. If we were to assume that half of the deposit consists of fives and the other half of tens, Uncle Billy should have 1,067 bills in his pile—534 fives and 533 tens. It looks to us like he barely has twenty.

DID YOU KNOW?: As Uncle Billy prepares his deposit, look for a starred flag on the wall. Thirty stars arranged in six rows, plus one larger star, lighter in color than the others, in the center. This is what's known as a "service flag." With its origins in World War I, services flags really took off in World War II. The concept was straightforward—families with a member serving in the armed forces during the war hung flags with a blue star. Over time, the practice evolved to replacing a blue star with a gold star if the family member died. This is where "Gold Star Mothers" comes from.

During World War II, the tradition expanded beyond individual families. Churches and businesses, for example, would create large flags for their communities. With that background, based on the number of stars, we think this service flag is meant to be one created by the bank, representing former bank employees serving or bank employee family members serving or both—thirty-one in all, with one fatality.

CLOSER LOOK: At the counter where Uncle Billy fills out his deposit slip, the day of the week is shown as Monday. (1:20:01) In fact, Christmas Eve 1945 actually did fall on a Monday, so kudos to the prop department for getting this one right.

CLOSER LOOK: The bank's "Information" counter is to the right of the front door. A Red Cross display resting on the counter shows a woman's profile below the Red Cross logo and reads, "Always Serving—Give Now—Your Red Cross Must Carry On."

JUST WONDERING: Earlier we wondered how Potter gets up to the Building & Loan offices, and here we have a similar question: How is he getting in and out of that carriage? Is he in the wheelchair while he's inside the carriage? Is there a ramp for the wheelchair? Whatever the process, the carriage is one of the more impractical rides we can think of for someone confined to a wheelchair.

RANDOM THOUGHTS: This scene contains one of the better curmudgeonly Potterisms. As Uncle Billy is sticking it to Potter in the bank lobby, Potter refers to his crosstown rival as "Slacker George." Here are a few other barbs from Potter: "Discontented lazy rabble" (referring to the working class of Bedford Falls); "Sentimental hogwash" (dismissing George's impassioned speech to the board); "A miserable little clerk" (referring to George); and "You're worth more dead than alive" (referring to George).

CLOSER LOOK: Some twenty-six years after we first saw Uncle Billy's reminder strings fail him, he's still making use of them. The string on his index finger is probably to remind him to stop off at the bank to make the deposit. And the one on his pinkie? Ah, if only it was to remind him not to hand the deposit to Potter.

RANDOM THOUGHTS: The $8,000 lost by Uncle Billy is substantial by any measure, but considering that $8,000 back in 1945 is equivalent to $120,000 today, there's no mistaking that Uncle Billy messed up big time.

CLOSER LOOK: As Uncle Billy heads to make his deposit, look for two more war-related, patriotic items on display. On the wall, left of the tellers' windows, hangs a plaque that reads, "We are Proud of the Men From This Organization Who are Defending the Cause of God, Humanity and America." This is an authentic plaque, created by a World War I veteran and sold during 1918 as a "National Honor Tablet" to American businesses and clubs as a way to show their pride in, and appreciation for, their members' war contributions. A smaller version, with modified phrasing, was available to homeowners.

To the right of Uncle Billy's selected window is another Red Cross advertisement. This one reads, "Always Serves—Give Now" and features service members and civilians, representative of Red Cross causes, flanking the centered uniformed Red Cross nurse. A larger version of this one shows up again in downtown Bedford Falls, and we'll point it out when the time comes.

CLOSER LOOK: On the front door is the bank's name—Bedford Falls Trust and Savings Bank. Below that are the bank's business hours and below that is a description of banking services offered, which reads, "Commercial—Savings—Escrows." (1:20:52)

Back at the Building & Loan

CAST ANECDOTES: We talked earlier about Jimmy the Raven's talents, and here we see his finest work of the film. As Thomas Mitchell (Uncle Billy) walks in the door, he raises his left arm as a perch and Jimmy nails his cue perfectly. Jimmy stays on Mitchell's arm all the way back into Uncle Billy's office, providing a few squawks along the way and adding to Uncle Billy's eccentricity but without ever interfering with the scene. Great acting, Jimmy!

CLOSER LOOK: Two war-related posters can be found in the Building & Loan during this scene. One is for the Red Cross and features the slogan, "On the Job—Always!" (1:17:37) The other is a plea to continue giving to another humanitarian aid-based organization that was originally called the War Chest and was later renamed, for obvious reasons, the Victory Chest. The poster reads, "Carry on…for Our Fighting Forces, Our Own at Home, Our Suffering Allies. Give. Victory/War Chest." (1:17:46) The community chest organizations that formed the War/Victory Chest were the precursor to the United Way.

HISTORY LESSON: Inside George's office we find a framed saying titled, "The Noble Structure." The specifics of the saying escaped us for years, but we have figured it out—it's the following quote from Calvin Coolidge:

> The man who builds a factory builds a temple, that the man who works there worships there, and to each is due, not scorn and blame, but reverence and praise.

Heady stuff, for sure, and delivered in Coolidge's typical lofty, academic prose. The quote dates to a speech Coolidge made at Amherst College several years before his presidency, and was aimed at conveying his high regard for labor and business, which seems to align well enough with Bailey sensibilities. While we don't know whose idea it was to add the saying to the set design of George's office, we can share the coincidental fun fact that Jimmy Stewart matriculated for a time with Coolidge's sons at Mercersburg Academy.

EXPLANATION REQUIRED: So what exactly is George doing for Violet in his office? Well, the script as it stood prior to filming provides the answer. The scene was to open with George typing out a generic letter of recommendation for Violet to help her in her job search in New York City. Look for the typewriter on George's desk. In a not-so-subtle hint as to why she's leaving town, Violet wryly suggests that George mention in the letter that "the good city mothers boycotted me and practically ran me out of town."

Instead George types: "The bearer, Miss Violet Bick, has been employed as a clerk by this company for the past two years. The undersigned is glad to recommend her for intelligence, ability and good character." As Violet watches over George's shoulder she points out the untruths, including her having "good character." All of this explains why the scene, as we know it, opens with George handing Violet a letter and Violet saying, "Character? If I had any character I'd…"

JUST WONDERING: Is George so geographically clueless after having been trapped in Bedford Falls all these years that he doesn't know where New York City is in relation to Bedford Falls? As George helps Violet get a fresh start in "New York" (meaning New York City), he hands her a few extra dollars and remarks "they charge for meals and rent up there just the same as they do in Bedford Falls." Unless Bedford Falls has relocated to New Jersey, New York City would be "down there" vis-à-vis Bedford Falls.

Uncle Billy Back at the Bank with George

RANDOM THOUGHTS: We know Uncle Billy's memory is shot, but his brain cramp involving the $8,000 is of epic proportion. First, Uncle Billy surely must know that he had the $8,000 inside the bank—he just counted it at the counter and even filled out a deposit slip. But he didn't have the deposit when he got to teller's window, which means the money is somewhere inside the bank. So it makes no sense to run out onto the streets with George on the theory that he dropped the cash on the way to the bank. And it makes even less sense to head home and start looking in all his secret hiding places. Think, Uncle Billy, think! You had the money at the bank!

Uncle Billy's Study

CLOSER LOOK: Have you spotted all of Uncle Billy's pets? It's no secret that Uncle Billy is a little quirky, but his study is just a few critters short of a zoo. In addition to Uncle Billy's consolatory squirrel, look for the following other animals as George reads Uncle Billy the riot act: a dog, a monkey, an owl, a mouse or two, and four birds, which our sources peg as small parrots. Uncle Billy's squirrel seems so cute, and believe it or not pet squirrels were a real thing back in the 1700s—Ben Franklin owned one named Mungo. But there are lots of reasons why it's a bad idea to have a pet squirrel, including razor sharp claws, wild tendencies that defy taming and very untidy habits. These animals were supplied by the animal trainer we mentioned earlier, Curley Twiford. The squirrel is almost certainly Curley's beloved Snoopy, who was another one of Curley's star performers and money makers.

CAST ANECDOTES: Now that we know that Snoopy the Squirrel and Jimmy the Raven share the same trainer and are close friends, wouldn't it be cool if they had had a scene together? Well, a year after *Wonderful Life*, Hal Landon (Marty) had a lead role in *Springtime in the Sierras*, and in it he has a scene with Snoopy on his shoulder and Jimmy the Raven on his arm. Yes, this was another film that Curley Twiford worked on, and we must say Snoopy's acting rivals Jimmy's.

EXPLANATION REQUIRED: During Uncle Billy's heated exchange with George, we learn that Uncle Billy is a widower. Though it's tough to hear through his hysterical sobbing, Uncle Billy cries, "I've gone over the whole house, even in rooms that have been locked ever since I lost Laura." To be sure, he's really torn this room apart. There are even drawers on the desk and floor that he's pulled out of cabinets.

CAST ANECDOTES: Thomas Mitchell, who plays Uncle Billy, had the Midas touch: nearly every film he appeared in was well received. In 1939 alone, Mitchell appeared in no less than five blockbuster films: *Mr. Smith Goes to Washington*, *The Hunchback of Notre Dame*, *Only Angels Have Wings*, *Stagecoach*, and, to top the year off, *Gone with the Wind* (as Scarlett O'Hara's father). Of these gems, *Stagecoach* actually won him the 1939 Academy Award for Best Supporting Actor. Other Mitchell film credits include Capra's *Lost Horizon* (1937) and *High Noon* (1952).

SOMETHING'S THE MATTER WITH DADDY

"Why did we have to live here in the first place and stay around this measly, crummy old town?"

—GEORGE BAILEY

George and Uncle Billy's frantic search for the bank deposit turns up nothing, and George returns home resigned to the fact that he's going to take the fall for Uncle Billy's epic blunder. Not even the vision of his lovely wife and kids preparing for a family Christmas Eve party can ease George's mind. And when a tearful George smothers his youngest son with hugs, Mary recognizes that something is amiss. Sure, George is a moody guy, but she's never seen him quite like this.

With each passing minute George gets more and more irascible. After some mean-spirited grousing in the kitchen ("Why did we have to have all these kids?!"), George heads upstairs to check on Zuzu, who caught a cold on the way home from school. Zuzu is busy caring for a flower, and when a few petals fall off, she asks daddy to fix it. George obliges by pretending to reattach the fallen petals, while secreting them into his watch pocket.

Any hope that George's visit with Zuzu might have a calming effect on him is quickly dashed upon his return downstairs. First he bawls out Zuzu's teacher on the phone, accusing her of causing Zuzu's sickness. Then he lays into each of the kids for, well, being kids. Then he goes ballistic and trashes his work area in front of the whole family. Finally, just as he seems to be gathering himself, he starts laying into the kids again! With this, Mary has seen enough. George too knows he's crossed the line, and before Mary can do the honors, he gives himself the boot and heads out into the night.

Probably the last place we'd expect to find George after leaving his home is Potter's office. But here he is, pleading with that "scurvy little spider" for a rather extraordinary favor—a loan of a mere $8,000. If only George's old pal Sam Wainwright was around, he would loan George the money in a heartbeat. Alas, he is overseas, so it's Potter or nothing. George swallows his pride and pleads for mercy. But George is in for a rude awakening. Potter has had it in for George and the Building & Loan for nearly two decades, and he's not about to let this prime chance to take them both down slip through his cold, clammy fingers. Before George can even get out the door, Potter is on the horn to the authorities alerting them that George has "stolen" Building & Loan funds.

Having received a healthy dose of reality from Potter, George now finds himself on the lam. So where does a man go in such a predicament? Why, the local watering hole of course! Sure, the sheriff will soon be on his trail, but when a man needs a drink, he needs a drink. So it's off to Martini's for a couple of stiff ones.

Martini's is a classic family style Italian restaurant. Mr. Martini greets his customers by name at the door, Nick pours a heavy drink, and the room is filled with the sounds of Italian arias. But George isn't paying much attention to the ambience—he needs help fast and seeks divine intervention between sips of bourbon.

For the time being, the only "answer" to his prayers comes in the form of a sucker punch from Zuzu's teacher's husband. Talk about bad luck! What are the odds of pulling up a bar stool right next to the man whose wife you bawled out on the phone just hours earlier? Bleeding from the mouth, George gathers himself as best he can, makes sure that he still has his life insurance policy, and, to Mr. Martini's dismay, heads back out the door. Moments later, George crashes his car into a tree and then scurries off into the night, staying just a few steps ahead of the law.

George Arrives Home on Christmas Eve

FILM ANECDOTES: While the film itself does not reveal the ages of the Bailey Children on Christmas Eve, the final script has Pete as nine, Janie eight, Zuzu six and Tommy three. George and Mary therefore had their first child in 1936, when George and Mary are around thirty and twenty-six, respectively. But Pete's age doesn't fit with the timing of Mary's first pregnancy, which she announced to George in June 1934. If we assume that Pete was born in January 1935, that would make him ten, almost eleven, on Christmas Eve 1945. We are going with the film, not the script, on this one.

CLOSER LOOK: George's return home on Christmas Eve gives us a good look at the downstairs layout for 320 Sycamore. Take a few minutes to tour the first floor using the floor plan we've created. Keep in mind that we have confined the floor plan to what we actually know about the first floor, so the footprint for the house would likely be larger. Also, the fact that this is a movie set accounts for some inconsistencies with the exterior of the house as well as the second floor. Finally, thinking back to their honeymoon, remember that George and Mary dined in what became the living room and slept in what became the dining room.

DID YOU KNOW?: The set for the Bailey house is filled with details that give it a real sense of home, right down to the doilies on the chair backs. (1:25:20) The doilies are called *antimacassars* and are a Victorian-era throwback used for keeping men's hair oil from staining the backs of chairs and sofas. Macassar was a brand of hair oil that was popular back in the day. While we doubt George is making use of Macassar oil here, his hair is pretty wet (owing to his having left his hat at the office) so the antimacassar does come in handy here.

CLOSER LOOK: There are more Bailey children's toys in this scene, some are harder to spot than others. The boys have on Santa masks of course, and Tommy's working a toy carpet sweeper while wearing a cowboy holster and gun. And there's a doll on top of the piano.

But the wildest toy we spied here is resting on the phone table of all places. It's a pull toy made up of a wooden doll attached horizontally to a set of rollers. Turns out this is an action figure in the form of a swimmer, with arms and legs that move in a swimmer's motion when the toy is pulled. Believe us, it took some out-of-the-box thinking to figure this one out, particularly since there's no pull cord to help narrow the field. The toy is called a Hustler Swimmer made by Frantz Manufacturing Company, and this is just one of dozens of creative pull toys the company made in the 1920s and early 1930s.

CAST ANECDOTES: We love Tommy's interplay with George in this scene, from his nightly check of his dad's pockets for gum and what not, to covering his dad with tinsel to being on the receiving end of an emotional hug. So perfectly done by Jimmy Hawkins and at just four-and-a-half-years-old. This film was just the beginning of Hawkins' long and impressive run as a child actor in both film and television. His film credits after *Wonderful Life* include a Jimmy Stewart film, *Winchester '73*, and a Capra film, *Here Comes the Groom* (1951). He transitioned to television with ease, early on starring in Gene Autry's long-running *Annie Oakley* series as Annie's pony-riding younger brother, Tagg. Later he reunited with Donna Reed in *The Donna Reed Show*, with regular appearances as the boyfriend of Reed's television daughter. With their shared experiences on *Wonderful Life* and *The Donna Reed Show*, Hawkins and Reed had a special bond and remained close throughout their lives.

FILM ANECDOTES: Throughout the scene, Carol Coombs, who plays Janie, is actually playing "Hark the Herald Angels Sing." Coombs' mother had her playing the piano at an early age, so the playing requirements of this role were a cinch. But think about it. Coombs knew the song well, but then had to regress to a sort of halting-yet-correct playing style to sell us on the notion that Janie is still getting the hang of it. Well done!

CAST ANECDOTES: Coombs' film resume spans from 1941 to 1957. Her appearances are all uncredited, except for one, *Wonderful Life*. But (sigh) as luck would have it, her name got misspelled as "Coomes" in the film's credits. She's in some very nice films, including the Humphrey Bogart crime drama *Knock on Any Door* (1949) and the Doris Day musical comedy *Tea for Two* (1950), in which she dances with a group of teenagers to, of all songs, "The Charleston." Coombs did make the transition to television, with appearances here and there through 1957.

CLOSER LOOK: Mary's artwork portraying George lassoing the moon is hanging on the wall in the living room just above the piano. (1:26:05) The last time we saw the piece was back in 1934 when it was hanging in George and Mary's bedroom on the night that Mary told George she was pregnant. (1:13:28)

DID YOU KNOW?: Were you aware that the Baileys have a pet? It's a bird. Look for it in its birdcage as George and Mary walk into the kitchen while Tommy excuses himself for burping. (1:26:45)

RANDOM THOUGHTS: Pete asks his dad how to spell two words: *frankincense* and *hallelujah*. While these words are by no means easy for a ten-year-old, knowing them surely would have made Pete competitive in the National Spelling Bee. The winning words for the National Spelling Bee from that era were surprisingly easy. *Therapy*, *initials*, *sacrilegious* and *semaphore* were all 1940s winners. Nowadays, your typical adult would be lucky to know the meaning of the Bee's winning word, let alone its spelling. Try using these modern-day winners in a sentence: *koinonia*, *cymotrichous* and *autochthonous*.

CAST ANECDOTES: Few actors have had an earlier, faster and busier start to a film career than Larry Simms (Pete). He wasn't even four when he appeared in *Blondie* (1938) as Blondie and Dagwood Bumstead's hilarious dead-panning, one-liner machine, Alexander "Baby Dumpling" Bumstead. It's remarkable what these films asked of Simms at such an earlier age; and boy did he deliver. By the time *Wonderful Life* was released he had already done a whopping eighteen *Blondie* films. After *Wonderful Life*, he did ten more. More than that, he's a huge part of these films, appearing in scene after scene and engaging in nothing less than sophisticated, adult comedy.

Among his few non-*Blondie* appearances was another Capra film, *Mr. Smith Goes to Washington*; it being the height of his *Blondie* run, the film credits even list him as "Baby Dumpling." This earlier appearance for Capra naturally led to him playing Pete. He was, to be sure, a film star, and *Wonderful Life* moviegoers would have been well aware that Pete was played by Baby Dumpling. You really have to see Simms' early *Blondie* films to fully appreciate his abilities.

CLOSER LOOK: We managed to solve a big mystery regarding a toy in Zuzu's room. On the floor, to the right of her bed, is the top of what looks like a game board. You can't see much of the board but at the top you can make out the phrase "STICK-EM" and the number "5". Well, through some serious sleuthing, and a little bit of luck, we were able to uncover the premise and backstory for this toy.

Turns out it's a target game. It's not an actual toy, but rather a made-up studio prop. You can see that the outer circle is worth ten points, and we can tell you that a bulls-eye is worth fifty points. There are animals scattered about the board—an elephant, a lion, etc.—but the only one you can see in the film is a leaping jaguar. Also, at the top, there's a policeman shooting a gun at a target in apparent simulation of the game. The "5" next to him signifies that you got five points if you missed the target circles but still managed to hit the board.

CLOSER LOOK: While we are talking props, here's another toy mystery we solved, and this time the toy is authentic. Also in Zuzu's room, on her nightstand, sits a very stoic-looking drummer boy. We discovered that this drummer boy is a plastic wind-up toy made in the 1930s by a Japanese toy company. He's mounted on a wooden stand and wearing a black hat, red coat, and white pants and suspenders. The side of the drum is red, trimmed in blue. Whenever Zuzu reached over to her nightstand and wound him up, he would sway his head back and forth while rapidly beating that drum for a minute or so.

JUST WONDERING: Why is there a crib in Zuzu's room? Hopefully it's for Zuzu's dolls. If it's for Tommy, then he is no doubt as unhappy about sleeping in a crib at his age as Zuzu is about sharing her princess room.

RANDOM THOUGHTS: There's actually a matching child's bedroom set in Zuzu's room, with a whimsical, cartoon flower design. The bed, nightstand, crib and dresser are all visible, and there's another dresser that's just out of the frame. As luck would have it, while viewing the original Blondie film to refresh on Larry Simms' early work, we spied the same style bedroom set in Baby Dumpling's bedroom. It's always fun to find common set design threads in films.

JUST WONDERING: So if Zuzu is the only one who sleeps in Zuzu's room, then where do Janie and Pete and Tommy sleep? As mentioned earlier, there are only two doors off the second floor hallway, one to Zuzu's room and one to George and Mary's room. Hmmm.

CLOSER LOOK: How many petals from Zuzu's flower end up in George's pocket? Slow motion reveals that three petals fall onto the bedcover, all of which are scooped up by George. (1:28:11)

CAST ANECDOTES: Karolyn Grimes, playing Zuzu, would have felt right at home on this set. In more than a few of her films Grimes' character was in bed, just as Zuzu is here. Her acting career focused on film, with some sixteen film appearances between 1944 and 1952. One of her best roles was in another holiday classic, *The Bishop's Wife* (1947), in which she shares some serious screen time with Cary Grant. And here are some other screen legends she worked closely with: Bing Crosby, Loretta Young, John Wayne, Fred McMurray, Angela Lansbury, Betty Grable and Gabby Hayes. Wow. We particularly love her winning ways in the Western *Albuquerque* (1948), with her plucky character surviving a harrowing runaway stagecoach incident with aplomb.

JUST WONDERING: Why is it that Zuzu and all the other kids in Bedford Falls are forced to attend school on Christmas Eve? And come to think of it, how did Zuzu's teacher know to call Mary Bailey to check on Zuzu's condition when Zuzu caught the cold walking home from school?

CLOSER LOOK: Just before George gets on the phone with Mr. Welch, you can hear Mr. Welch yelling something. The official script has the line as, "Now, who do you think you are?" However, a careful listen reveals that Mr. Welch actually yells, "Hey, you! I'll knock your block off!" Sure enough, just a few scenes later Mr. Welch makes good on his promise and decks George.

CLOSER LOOK: What exactly does George destroy during his tirade? It's his work area, which contains various models, including a bridge, a skyscraper, and some residential homes. As he goes ballistic, look for his air-raid warden's helmet hanging off to the right. (1:30:30)

CLOSER LOOK: Above George's work area hangs a portrait of President Abraham Lincoln, which means we can celebrate the fifth and final addition to our U.S. presidents list. Below Lincoln are headshots of Eustace, Ma Bailey, Mary, Harry and Uncle Billy. As we mentioned earlier, this photo of Ma Bailey pops up in a few other places, including in this scene atop the piano (1:30:38), in Uncle Billy's study (1:24:21) and on George's desk during the bank run. (53:29).

These photos were taken connection with *Wonderful Life,* with the actors posing in character. A bespectacled Eustace is, appropriately enough, wearing an accountant's visor and holding a pencil to his mouth as if in deep numerical thought. He's wearing the same outfit he has on in 1928 on the day the Building & Loan board voted Potter down.

Ma Bailey is in a print dress that's similar to, but not quite the same as, the one she's wearing on the night of the graduation dance. Mary has on a sweater similar to the one she wears on moving day for the Martinis. Harry is wearing a military uniform. And Uncle Billy's getup closely tracks his appearance in 1919. The photo in between Mary and Harry shows a golfer finishing his swing. We've never thought of George as the golfing type, but, who knows, maybe he and his pals liked to tee it up.

CAST ANECDOTES: Two Jimmy Stewart photos pop up here. One we've seen before—it's his 1928 yearbook photo. But the other one is new. It shows Jimmy posing at a table with his sisters, Mary and Virginia, all pretending to be reading a book. Look for these photos as George wrecks his work station. The yearbook photo is above Uncle Billy's photo; the siblings photo is below Harry's photo. That makes four Stewart photos in *Wonderful Life*...and we're still looking!

JUST WONDERING: What was Mary going to say to George just before he left the house? Having seen enough of his tantrum, Mary says, "George, why must you torture the children? Why don't you..." Surely she wasn't going to tell George to "go jump off a bridge," was she?

RANDOM THOUGHTS: With Zuzu being in bed, Karolyn Grimes was not in this heavy scene, which may have been an okay break in the moment. The other three child actors confirmed that it was pretty darn scary for them to watch, and interact with, Jimmy Stewart here. Carol Coombs remembered that it wasn't hard to get the tears flowing. And poor Larry Simms must have been wondering what the heck he had gotten himself into. He'd spent eight years acting on the household sets of the *Blondie* series, cracking jokes in a screwball comedy environment, and here he is on the set of the Bailey household getting yelled at by Jimmy Stewart in a Christmas Eve scene. Thankfully, filming for the Christmas Eve celebration scenes started just a few days later, so happier times on the set were just around the corner.

EXPLANATION REQUIRED: Uncle Billy's phone number—BEdford 247—is typical for that era in that it makes use of a "telephone exchange name." Typically the exchange name would be the name of the town or the street on which the telephone company was located. The first two letters of the exchange name would correspond to the first two digits of the phone number, with letters being translated to numbers based on how the numbers appear on the telephone dial. So Uncle Billy's phone number is 23-247. Check out our map of downtown Bedford Falls—left of the courthouse is the Telephone Exchange Building. And you can see the building when Uncle Billy walks by the courthouse on Christmas Eve.

FILM ANECDOTES: Want to see 320 Sycamore in another film? Then *The Magnificant Ambersons* (1942) is your ticket. This was Orson Welles' first picture after *Citizen Kane*. Set mainly in the early1900s, it tells the tale of a prominent family's slow decline as America modernized—something akin to Potter sticking with his horse and carriage all those years. You will instantly recognize the house used for 320 Sycamore, though the version shown in *Wonderful Life* is wider. And as a huge bonus, a drugstore scene makes use of the same set used for Gower Drugs. The exterior and interior drugstore shots are so similar to Gower Drugs that you'll be expecting Mr. Gower to walk out of the back room.

320 SYCAMORE

1. Window where Bert and handyman hang posters on George and Mary's wedding night, and where Bert and Ernie serenade the newlyweds.
2. Where Mary stands when George arrives at the bridal suite.
3. Where George stands bewildered upon arriving at the bridal suite.
4. Location of George and Mary's bed in the bridal suite.
5. Where George hugs Tommy.
6. Location of the butterfly collection framings.
7. The Bailey family Christmas tree.
8. Location of Mary's "George Lassos the Moon" framing.
9. Where Tommy excuses himself for burping.
10. Location of the Bailey's birdcage.
11. Location of Zuzu's room (on second floor at the top of the stairs).
12. Where George and Mary talk on the phone with Zuzu's teacher.
13. George's work area.
14. Where George hugs his wife and kids upon returning home.
15. Location of tables where George's friends and family make their donations.

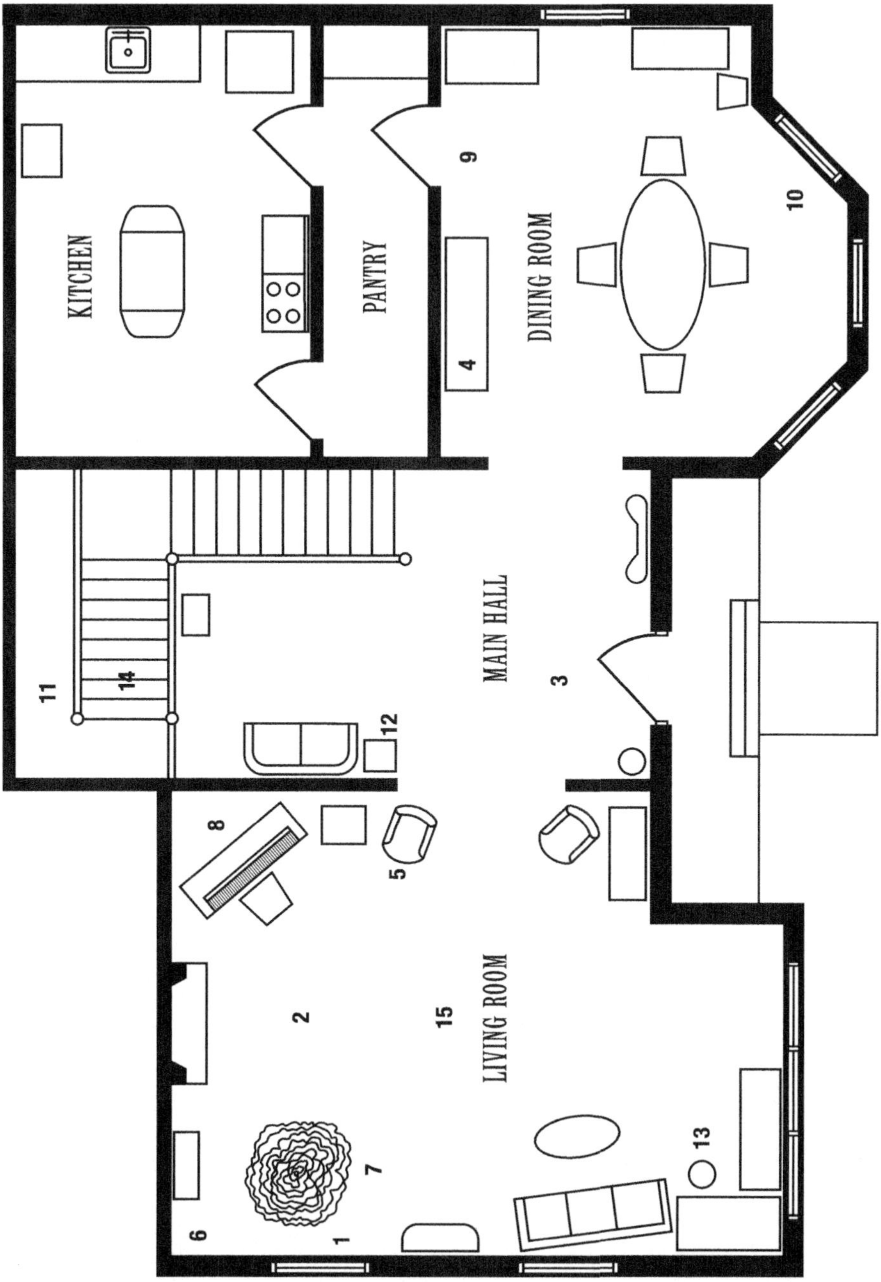
KITCHEN
PANTRY
DINING ROOM
MAIN HALL
LIVING ROOM
1
2
3
4
5
6
7
8
9
10
11
12
13
14
15

CAST ANECDOTES: Just like the Baileys, both Donna Reed and Jimmy Stewart raised two boys and two girls. Reed's children were all from her second marriage. In a super fun confluence of big life events, Reed and Tony Owen adopted their first child during the filming of *Wonderful Life*. After Reed convinced director Frank Capra to give her a few days off, she and her husband traveled all the way from Los Angeles to Chicago (no small feat back then) to unite with their new baby girl. And, put this in the category of you can't make this stuff up, her first day back on the set found her shooting scenes for the Bailey family montage, in which Mary Bailey is shown caring for her newborn baby, Pete. Well, she certainly had done her homework for the scene.

As for Stewart, when he married in 1949, his wife Gloria had custody of her two boys from a previous marriage, and Stewart became a father to both of them. In 1951, Gloria gave birth to twin girls. Their oldest son, Ron McLean, became a Marine and served in the Vietnam War. They lost him to the war in 1969, and for his combat gallantry he was awarded the Silver Star posthumously.

George Pays Potter a Visit

JUST WONDERING: Why is George under the impression that his life insurance policy is his only asset? Has George forgotten that he and Mary own a house? Surely it has appreciated some in the thirteen years since they first moved in.

JUST WONDERING: How did word get "all over town" (according to Potter) that George loaned money to Violet? First, George had only met with her a few hours earlier. Second, Potter's informant was almost certainly Mr. Carter, the bank examiner, but he could not have known what transpired between George and Violet because their conversation occurred in George's office behind closed doors.

DID YOU KNOW?: While Potter may be a shrewd businessman, his knowledge of the law is somewhat lacking. As a board member of the Building & Loan, he certainly has the right to report George to the authorities. But he does not have the power, as he suggests, to personally "swear out" a warrant for George's arrest. Only a judicial officer can do that after a proper hearing.

Also, Potter rattles off three crimes that George has purportedly committed: manipulation, malfeasance and misappropriation of funds. Of these, only misappropriation of funds, more commonly known as embezzlement, is really applicable to George. By the way, in order to tag George for the crime of embezzlement, the prosecution would have to prove that George was knowingly involved in the misdirection of funds. That means George's best defense would be to blame it all on Uncle Billy.

Martini's

EXPLANATION REQUIRED: Visually, all of our attention here is on George settling down at the bar. But as he does so, some bonus dialogue floats through the air, providing us with a little insight into the menu at Martini's:

MR. MARTINI (to Patron): "Ah, Merry Christmas! I'm glad you come."

PATRON: "Same to you! How about some of that good spaghetti?"

MARTINI: "We've got everything!"

Hey, Mr. Martini, we'll take an order of that good spaghetti too!

MUSIC NOTES: While George sits at the bar, two Italian songs are played. The first is "Vieni, Vieni," a lively number that hit the top of the charts in 1937 on the vocals of Rudy Vallee. The lyrics that you hear as George prays are:

Vieni, vieni, vieni, vieni, bella, bella, bella, bella accanto a me
Vieni, vieni, vieni, vieni, bella, bella, bella, bella accanto a me
Paola, mia rondinella, sei la piu bella, sei nel mio cuore
Ah, Paola, voglio cantare, una canzone, d'amore.

All of this translates to:

Come beautiful one beside me
Come beautiful one beside me
Paola, my little swallow, you're the most beautiful, you're in my heart
Ah, Paola, I want to sing a song of love.

The second song is "Santa Lucia," an ode to the city of Naples and its Santa Lucia district. Only the first line of the song's first verse can be heard before George gets popped by Mr. Welch. It goes, *Sul mare luccica l'astro d'argento*, which translates to, *On the sea shines the silver star.* The unheard portion of the same verse has a local boatman ensuring calm waves and favorable winds to anyone who desires to take a spin in his quick little boat.

CAST ANECDOTES: If you find yourself mesmerized by the sweet, lilting voice of the soprano singing in Martini's, there's a good reason. The singer here, Adriana Caselotti, was the voice of Snow White in Walt Disney's classic *Snow White and the Seven Dwarfs* (1937). Her voice has a youngish, operatic and bygone-era quality to it that is utterly entrancing. Indeed, that youthful sound is exactly what Walt Disney was looking for when he cast her as Snow White as a teenager. What a treat to hear her in Martini's, and for two songs at that. She's also visible for a few seconds, behind George as he sits at the bar. (By the way, she's singing duets here and we believe her singing partner is a fellow named Muzzy Marcellino, who was known for his ability to whistle a tune.)

Her post-Snow White film career is somewhat limited as Disney apparently kept a tight rein on her activities in an effort to protect the *Snow White* property. Interestingly, we just learned (while discussing the Bedford Falls theater marquee) that *Wonderful Life* distributor RKO Radio Pictures was also the exclusive distributor of Disney cartoons, so it makes perfect sense that Caselotti, an invaluable Disney asset, would appear here in an RKO picture. Now, not to be outdone by Caselotti's performance at Martini's, Nick's in Pottersville also employs a music legend for its Christmas Eve entertainment. We will let you know who that is when we get there.

FILM ANECDOTES: Of all the dramatic scenes Jimmy Stewart nails in this film, this one in Martini's stood out the most to him. Stewart often explained that he cried in this scene, and a tear definitely falls from his right eye. (1:34:51) Stewart said he was so emptied by the first take that he didn't want to do any more. This presented an interesting situation. They shot the first take with a single wide-angle shot, and now they wanted close-ups to increase the intensity and humanity of the moment. As a creative work-around, Capra used the first take, creating a zooming effect by gradually tightening the framing to the desired close-up. We're sure glad they did it that way. It is one powerful scene.

RANDOM THOUGHTS: At Martini's we find George in the midst of his "Bedford Falls" crime spree. With a warrant out for his arrest for embezzlement, George downs several drinks, gets into a scuffle (disorderly conduct), speeds off in his car (drunk driving; reckless driving), plows the car into a tree (destruction of property), and then runs off into the night (leaving the scene of an accident). Can't wait to see whether George can top this performance in Pottersville!

DID YOU KNOW?: The featured beer at both Martini's and Nick's is Schlitz. Both establishments have a neon sign in the window that reads "Schlitz—In Bottles." (1:35:27; 1:50:29) In 1945, Schlitz Brewing Company was one of the largest breweries in the country (along with Pabst and Anheuser-Busch). Two decades earlier, however, business wasn't so hot as breweries struggled to survive Prohibition.

Desperate for sales, Schlitz and the other big breweries turned to near beer as a means of generating revenue. But near beer never really caught on, largely because the real stuff was readily available in bootlegged form. It also didn't help that the breweries all adopted goofy names for their near beers, like Famo (Schlitz), Bevo (Anheuser-Busch), Pablo (Pabst), Vivo (Miller), and Lux-O (Stroh), which to us sound more like the names of long lost Marx Brothers than a cold brew.

After Prohibition was repealed in 1933, the large breweries had no trouble rebounding. In the first year back, production was around 30 million barrels; and by 1945, when thirsty servicemen were returning home in droves from the war, production had soared to 80 million barrels.

CLOSER LOOK: "The Schlitz—In Bottles" sign is a nice piece, and we spied another one in Jimmy Stewart's *Call Northside 777* (1948). But this is not the only Schlitz advertisement in Martini's. As Mr. Welch insists on paying for his drink, you can see a round Schlitz beer sign hanging at the end of the bar. This is an authentic sign made by a Pennsylvania company that specialized for a time in reverse-painted glass beer signs for display in bars, and their Schlitz sign was a top-shelf offering. It's really more artwork than an advertisement, with rich colors—a deep blue background with gold lettering—and the classic Schlitz world globe logo in the center.

CAST ANECDOTES: The colorful Mr. Martini is played by William Edmunds, who was typically cast as a heavily accented foreign gentleman—Italian, Spanish, even Hungarian. If he looks familiar to you, perhaps you remember him from his brief appearance in another American classic, *Casablanca*, where for all of eight seconds in Rick's Café the screen is his as he gives instructions to a man seeking illegal passage out of *Casablanca.*

You can also find Edmunds in *The Shop Around the Corner* (1940, starring Jimmy Stewart), *For Whom the Bell Tolls* (1943), *House of Frankenstein* (1944), *The Three Musketeers* (1948) and *The Caddy* (1953), a Dean Martin and Jerry Lewis screwball comedy. The Caddy is of added interest not only because it stars a resplendent Donna Reed as Dean Martin's love interest, but also because it features, coincidently enough, the actress who plays Mrs. Martini in *Wonderful Life*, Argentina Brunetti.

JUST WONDERING: Sure Mr. Martini advertises that he serves Schlitz in bottles, but does he actually do so? Absolutely. George's soon-to-be-nemesis, Mr. Welch, is enjoying a bottle of Schlitz at the bar. You can see the iconic Schlitz world globe logo on the neck label, plus the top of the body label, when Mr. Welch gets wise to who's having a drink next to him. (1:35:12)

EXPLANATION REQUIRED: When we spied the right edge of a commercial machine by Martini's front door, we assumed it would turn out to be Mr. Martini's jukebox. After all, at the end of the film Mr. Martini says he "busted the jukebox." But a closer look reveals that the machine is actually an automatic cigarette vending machine. It's made by the Rowe Manufacturing Company, and the vending buttons, dispensing slot and chrome work all match up with a 1930s Rowe model. We have not yet found a jukebox in Martini's, so we either have to take Mr. Martini's word for it that he has one, or he actually busted the cigarette machine.

CLOSER LOOK: Another minor film gaffe of the scene inconsistencies variety occurs during this brief scene. When George crashes his car after leaving Martini's, the car hits the tree head-on, coming to rest just short of it. (1:37:36) However, in the next shot the car is situated off to the side of the tree and past it.

JUST WONDERING: How is it possible that the owner of the tree George crashes into doesn't know George? He's no doubt one of the town's more visible figures, with an office right up on the main strip and a family business that's been building homes for Bedford Fallsians since 1903. Guess he's never heard of Potter either. Anyway, we like to think of this irascible homeowner as being the one townsperson who pretty much acts the same in Bedford Falls and Pottersville.

GEORGE "SAVES" CLARENCE

"I don't know whether I like it very much being seen around with an angel without any wings."

—GEORGE BAILEY

Finally, our retrospective of George's life has come to an end. The angels told us at the very beginning of the film that George would arrive on the bridge contemplating suicide at precisely 10:45 P.M. What they didn't tell us is that it would take us filmgoers an hour and forty minutes to get there! Anyway, as George peers over the railing to the icy waters below, there's not much doubt that he's serious about this suicide thing.

Don't do it, George! You can't do it! Sure, losing the deposit money was a tough break, but things aren't really that bad! You've got great kids. Your wife is amazing. What are we missing here? And how can you possibly be buying into Potter's "you're worth more dead than alive" malarkey? Are you really going to let Potter have the satisfaction of sending you and your dad to your graves?

It's going to take a miracle to save George now. And lo and behold, here comes our man Clarence. Up until now we've only heard Clarence, but here we get our first glimpse of George's guardian angel as he lurks in the shadows atop the bridge, waiting for just the right moment to leap into action. Clarence surmises that if he jumps into the water first, George's benevolent nature will lead him to rescue Clarence. Sure enough, just seconds after Clarence hits the water, George dives in after him and pulls him to safety.

After the "rescue," George and Clarence dry off in the tollhouse. When Clarence tries to explain that he is George's guardian angel, George is understandably a bit skeptical. Clarence quickly realizes that it's going to take some doing to convince George that he really is worth more alive than dead. So when George laments that he wishes he'd never been born, Clarence gets an idea. How about showing George what life would be like if he truly had never been born? And so it shall be.

George on the Bridge

RANDOM THOUGHTS: If George is thinking he can take his life while preserving his family's ability to collect on his insurance policy, he may first want to check to see if the policy has a coverage exclusion for suicide. (Nowadays, policies typically cover suicide but even then, there's typically a coverage exclusion window of a year or two.) Beyond that, it's not a great plan to have the policy in your pocket. It tends to indicate the circumstances, plus it might get lost, complicating matters for your family.

CLOSER LOOK: Take a moment using slow motion to examine George's improbable dive off the bridge. (1:39:13) From a considerable height, and with his feet supposedly on the ground, George somehow vaults over the railing for a perfect headfirst dive. We're guessing that the stuntman performing the dive made use of a trampoline.

RANDOM THOUGHTS: In case you're wondering just how prodigious the dive is, we've done the calculations for you. We timed the dive at about 1.5 seconds, which means that George takes off from about 11.25 meters (37 feet) above the water. By comparison, the Olympic platform diving distance is 10 meters (32.75 feet).

DID YOU KNOW?: More than twenty-five years after rescuing Harry, George's water rescue techniques remain unorthodox, yet effective. Again, George should have tried to avoid jumping into icy waters and looked instead for a flotation device on the bridge. Even so, his dive was anything but safe. The proper method for diving into water from any substantial height is feet-first—not head-first—with your body vertical, toes pointed, and hands protecting your midsection. And regardless of whether he dove head-first or feet-first, George could easily have hit one of the many ice floes lurking in the water, and that, friends, would not have been pretty.

JUST WONDERING: What do you suppose is the name of the river on which Bedford Falls is located? We're going to play it safe here and guess that it's the Bedford River. By the way, Bedford Falls is in Bedford County. We know this from the local gas company's storefront signage, "Bedford County Gas Co." For the location of that business, check out the map of downtown Bedford Falls.

CLOSER LOOK: Look for the sign on the bridge behind the tollhouse keeper as he walks outside to investigate. It reads, "Avoid Delay—Have Exact Fare Ready." (1:39:28) The following other signs are visible as George reaches the bridge at the beginning of the scene: "Trucks Over 15 Tons Excluded," "Tractors with Lugs Prohibited," and "Pedestrians Only." (1:38:25) Lugs are basically cleats on tractor tires designed to provide traction. They're great in soil, but tend to wreak havoc on pavement.

RANDOM THOUGHTS: That is one powerful flashlight the tollhouse keeper has there. From the bridge, the flashlight casts a beam down on George and Clarence rivaling that of an air-raid searchlight.

FILM ANECDOTES: The special effects for the film were a huge undertaking, particularly when it came to the snow scenes. For winter scenes they used traditional methods to simulate ground snow, including hundreds of tons of plaster, gypsum, and shaved ice. But director Frank Capra was looking for a new way to simulate falling snow; the most common method until then had been bleached corn flakes. So Capra's special effects gurus drummed up a concoction of fire retardant foam and soap, which, when shot through a hose, resulted in a pretty decent simulation. The stuff was a bit messy for the actors though, as you can see in this scene. When George and Clarence are floundering in the water, both men have "snowflakes" caked on their faces. (1:39:36)

George and Clarence Recover in the Tollhouse

DID YOU KNOW?: In the tollhouse, Clarence does his best to salvage his copy of *The Adventures of Tom Sawyer* by Mark Twain. Born in 1835, Twain published this American classic in 1876, based on his own life experiences growing up in the small lazy river town of Hannibal, Missouri. Don't bother searching for some hidden or symbolic meaning involving the use of the book—Capra used it simply because he liked it.

RANDOM THOUGHTS: As Clarence explains that he saved George from committing suicide, the tollhouse keeper says, "It's against the law to commit suicide around here." Actually, at that time it was not a crime in New York to commit suicide, perhaps due in part to the futility of enforcing the law on a person who is, well, dead. And while New York did at one time have a law that made it a crime to attempt to commit suicide, the law had been repealed decades before the year that this scene is set in. So George can take comfort in knowing that he has one less crime to worry about.

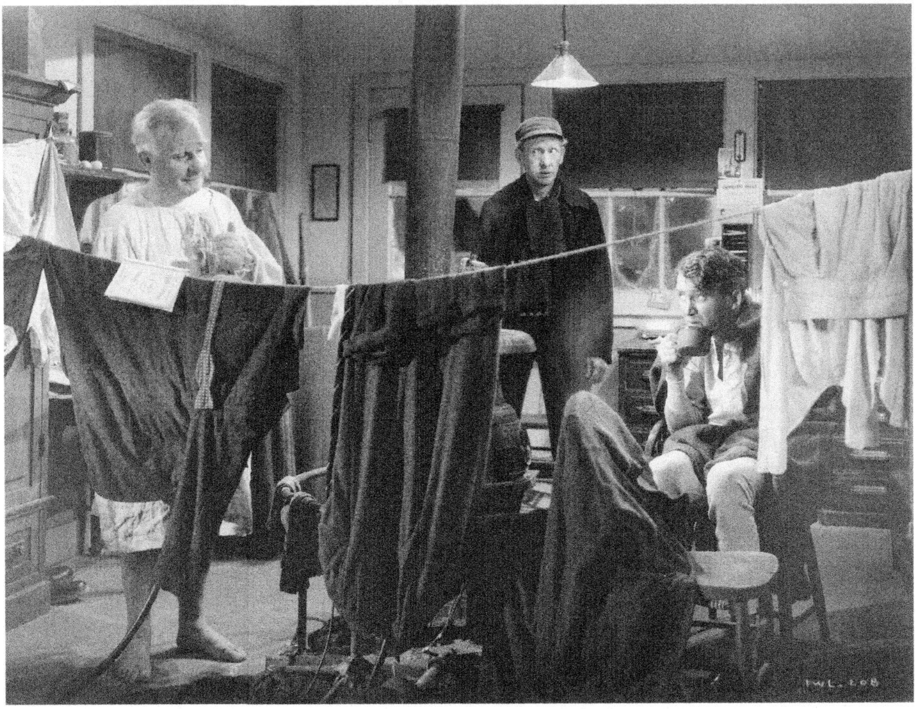

CLOSER LOOK: Here are some items to look out for in the tollhouse. First and foremost, the tollhouse keeper has a coin changer on his belt. We can imagine the traffic jams on the bridge as he fumbles with the change. There's also a photo of an airplane nose and prop (by the door), a photo of a horse, a copy of *Star Western* magazine, a New Jersey phone directory, a safe, a photo of men posing with a big game fish, a soup can or two, and a notice labeled "Important."

This New Jersey phone directory is the same one that shows up in Gower Drugs in 1919. The New Jersey part still makes no sense, nor does the fact that the same phone book is in scenes set twenty-seven years apart. *Star Western* was an actual pulp magazine published in the 1940s. The edition visible in the tollhouse is authentic and dates to August 1946. The tollhouse scenes were filmed in the last days of July 1946, which means this edition is hot off the presses. And yet here it is in a December 1945 scene, having slipped passed the prop team's continuity check.

POTTERSVILLE

> "Hey, look, mister. We serve hard drinks in here for men who want to get drunk fast. And we don't need any characters around to give the joint atmosphere. Is that clear? Or do I have to slip you my left for a convincer?"
>
> —NICK

George doesn't know it quite yet, but he is now in Bedford Falls' alter ego, a wild and woolly town called Pottersville. It seems that without George around to keep him in place, Potter was able to overrun Bedford Falls and turn it into a real sleazeball of a town.

One of George's first clues that he's not in Bedford Falls comes when he and Clarence return to where George crashed his car. The car is nowhere in sight, and the tree he hit is unscathed. Hmmm. That's weird. Undaunted, George continues down the road with Clarence. By now George is worn out from all the fighting and rescuing and walking, and could go for a comfortable bar stool and a stiff drink. So it's back to Martini's...or so George thinks. This is Pottersville, and in Pottersville there is no Martini's, only the rough and tumble Nick's.

Now don't get us wrong—we love Martini's. But Nick's is one cool joint too. The place is packed with Pottersvillians (no pun intended), there's a guy playing boogie piano in the corner, and the crowd looks like they're ready to roll all night long, even if it is Christmas Eve! Sure, the Pottersville version of Nick could be a little friendlier, but we'll forgive him as long as he keeps the drinks coming.

To George the place is a little edgier than usual, but he doesn't seem too concerned as he and Clarence belly up to the bar for a few pops. Unfortunately, Clarence's quirky ways catch Nick's attention, and before long Nick concludes that they're both trouble and gives them a choice of sorts—they can leave Nick's going "through the door or out the window."

Outside Nick's, George starts to realize that things are quite different. Where was Martini? Why was Nick so ornery? What was the deal with Mr. Gower? And how in the heck does this little fella Clarence know about Zuzu's petals? While George chalks it all up to a "funny dream," he's in for even more surprises.

Welcome, George, to downtown Pottersville! No small-town charm to be found here—just neon signs, glitz, and a shady nightclub every half a block or so. Dazed and confused, George desperately searches the town for signs of "his life," making stops at the former site of the Building & Loan, his home, his parents' home, and Bailey Park. Each stop offers a frightening glimpse of how life has evolved in his absence. Eventually George gets around to asking what's become of Mary. Clarence isn't supposed to tell, but under pressure from George he finally comes clean.

It turns out that Mary never married, and what's more she is—brace yourself—a librarian. George tracks her down as she's closing shop for the night, convinced that she of all people will recognize him. Predictably, George's overtures don't go over too well with the Pottersville Mary. And who could blame her for being positively horrified, what with a deranged-looking man chasing her down the street, grabbing her by the arms, and demanding to know "What's happened to us?" and "Where's our kids?" So when her inevitable screams for help attract a crowd—and the police—George finds himself a fugitive in Pottersville too.

George Heads Back to His Car

EXPLANATION REQUIRED: The exchange between George and the homeowner contains a curious line. When George's car isn't around, he asks the homeowner where it is. The owner inspects the tree where George says he crashed the car. Seeing no damage, he gives George a quizzical look, takes a whiff of his breath, and replies, "You must mean two other trees." Of course, there's only one tree and George never refers to two trees. So this is just the home owner's way of saying "You're drunk, buddy, and I don't know what the heck you're talking about."

CAST ANECDOTES: J. Farrell MacDonald plays the homeowner. He was one of a handful of actors in this film who got their start in silent films. His distinctive, gravelly voice (you don't even have to see his face to know it's him) helped him pivot to talkies. We like him in John Ford's Western classic *My Darling Clementine* (1946) as the barman and in *Maybe It's Love* (1935) as an affable New York City cop with an Irish brogue, who tells Henry Travers' character to "pipe down." As for his silent films, he's in *Sunrise* (1927), which many regard as the best silent film ever made. Trust us, you will not recognize him with hair.

Nick's

MUSIC NOTES: The man playing piano at Nick's is boogie-woogie piano legend Meade "Lux" Lewis. In 1938, a then little-known Lewis and two other barrelhouse piano men performed at Carnegie Hall and unwittingly triggered a boogie-woogie craze that lasted through the war's end. Lewis relocated to Los Angeles around 1941 and was fresh off a tour with jazz legends Lester Young and Colman Hawkins when tapped for *Wonderful Life*. He epitomizes coolness here in his bowler and all-plaid outfit, chomping on a cigar with a beer sloshing atop his rough upright piano. Lewis plays for almost three minutes before Nick stops things, and then gets some bonus screen time as Nick gives out wings at the register.

RANDOM THOUGHTS: While sitting at the bar, George asks Clarence how old he is, and Clarence replies, "Two hundred and ninety three…next May." That means that the 292-year-old Clarence was born in May 1653, just thirty-two and a half years after the Mayflower reached the shores of Massachusetts.

RANDOM THOUGHTS: Well, Nick and Clarence definitely don't hit it off, but you can't say they have nothing in common. They are both wearing polka dot bow ties.

CLOSER LOOK: So how much different is Nick's from Martini's? A lot! Martini's is a homestyle restaurant and bar, with a cozy, country farmhouse vibe. Nick's is strictly a bar, catering to folks who want to get drunk fast. Nick's is smoky and loud and has cigarette girls, a bouncer and no-nonsense cocktail waitresses. Nick likes his sports and gambling—there are plenty of boxing and horseracing photos strewn around the joint and there's a slot machine in the back. And don't forget the entertainment. You will not find a soprano singing songs from the old country here, just hard driving blues and jazz. Now, one similarity we do see is that Nick's has some Christmas decorations—look for a wreath on the front door and "Merry Christmas" scrolled on the bar mirror.

CLOSER LOOK: Here are a few liquor bottles visible in Nick's: VAT 69, Delano wine, Johnny Walker, a bottle of Kentucky Straight Bourbon Whiskey, G&W Whiskey (actually a cardboard advertisement) and plenty of classic straw-wrapped Italian wine bottles.

RANDOM THOUGHTS: If you're looking for a more authentic viewing of *Wonderful Life*, try firing up a batch of one of Clarence's two favorite holiday beverages: mulled wine and a flaming rum punch. These drinks are not for everyone, and given what a hassle they are to make, it's no wonder Nick gave Clarence the hairy eyeball.

MULLED WINE: Mulled wines are from medieval times and were thought to have "medicinal" qualities (it's called a buzz!). Mulled just means heated and spiced, and there are any number of ways to make this stuff—here's ours:

1/2 cup brown sugar
12 whole cloves
1/2 tsp. ground cinnamon
1/4 tsp. ground nutmeg
2 cups water
peel from 1 lemon (yellow part only)
peel from 1 orange (orange part only)
1/4 cup strained lemon juice
1 bottle (750ml) of a full-bodied red wine

Place sugar, spices, water, and peels in a saucepan and bring to a boil. Reduce heat and simmer for 5–7 minutes. Strain and return to pan. Add warmed lemon juice, then the wine, and reheat the whole thing, but DON'T BOIL—it'll ruin the wine. Serve in mugs, and add more cinnamon (we recommend a cinnamon stick) if, like Clarence, you prefer it "heavy on the cinnamon and light on the cloves."

FLAMING RUM PUNCH: Don't let this discourage you from making it, but the drink sounds way cooler than it actually is, plus making it has its challenges. First, to achieve the flaming part you have to use rum that's at least 80 proof, which may have you carting granny off on a stretcher. Second, for the most part you can only generate a flame by lighting the rum separately, before diluting it with the nonalcoholic mixers. Finally, high-proof liquors can put off a formidable flame, so igniting the rum is not for everyone and definitely calls for caution in a controlled environment. The objective here is to enjoy a holiday cocktail without setting your hair on fire. Keeping all this in mind, here is what you'll need:

4 cups apple cider
1 cup fresh lemon juice
2-3 tbsp. sugar
6 cinnamon sticks
12 whole cloves
3 cups rum
2 cups water

Throw everything but the rum into a large saucepan and heat to simmer for five or so minutes. Pour the heated concoction into a punch bowl and add rum. If you're up for the flaming part, first make sure there is nothing flammable around the punch bowl—ignited rum definitely has the ability to set other things ablaze immediately upon contact. Pour a few ounces of heated rum into a long-handled ladle. Turn the house lights down and ignite the ladled rum over the punch bowl using a long-stemmed match. Enjoy the modest show before dousing the flame by immersing the ladle in the punch. Now, can you imagine Nick trying to make this?!

EXPLANATION REQUIRED: After George keeps calling Nick by name, Nick responds that he doesn't know George "from Adam's off ox." This is just a derivation of the more common phrase, "I don't know you from Adam," that is, "Who the heck are you?" The term off ox refers to the ox on the right-hand side of a two-oxen team, farthest away from the driver (who typically stands to the left of the team).

DID YOU KNOW?: As Nick waits on George and Clarence, he is about to open a bottle of liquor called King. (1:49:32) It may look like a prop but King is an actual brand of liquor. King Blended Whiskey was a popular brand in the 1940s, bottled by Brown-Forman, the current manufacturer of Jack Daniels. King's ads through the years used the slogan, "Be Right—Drink Light" and portrayed various folks having a good old time drinking King while enjoying their favorite outdoor activities. Who says whiskey and ice skating don't mix?

CLOSER LOOK: In front of George on the bar counter is a box of Lite King brand matches. This was an actual match brand made by the Pacific Match Company in Tacoma, Washington. Lite King matches also show up in Peter Bailey's office during the board meeting that takes place after his death. No relation to King whiskey, but a very nice tie-in.

RANDOM THOUGHTS: When Mr. Gower gets thrown out the door he manages to scamper away pretty quickly. Even though George and Clarence follow just a few seconds later, Mr. Gower is nowhere to be found.

CLOSER LOOK: We have some more continuity issues for you. Keep an eye on how George and Clarence are positioned as they are collared by the bouncer—looking out the door, Clarence is on the left and clearly in front of George. Now let's go to the exterior shot of them flying out the door and into the snow—the two have now switched positions, with George on the other side of Clarence and in front of him. Thankfully, the ensuing close up of the two in the snow has them oriented to the exterior shot, thereby avoiding a far more noticeable "double switch."

Next, Clarence is shoved to the door with *The Adventures of Mark Twain* in his left hand. But once outside and launched, Clarence has the book in his right hand. The ensuing close up of George and Clarence in the snow shows Clarence clutching the book in his right hand. A bit of a mixed bag, but overall a decent effort at maintaining continuity.

FILM ANECDOTES: And while we are here, the two men flying out the door are definitely stuntmen. While it's no surprise that the then-seventy-two-year-old Henry Travers would not be doing his own stunts, Jimmy Stewart probably could have taken this one on. Ah, but they do land pretty hard, so perhaps it wasn't worth the risk of having to write into the script a broken wrist for George Bailey. Anyway, the stuntman for Clarence does show his worth by holding on to that book despite a very rough landing.

DID YOU KNOW?: Outside Nick's, Clarence reminds George that he has no 4F card. During World War II, men between the ages of eighteen and sixty-five were required by law to carry a draft card, which included their draft classification. (We noted earlier that the 4F draft classification meant that the individual was unfit for military service, which George was on account of his bad ear.) And even though the war has been over for more than three months now, George would still be required to carry his draft card as the Selective Service Act did not expire until March 1947.

CAST ANECDOTES: The role of Nick is played by Sheldon Leonard, a New York native who was a natural at playing tough New York gangster types. He's fun to watch in that role in Capra's *Pocket Full of Miracles* (1961), and we love him as a shady character in *Another Thin Man* (1939). After retiring from film, Leonard carved out a highly successful career as a television producer, with several hit sitcoms to his credit, including *The Andy Griffith Show*, *The Danny Thomas Show* and *The Dick Van Dyke Show*.

Downtown Pottersville

CLOSER LOOK: Finally, we get a glimpse of the late-night scene in downtown Pottersville. Who would have thought that life could be so different without George, but here's proof. Check out the map of Pottersville and the accompanying index for store locations as well as the location of various events that occur during George's brief but memorable tour through downtown.

CLOSER LOOK: Judging from the signage, downtown Pottersville is one oppressive place. Look for these cautionary signs that appear in the background as George staggers through town: No Parking, Keep Moving, No Left Turn, No Dog Allowed, No Loitering, Keep Off The Grass. What exactly can you do in this town without getting arrested?

RANDOM THOUGHTS: While George may be horrified by what's become of his hometown, there's no denying that the drinking establishments sound pretty cool. With catchy names like the Indian Club, the Blue Moon, the Bamboo Room and the Midnight Club, they all appear to warrant further investigation. Mai Tais at the Bamboo Room, anyone?

CLOSER LOOK: How else does downtown Pottersville differ from Bedford Falls? Well, Gower Drugs is now a pawnshop called the Imperial Loan Co. (the storefront signage reads "Pawn Broker—Loans"), the entrance to the Building & Loan now leads up to a nightclub called Dreamland, the florist shop is now the Cut Rate Liquor Store, and instead of *The Bells of St. Mary's* the theater now hosts a raunchy burlesque act called "Georgia's Sensational Striptease Dance." For other differences, compare our downtown Bedford Falls and downtown Pottersville maps.

CLOSER LOOK: Things are so upside down in Pottersville that there are no less than two bars on the same block as the public library: the Midnight Club and the Blue Moon. The Midnight Club's offerings are enough to make a librarian blush, with signage boasting, "20 Beautiful Hostesses—Romantic Atmosphere." The Blue Moon is more of a shot-and-a-beer type place. As with most Pottersville establishments, it's packed late on Christmas Eve.

Downtown Pottersville

1. George stands by "Pottersville" sign (shot looking toward the courthouse).

2. George stands outside the entrance to Dreamland and watches Violet get arrested.

3. George flags down Ernie's cab.

4. Ernie spots Bert in front of the theater, signaling him to follow his cab (shot looking toward the courthouse).

5. George accosts Mary on the sidewalk.

6. George punches Bert, Bert fires shots at George (shot looking toward the courthouse).

7. Bert gets into his police car to chase after George. (Bert pulled up to the bar going the wrong way on the boulevard, and speeds off toward the courthouse still going the wrong way.)

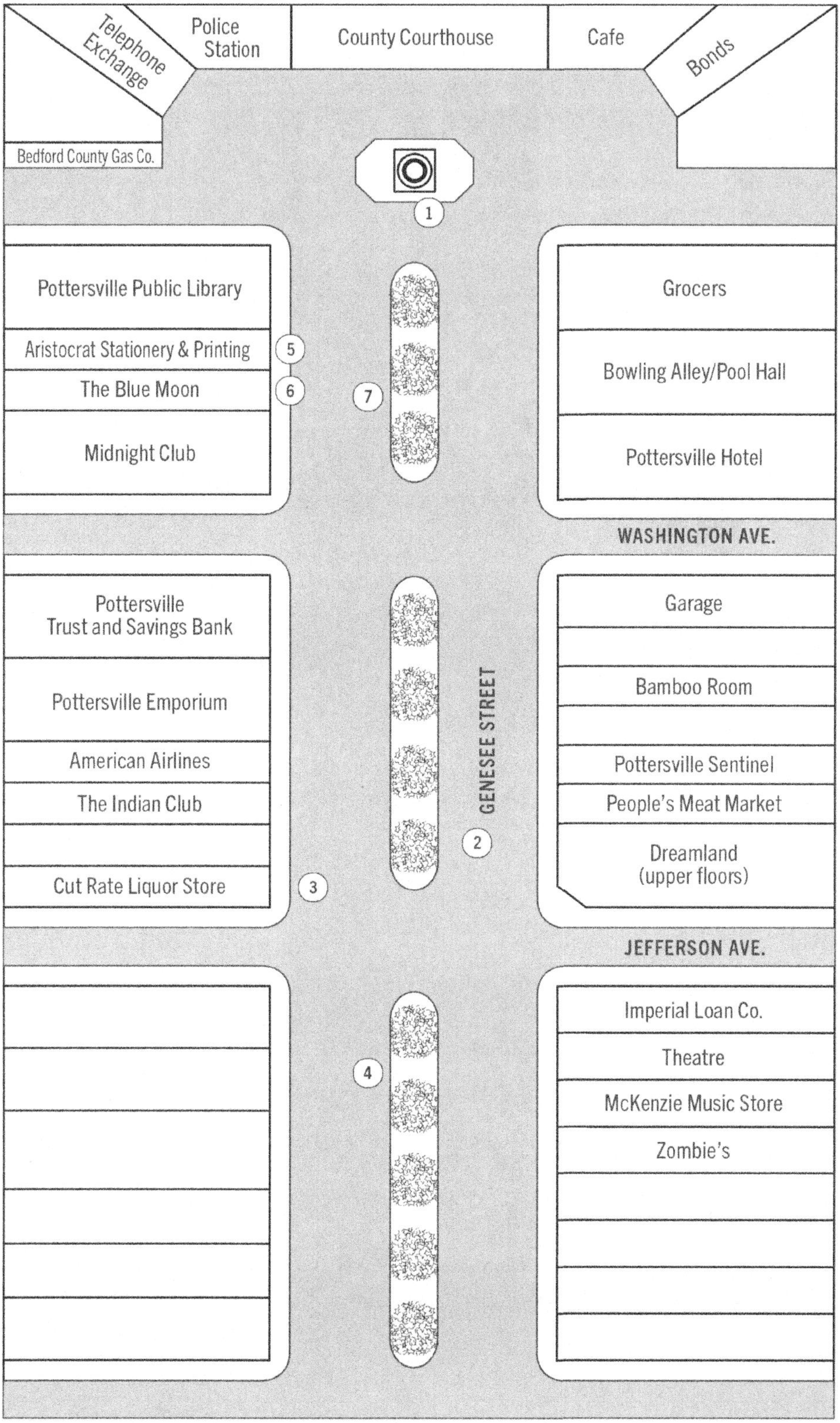

Telephone Exchange
Police Station
County Courthouse
Cafe
Bonds
Bedford County Gas Co.
1
Pottersville Public Library
Aristocrat Stationery & Printing
5
The Blue Moon
6
7
Midnight Club
Grocers
Bowling Alley/Pool Hall
Pottersville Hotel
WASHINGTON AVE.
Pottersville Trust and Savings Bank
Pottersville Emporium
American Airlines
The Indian Club
Cut Rate Liquor Store
3
GENESEE STREET
2
Garage
Bamboo Room
Pottersville Sentinel
People's Meat Market
Dreamland (upper floors)
JEFFERSON AVE.
4
Imperial Loan Co.
Theatre
McKenzie Music Store
Zombie's

CLOSER LOOK: Here's some other signage from the hardscrabble streets of Pottersville—see if you can spot them:

- Whiskies—Barrel Wine
- Bowling Alley—Pool Tables—Pool–Billiards—Fights Every Wednesday Nite—Free Bowling Instruction—Pocket Billiards
- Pottersville Hotel
- Liquor and Wines—Wholesale Only
- Sentinel—A Progressive Newspaper
- 20 Gorgeous Girls—Girls, Girls, Girls—8 Acts All Star Cast—A Chorus with Atomic Energy—Burlesque
- Zombie Cocktail Lounge
- Indian Club—Class Lessons—Easy Methods—Dancing Lessons

EXPLANATION REQUIRED: Though we are never told why Violet gets arrested, the official script reveals that she is a "tart," that is, a call girl. Listen closely to Violet as she struggles with the cops. She says, "That sailor's a liar! I know every big shot in this town! I know Potter and I'll have you kicked off the…" One cannot help but wonder how she has come to know Potter.

320 Sycamore, Pottersville, New York

CLOSER LOOK: At the very beginning of the guide we noted that Bert's Christmas Eve prayer for George is accompanied by a shot of a house, presumably Bert's and somewhere in Bedford Falls. (1:41) Well, in this scene we learn that the house is located on a familiar street. As Pottersville Ernie and George pull up to 320 Sycamore, take a close look at the house next door. (1:54:50) That's Bert's house all right. In fact, the two shots are taken from the same spot, as is confirmed by the street lamp that appears in the foreground of both shots.

While it would be nice to think that Bert and his wife are the Bailey's next-door neighbors, director Frank Capra probably did not intend for this to be so. Rather, Capra probably needed a wintertime shot to go with Bert's prayer, and with limited wintertime footage at his disposal, simply used footage of another house on the Sycamore Street set.

FILM ANECDOTES: But there's an even bigger story relating to the house next door to 320 Sycamore. You see, the house show in Bert's prayer is the same house used in the film for Mary Hatch's house. When George is "picketing" in front of Mary's house, this is the house he's in front of. To put it another way, on the Encino Ranch backlot, the houses used for 320 Sycamore and Mary Hatch's house are right next to each other. How cool is that?!

CLOSER LOOK: While George frantically scrambles around inside 320 Sycamore during the unborn sequence, look for the graffiti on the wall—a heart with an arrow through it, and "Jerry + Toni" scrawled in the heart's center. (1:55:33)

JUST WONDERING: Is that George we hear trying to get out of this jam by laying blame on Clarence? As Bert closes in on him at the Granville house, George blurts, "Bert, listen, it's that fellow there! He's says he's an angel. He's trying to hypnotize me!" Desperate times call for desperate measures, we suppose. No worries though, just a few seconds later Clarence makes himself a legitimate arrest target anyway by biting Bert.

Ma Bailey's Boarding House

CLOSER LOOK: Just to make sure there wasn't a glaring oversight, we compared the Bedford Falls version of Ma Bailey's front porch (shown at the "welcome home" party for Harry and his new bride) with the Pottersville version. Yep, they're the same, except for the fact that Ma Bailey's Boarding House desperately needs a coat of paint.

The Town Cemetery

CLOSER LOOK: When it came time to create Harry Bailey's gravestone, someone on the prop team forgot to do the math. Clarence informs us that Harry fell through the ice and drowned at the age of nine. If Harry was born in 1911, as his gravestone indicates, he would not turn nine until 1920. Yet the gravestone has Harry down for dying in 1919. Good effort, but not quite.

Also, keep an eye out for a continuity gaffe here. In the first shot of the gravestone Harry's year of death is clearly visible. But seconds later the date is covered by snow, forcing George to go digging.

CLOSER LOOK: Harry's gravestone isn't the only Bailey gravestone in this scene. Just to the left is the gravestone of Peter Bailey. (You will have to trust us, as this is not legible in regular viewing mode.) The gravestone states that Peter died in 1928, which is the same year he died in Bedford Falls. That's certainly an interesting parallel in an alternate universe, and it's good to know George's absence in Pottersville didn't take any years off of Peter's life.

FILM ANECDOTES: George and Clarence stumble onto the cemetery while looking for Martinis house in Bailey Park. Both wonder if this is Bailey Park, but there's an easy way to tell. The big tree at the entrance to the cemetery is the same one that we see on moving day for the Martinis at the entrance to Bailey Park.

Mary Closing the Library

JUST WONDERING: What in the world is Mary Hatch doing at the library after 11 P.M. on Christmas Eve? Remember, according to the angels, George is on the bridge contemplating suicide at precisely 10:45 P.M.

CLOSER LOOK: As Mary leaves the library, she is holding a Christmas wreath in her right hand. (1:59:50) But when she turns around the wreath is no longer there. (1:59:55) Is this another Christmas wreath-related film gaffe? Actually, we don't think so. Instead, we're thinking that some tight editing eliminated a portion of the scene where Mary hangs the wreath on the library's front door. Look for the wreath behind Mary as she walks toward the street. (1:59:55)

FILM ANECDOTES: Decades after making the film, director Frank Capra confided that the one aspect of the film he wished he could change was its portrayal of the Pottersville Mary. Capra conceded that he should have made her strong and independent, and not a feeble stereotypical spinster. Hard to disagree with him on that one!

JUST WONDERING: How did Capra resist using the obvious plot twist of having Mary unhappily married to huckster Sam Wainwright (who would, of course, be broke because George wasn't around to give him the idea for making plastics from soybeans)?

CLOSER LOOK: There are no signs outside the bar Mary runs into to identify it, but we can tell you that it's the Blue Moon. The façade in this scene matches with the shot of the Blue Moon we just saw when George arrived in downtown Pottersville. (1:52:51) Also, check out the map of Pottersville for the bar's location, just down the block from the library.

CLOSER LOOK: It's good to see that George's absence has not affected the friendships of Building & Loan shareholders Tom, Ed and Charlie. These three appear together in the Blue Moon. George addresses them by name, and while we don't think they say anything, there are a couple of funny cracks in here directed at George, like "I'm gonna hit 'em over the head with a bott'el" and "You need a straightjacket." Okay. Tom, Ed, Charlie. You guys may not realize it, but we will be seeing you all shortly at 320 Sycamore, Bedford Falls.

RANDOM THOUGHTS: George's crime spree in Pottersville is no less impressive than the one in Bedford Falls. After getting tossed out of Nick's, George stomps around 320 Sycamore in the presence of a police officer (criminal trespass), flees the scene while Bert is trying to arrest him (resisting arrest), grabs Mary outside the library (battery), punches a police officer (aggravated battery—a felony) and flees the scene again (resisting arrest). George better hope Clarence bails him out of this mess or he's going to be doing some serious time in the Pottersville jail.

CLOSER LOOK: After George punches Bert and takes off on foot, Bert whips out his revolver and cracks off all six shots at his disposal. Keep your eye on the neon sign way at the end of the block that reads, "POTTERSVILLE." As Bert unloads his gun, the S, V, and I in "POTTERSVILLE" go dark, giving the appearance that one of Bert's shots hits the sign. (2:01:03) Years later, though, Capra explained that the electrical outage was not planned, but rather just happened to coincide perfectly with what transpired on film.

FILM ANECDOTES: Earlier we pointed out Bert's summer police vehicle of choice, a motorcycle. And here we see Bert's all-season ride. In Pottersville and Bedford Falls he drives a Ford Deluxe four-door, likely from 1941. This was a very popular pre-war car for both civilian and police use. Incidentally, this car is one of the later model cars that you'll find in the film—1941 was the last year of full production before war needs restricted and then ended consumer automobile production.

RANDOM THOUGHTS: Is Bert acting within the law when he shoots at George? Nowadays, police officers generally do not have the authority to use deadly force to "apprehend" an unarmed fleeing suspect. But back then the laws were not so restrictive on this front, and New York had laws on the books that authorized the use of deadly force to apprehend a fleeing suspect known to have committed a felony, which in this case would have been battery on a police officer. Still, Bert's judgment is highly questionable given that he has no reason to believe that George is carrying a weapon, and, more important, the streets are teeming with innocent bystanders. Had Bert hit someone besides George, he would have had some serious explaining to do.

GEORGE WANTS TO LIVE AGAIN

"Zuzu's petals! Zuzu's...they're...they're here, Bert! What do you know about that! Merry Christmas!"

—GEORGE BAILEY

With the gun-wielding Pottersville Bert hot on his trail, George makes his way back to the bridge where this whole nightmarish "never been born" thing began. Apparently one hour in Pottersville is more than enough to convince George that his life really wasn't all that bad after all.

Just one problem. Clarence, the most likely candidate to get him out of this mess, is nowhere to be found. As George urgently pleads for Clarence to intervene, Bert finally catches up with George, and seemingly the stage is set for another fight.

But hold on a minute here. Did Bert just call George by name? Is George's mouth bleeding again from that punch from Mr. Welch? And what about Zuzu's petals? They're there! Hurray! Yes, friends, Clarence comes through in the nick of time, delivering George safely back to Bedford Falls just before he is to incur the wrath of Pottersville Bert.

Now all George wants is to be reunited with his family, and he sets off on a mad dash back to 320 Sycamore, taking time out of course to say "Merry Christmas" to a few people and things along the way. So what if the sheriff is waiting for him there? George has his life back again and that's all that matters.

Thankfully, while George was stumbling around Pottersville in a daze, Mary was back in the real world trying to figure out how to keep him out of jail. Even though it's five minutes to midnight, George's house is soon packed with friends and family, all of whom are eager to contribute to George's cause. And when the sheriff rips up the warrant and makes an offering himself, we know for sure that George is off the hook.

Now all we need are a couple of cappers for the film, and George's brother Harry provides the first. Upon receiving word of George's plight, Harry flies home in a blizzard, gets picked up at the airport by Bert, and arrives just in time to give a short but poignant toast: "To my big brother George. The richest man in town!" Then, moments later, a bell rings on the Bailey's Christmas tree, letting us all know that our old friend Clarence finally did get his wings. Attaboy, Clarence!

George Returns to the Bridge

CLOSER LOOK: We've got two minor film gaffes for you involving Bert and his squad car. When the film cuts to Bert's squad car rounding the turn onto the bridge, notice that it's not snowing yet, meaning that Bert and the car are still back in Pottersville. (2:01:41) Yet the car's siren isn't blaring, as it was when the chase began.

Seconds later Bert stops his car on the bridge and immediately gets out of the passenger side of the car. (2:01:57) This would only make sense if Bert had been riding shotgun with a partner, but we know that when the chase begins Bert is at the wheel and by himself.

George Runs Home

RANDOM THOUGHTS: On his triumphant jaunt through downtown George takes an interesting route. Using our handy map of Bedford Falls, let's track his progress. George starts out in front of the county courthouse by the "You Are Now in Bedford Falls" sign. He then heads down Genesee Street, first waving to some folks in front of the library. He then runs a full block and a half, down to the Bijou Theatre. Next, he backtracks one full block to greet the Bedford Falls Emporium and the Building & Loan. Finally, he heads back up the same block to pay Potter a visit at the Bedford Falls Trust and Savings Bank. Now the only question is, which way is 320 Sycamore from here?

CLOSER LOOK: As George runs past the Bijou, look for signage in the window of the theater's next door neighbor, McKenzie Music Store. Conveniently, the store boasts "MUSICAL Instruments OF ALL KINDS." That being the case, it's a safe bet Bert the cop bought his accordion here.

CLOSER LOOK: Curious as to what the Bedford Falls Emporium is all about? It's really just your garden-variety department store, and if you pause the film as George runs by the store, you'll learn from its signage that the Emporium offers a wide array of household products, including shoes, lingerie, gowns, uniforms, hats, silverware and cut glass. (2:03:08)

FILM ANECDOTES: The set design team wasn't just satisfied with the Bijou's real-world reference to *The Bells of St. Mary's*. They also hung actual movie posters from the film outside the Bijou. Look for two prints of the same poster here, at the bottom of the screen as the marquee flashes by, in the "Now Showing" movie poster display cases. The posters feature Bing Crosby and Ingrid Bergman's names above side-by-side illustrations of their cheerful faces. Crazy thing is, Henry Travers also had billing in *The Bells of St. Mary's*, and his name appears at the bottom of the very poster shown at the Bijou. This means there was very nearly a prop in *Wonderful Life* that included a reference to one of the actors in the film.

CLOSER LOOK: Just to the left of the Building & Loan entrance is one more Red Cross sign. This is a larger version of one by the teller's window when Uncle Billy tries to make the deposit.

FILM ANECDOTES: Interestingly, the film gives no hint that Potter will pay for his thievery. In this respect, the film breaks from Hollywood protocol, which at the time encouraged films to show criminals being caught and punished. Director Frank Capra apparently considered several alternative scenes involving Potter at the end of the film. The script as it stood before filming had Clarence appearing in Potter's office to lecture him on what an evil man he was. An earlier script had Potter standing dejectedly on George's front porch, trying in vain to join the festivities. But in the end Capra wisely left it to the audience to decide Potter's fate.

RANDOM THOUGHTS: What exactly is Potter's crime, you ask, and how did it come to be? Larceny is the best bet. While it's true that Potter did not physically take the money from Uncle Billy, the law nevertheless considers mislaid property to be constructively in the possession of its rightful owner; that would be Uncle Billy, or more precisely, the Building & Loan. So when a person finds mislaid property and retains it despite knowing full well who the rightful owner is, the crime of larceny can arise.

Potter's best defense would be that he never intended to keep the money; rather, he was going to return it once he sorted out what had happened. Yet Potter knew later that same evening (through George) that the Building & Loan had lost the precise amount that he had found. Factor in Potter's interactions with Uncle Billy at the bank, and a reasonable person in Potter's position should have known that the money belonged to the Building & Loan.

By the way, if Potter is charged with a crime he had better hope that he's taken good care of his bodyguard all these years, because he knows everything. And he may want to consider waiving his right to a jury since the Bedford Falls jury pool will likely be stacked with locals who would dearly love to pay back Potter for his slumlord ways.

MUSIC NOTES: Playing throughout George's downtown run, as well as his reunion with his family at 320 Sycamore, is a fantastically uplifting score cue. But the cue was not scored for *Wonderful Life*, nor is it by the film's composer Dimitri Tiomkin. Rather, one of Tiomkin's contemporaries, renowned Hollywood composer Alfred Newman, is behind this short but powerful cue titled, "Hallelujah." Newman wrote it for another RKO film, *The Hunchback of Notre Dame.* There, the cue is prominently featured as Quasimodo saves Esmeralda from being hanged and then again at the end of the film. Newman's score for *The Hunchback of Notre Dame* received high praise, including an Academy Award nomination for Best Score, and "Hallelujah" was a definite highlight.

Earlier we discussed how upset Tiomkin was that cues of other Hollywood composers ended up in the score. This Newman cue is exactly what Tiomkin was talking about, and adding to the insult, Newman's cue is front and center in a key scene.

We will say that this seems like Capra just being Capra and making a call for the good of the picture. We're guessing he fell in love with this well-known cue, and saw it as the perfect vehicle for accentuating the pure joy he sought to convey. He knew both composers well, as both had worked on Capra's World War II *Why We Fight* series, and probably figured any hurt feelings would be quickly forgotten.

George Comes Home Again

MUSIC NOTES: We were surprised and delighted to discover that during the "Hallelujah" cue George actually exclaims, "Hallelujah!" This turns out to be a handy way to remember the name of the cue.

RANDOM THOUGHTS: Greeting George at the door is the bank examiner (Mr. Carter), the sheriff, a reporter and a photographer. Look for the sheriff's badge pinned on his shirt (just before George arrives) and for the reporter's pen and note paper (just after). The photographer actually takes photos throughout the gathering. Imagine the feel-good "Christmas miracle" story that's going to appear in *The Bedford Falls Sentinel* tomorrow, complete with photos of Uncle Billy at the collection basket and George and Zuzu by the Christmas tree.

FILM ANECDOTES: George calls Zuzu his "little ginger snap," and it turns out he calls her that for good reason. Zu Zu was the name brand of a popular ginger snap cookie sold by The National Biscuit Company (today's Nabisco) starting around 1901. The ad campaign featured a clown mascot, dressed in a star-covered, pajama-style clown suit with matching pointed hat, imploring everyone (read: kids) to "Say Zu Zu to the grocer man!" These ginger snaps were wildly popular during George's childhood and were still on the shelves in 1945, though by then Nabisco wasn't putting much behind the brand. Moviegoers back in 1946 would absolutely have gotten the Zu Zu/ginger snap reference.

JUST WONDERING: Is Zuzu her real name or is it a nickname? If it's her real name then George and Mary made a bold move, naming their daughter after a name-brand cookie.

RANDOM THOUGHTS: Remember our discussion earlier about straw hat etiquette and whether Uncle Billy should have been wearing one in early May? Well, here he is wearing a summer straw hat in December. In the 1920s that might well have earned him a hat stomping, but here in 1945 he's probably just getting the occasional quizzical look. No worries, he's used to it.

CLOSER LOOK: Quite a few Building & Loan shareholders come to George's rescue on Christmas Eve. Here are the main ones appearing in both scenes:

- Tom—He talks over Uncle Billy saying, "What is this, ah, another run on the bank?!" During the bank run he demands all $242 he has on deposit.
- Unnamed Building & Loan Shareholder (Round Glasses)—He comes in right behind Tom and says, "Here you are George, Merry Christmas!" We pointed out earlier that he's in the interior and exterior bank run scenes, but with no lines.
- Ed—He arrives just after Tom but has no lines. During the bank run he asks for $20 of his $300.
- Mrs. Thompson—Just before Mr. Martini approaches the basket, she tells George, "Merry Christmas! Thanks for everything!" as she waves and backs away from the basket. During the bank run she asks for $20 after commenting that it's George's own money.
- Charlie—He arrives behind Mr. Martini and at the basket says, "I wouldn't have a roof over my head if it wasn't for you, George." During the bank run he tells George he wants all of his money, saying, "Then I'll take mine now!"

- Mrs. Davis—She arrives with Charlie and appears over Charlie's shoulder as he thanks George, but has no lines here. During the bank run she asks for $17.50.

- Unnamed Building & Loan Shareholder (Dark Coat)—He steps up to the donation basket just as Ernie says, "The line forms on the right." In a foreign accent he tells George, "There's more coming George, Merry Christmas and God bless you!" During the bank run he's up against the counter, screen left, in a rain slicker and matching rain hat.

FILM ANECDOTES: This is one of several scenes that make use of movie prop money. Others include the bank run scene, Uncle Billy's bank deposit debacle, Violet's Christmas Eve day goodbye and Nick's. While it's no shocker that the money used in these scenes is fake, you may be surprised to learn that you are looking at fake Mexican pesos. Yep, Hollywood studios had to steer well clear of prop money that even remotely resembled U.S. currency, and their solution was to use rough reproductions of old Mexican pesos.

Here the prop team used at least two common Mexican pesos prop variants. The ones in this scene have "El Estado de Sonora" centered above a portrait of someone who is definitely not a U.S. president. You can even see "Pesos" on a few bills. When Mary fans the honeymoon kitty in the back of Ernie's taxi you can see, clear as day, a fake $10 pesos note with "El Estado de Chihuahua" on the front and "Diez Pesos" right below it. When Uncle Billy thumbs his deposit, a few $5 pesos notes flick by.

FILM ANECDOTES: With Mr. Martini shouting, "And I busted the juke box too!," it's fair to say that he must have done something else. Indeed, before filming Mr. Martini was to say, "I got all the money out of the cash register—and I broke the juke box too!" We think actor William Edmunds delivered both lines, but the first one got clipped in the final edit.

EXPLANATION REQUIRED: Mrs. Hatch has her own donation backstory. She breaks into her emergency cash, stashed in a cookie jar. She's holding the cookie jar when she walks in the front door with Uncle Billy and others at the beginning of the party. And film stills from the scene show Mrs. Hatch holding the same cookie jar.

FILM ANECDOTES: We're not sure exactly what snow substitute Capra used in these interior shots. For the most part, the "snow" rested nicely on the coats and hats of the actors, but when Mr. Gower makes his contribution look for a few stray "snowflakes" defying gravity and floating like feathers around Mr. Gower's hat.

CLOSER LOOK: We just mentioned that there are no U.S. presidents to be found on the currency in the collection basket, but there is one image of a president hiding in the pile. During Mr. Gower's offering, look for a portrait of George Washington on the side of a tin canister. This is an early 1900s tobacco tin made by the R.J. Reynolds Tobacco Company for its George Washington brand cut plug tobacco, repurposed here as someone's savings container. Unfortunately, this does not expand our U.S. presidents list as we already had a George Washington sighting in Peter Bailey's office.

EXPLANATION REQUIRED: As Violet speaks to George, an apparently smitten Ernie mutters to himself, "Vi-o-let Bick, Mer-ry Christmas, missy!" And during her exchange with George, Violet can be heard saying, "Here you go Georgie Porgie." We heard Violet use this nickname earlier, on the night George ran into Violet downtown before calling on Mary.

DID YOU KNOW?: Now, remember Uncle Billy's embarrassing exchange with the bank teller this morning? Thanks to Uncle Billy, we learned that the teller's name is Horace, but we never really got a good look at him. Well, great news! Horace is here tonight and in the thick of things. He's generally screen left during the festivities, but the best view of him is when Annie makes her contribution—he's just off of Annie's right shoulder, in an overcoat and scarf, with slicked-back grey hair. You can find the actor playing Horace, Eddie Fetherstone, in several Capra films, and we like him in *Movie Crazy* (1932), playing an assistant director who oversees filming of a scene gone sideways.

EXPLANATION REQUIRED: Mr. Partridge donates his pocket watch on a whim, and the move is a real crowd pleaser. We can tell it's an Elgin brand pocket watch, with an ornamental fob on the end of the chain. This makes sense given that for years Elgin made as many as half the pocket watches sold in the U.S.

In giving this piece away, Mr. Partridge is getting with the times, so to speak. Pocket watches began losing favor to wristwatches during World War I. Wristwatches had been more of a feminine accessory but it turned out they were super handy in military settings. By the time World War II came along, pocket watches were an old timey thing.

It's fun to think that perhaps one of the actors or a crew member supplied the pocket watch for the scene. Whatever the case, somebody out there surely has this watch, tucked away in a closet or drawer, with no idea that they own a special piece of American film history.

CLOSER LOOK: Funny thing about the watch. When we first see the face it shows 11:20, well behind the time on the grandfather clock in the entrance hall, which reads 11:55. A few seconds later, during "Hark the Herald Angels Sing," we see it's more properly set to 12:05, meaning it's Christmas. Yay, all is well…except that before the song is even over the watch is back to 11:20. Dang, it is not easy managing props.

DID YOU KNOW?: And while we're identifying hardware, The Bevin Brothers Manufacturing Company in East Hampton, Connecticut, stakes claim to being the maker of the bell on the Christmas tree. East Hampton was so deep into bell making that it became known as "bell town." And the company has been around so long that sleigh bells were once its specialty, back when sleigh bells were a key safety feature for sleighs (think: car horn).

EXPLANATION REQUIRED: The script called for Uncle Billy to say a quick prayer to himself by the tree and he does appear to do so, just before getting a big hug from Ma Bailey.

JUST WONDERING: Mr. Carter, the bank examiner, joins in the fun and makes a donation while merrily singing. But does his family know about his change in plans? He told George earlier in the day at the Building & Loan that he wanted to finish up so he could be with his family on Christmas in Elmira, New York. Looks like he will just have to leave first thing in the morning.

CLOSER LOOK: As Ernie reads Sam Wainwright's telegram, the man appearing just over Ernie's right shoulder is the most improbable of guests. Yes, it's Mr. Welch! Just two hours ago this guy punched our hero in Martini's, and yet here he is now in George's living room celebrating with George's friends and family. Somebody needs to give this guy the boot.

FILM ANECDOTES: Mr. Welch's surreptitious presence can be explained by the fact that the script at one time called for him to apologize to George at the party by offering up the following words of atonement: "I'm sorry, George. It was all a mistake." A mistake, Mr. Welch? We don't think so. George insulted you and your wife, and you clocked him. Pretty simple.

DID YOU KNOW?: Another man shows up at the same time Mr. Welch does, only with no hint as to who he is. Unlike Mr. Welch, who drifts into the background, this guest retains his prime spot amidst the main characters for the rest of the scene. Who is this mystery man? Was he in part of a scene that got cut? Was he an extra who somehow slipped into the foreground?

None of the above. He's the man who helps Bert hang tropical-themed advertisements at the Granville house on George and Mary's wedding night, a role that is often described as the "bill poster." But it's nearly impossible to make out the bill poster in that scene—it's dark out, he's soaking wet and he's wearing a painter's cap. And while the bill poster has a distinguishing squeaky New York City accent, he doesn't speak on Christmas Eve. So it's not at all surprising that he's not familiar to us here.

CAST ANECDOTES: Actor Garry Owen, who plays the bill poster, was in fact a Capra favorite. Capra tapped Owen to provide similar comic relief in *Meet John Doe* (frustrated sign painter) and *Arsenic and Old Lace* (patient but frustrated taxi driver). Of his non-comedy roles, his portrayal of a cop in the film noir classic *Mildred Pierce*, talking Joan Crawford out of jumping off the pier, cannot be beat.

JUST WONDERING: Where in the heck does Bert's accordion come from? Does he carry it around in the trunk of his squad car just in case? If he stopped by his house to get it, he sure covers a lot of ground at the end of the film. Remember, after tracking down George on the bridge, Bert also picks Harry up at the airport.

RANDOM THOUGHTS: It's now time for a head count to determine who is missing from the film's final scene. Here's a list of characters who are not there:

SAM WAINWRIGHT: He's in Europe and had to be out of reach, otherwise he'd have been around to loan George the money.

MARTY HATCH: Whereabouts unknown. Last seen crossing the bridge at Remagen.

JOE "THE LUGGAGE GUY" HEPNER: Maybe it's just too painful for George to be friends with the owner of a store specializing in travel.

RUTH DAKIN BAILEY: She's probably back in Buffalo—a real-life Buffalo gal—wondering if Commander Harry Bailey has any interest in returning to work at her father's glass factory.

PETER BAILEY: May he rest in peace, but surely he's present in spirit.

NICK: Somebody has to close up Martini's.

CLARENCE: But that bell on the Christmas tree didn't ring all by itself.

CAST ANECDOTES: Earlier we mentioned that we have always wondered why Ruth Dakin Bailey wasn't in the Christmas Eve scenes. Under normal circumstances, Ruth would have been in Washington D.C. for the medal ceremony (how could a spouse miss that?!), and it would have been no issue to simply have her fly home with Ma Bailey. Well, actor Virginia Patton recalls a very practical reason—she had the mumps. (If you're scoring at home, she's the second actor in the film known to have had the mumps during filming). Indeed, her bout with the mumps spanned her birthday, June 25, and, sure enough, filming for the Christmas Eve gathering took place on the same day as her birthday.

CLOSER LOOK: Harry shows up at George's house wearing his military uniform. The film's costume designers were actually on the ball here, as the rank insignia shown on the shoulder boards of Harry's uniform—three broad gold stripes and a star—is proper for a Navy commander. (2:08:22)

CLOSER LOOK: On this first Christmas Eve since the end of the war, Ernie is wearing a shirt from his military days. Check out the patch on his left sleeve—it's a U.S. Army Air Force patch worn during World War II; it's known as the "Hap Arnold" emblem. (2:07:53) Being in the Air Force doesn't seem to quite mesh with his wartime backstory of being a paratrooper, but hey, the war's over, we're moving on. Anyway, we love the patriotic gesture, but is that a military-issue bow tie he's wearing with it?

EXPLANATION REQUIRED: Mary says, "And Mr. Martini how about some wine?! An earlier script included more lines for Mary here. Before asking Mr. Martini about wine, she was to quickly point out that it's approaching midnight, cue Janie to start playing, and ask Tilly and Annie to serve punch. But it all got cut, and that's why her line starts with *and*. No matter, though. Janie, Tilly and Annie got the message. Janie starts playing, and look for Tilly and Annie easing their way through the crowd carrying a punch bowl and handing out glasses.

CLOSER LOOK: A few things to look for here as Janie starts in on "Hark the Herald Angels Sing." First, she's looking at legitimate sheet music for the song. You can just make it out (bottom of the right-hand page) both here and in the first shot of her practicing. Next, look for a framed photograph of George and Mary resting on the piano. We believe Mary is wearing the same dress she has on in the war montage, serving as a USO hostess.

RANDOM THOUGHTS: Well, all of that practice by Carol Coombs, er Janie, sure paid off—she really nails the song at the party. And boy did she get a lot of practice. Janie is playing when George walks in the door on Christmas Eve and she plays all the way through until George tells her to stop. You can even hear her when George is in the kitchen and upstairs in Zuzu's room. All in all, she practices uninterrupted for five minutes and forty seconds. Add another forty seconds for her performance at the party, and that's a lot of film time Carol enjoys, in a fun and rather unconventional way.

JUST WONDERING: Harry has been married over thirteen years now and he's around thirty-six years old, so do he and Ruth have kids yet?

CAST ANECDOTES: While you may associate the Bailey kids with the end of the film, don't forget that Carol Coombs and Karolyn Grimes took part in the very first scene. As George's friends and family pray for him, Carol's line as Janie is,

"Please, God, something's the matter with daddy." Karolyn's as Zuzu is, "Please bring daddy back." So both girls put in some extra work recording their lines, apart from their 320 Sycamore scenes.

DID YOU KNOW?: George is not only the richest man in town, he's also the luckiest. Despite the valiant efforts of his friends, George should still be spending the night in jail. Earlier that evening, a judicial officer issued a warrant for George's arrest. The warrant alleged that George stole money from the Building & Loan. Of course, just because his family and friends give him enough money to replace the allegedly stolen money doesn't mean he's off the hook. Otherwise, bank robbers could sleep easy knowing that if caught they could always offer to pay the money back. So, for the time being anyway, George is the beneficiary of an error in judgment by the sheriff.

CAST ANECDOTES: Director Frank Capra loved casting actors that had previously appeared in his films, and he was true to form when it came to casting *Wonderful Life.* For example, here are nine actors from *Wonderful Life* that also appear in Capra's 1938 film *You Can't Take It With You*: Jimmy Stewart, Lionel Barrymore (Potter), Samuel Hinds (Peter Bailey), H.B. Warner (Mr. Gower), Ward Bond (Bert), Stanley Andrews (Mr. Welch), Charles Lane (Potter's rent collector), and Edward Keene (Building & Loan shareholder Tom) and Jimmy the Raven.

And Capra's 1941 film *Mr. Smith Goes to Washington* features these *Wonderful Life* actors: Jimmy Stewart, Thomas Mitchell (Uncle Billy), Beulah Bondi (Mrs. Bailey), H. B. Warner, Larry Simms (Pete Bailey), Dick Elliott (the grumpy neighbor), Stanley Andrews and Charles Lane.

CAST ANECDOTES: Jimmy Stewart first made a name for himself playing characters not dissimilar from his own persona. After several solid pictures, Stewart went on a roll, starting with Frank Capra's *You Can't Take It With You.* The film won Best Picture in 1938 and solidified his status as a rising star. Just one year later he teamed up with Capra again for *Mr. Smith Goes to Washington,* earning a nomination for Best Actor. The year after that, he won Best Actor for his performance in *The Philadelphia Story*, which some say was a "make good" award for his not having won for *Mr. Smith.*

After a five-year hiatus from acting brought about by the war, *It's a Wonderful Life* launched his "second career." In the years that followed, Stewart proved himself proficient in every genre thrown his way, from Westerns (*Destry Rides Again, Broken Arrow, Winchester '73, The Man from Laramie, The Man Who Shot Liberty*

Valance) to thrillers (*Vertigo*, *Rear Window*) to dramas (*Anatomy of a Murder*) to comedies (*Harvey*).

In contrast, Donna Reed's film resume is far less diverse than Stewart's, in part because she was typecast early in her career as the innocent good girl. The one notable exception was *From Here to Eternity* (1953), where she was, somewhat improbably, cast as a call girl. The film—a gritty tale of love and war in Hawaii in the days before Pearl Harbor—was a box office hit, due in no small part to stellar performances by Reed, Frank Sinatra, Montgomery Clift, Deborah Kerr and Burt Lancaster.

And as these things go, this breakout role earned Reed her first and only Academy Award (Best Supporting Actress). Yet Reed's performance did not translate into better roles, and after enduring a string of projects that were beneath her talents, in the late 1950s she made the move to television via *The Donna Reed Show*.

Several of Reed's more notable performances came in the years surrounding *Wonderful Life*. In 1945, Reed had a high-profile appearance in *The Picture of Dorian Gray* (1945), which did quite well at the box office despite the fact that it is one painfully slow film. Reed then appeared in *They Were Expendable*, playing a World War II nurse who falls for John Wayne. Her performance in this film apparently convinced Capra to cast her in *Wonderful Life*.

After completing *Wonderful Life* in the summer of 1946, Reed starred in *Green Dolphin Street*. The film has Reed playing a young lass who, through a bizarre set of circumstances, ends up on the other end of the purity spectrum from her character in *From Here to Eternity*. Interestingly, *Green Dolphin Stree*t ended up trouncing *Wonderful Life* at the box office in 1947, ranking 10th on Variety magazine's list of top grossing films for the year, compared to 26th for *Wonderful Life*.

MUSIC NOTES: Yet another falling-out between Capra and score composer Dimitri Tiomkin concerned the film's final song. Tiomkin selected "Ode to Joy," which he viewed as a good thematic fit. But Capra saw things differently and without consulting Tiomkin substituted "Auld Lang Syne." While "Ode to Joy" is a great song, we are siding with Capra on this one.

CLOSER LOOK: George's friends are even more generous than you think. Pause the film on Clarence's literary gift as it rests in a pile of money and you can see a $10, a $100 and, oh my, a $1,000 bill. If only this wasn't Mexican pesos prop money.

FILM ANECDOTES: You be the judge as to whether Ward Bond is actually playing that accordion. We mentioned that Jimmy Stewart knew how to play the accordion, but we came up empty on the same for Bond. Whatever the case, there's definitely an accordion playing during "Auld Lang Syne."

RANDOM THOUGHTS: It's fun to watch Janie and Pete hanging beneath the joyous adult commotion, enthralled by the growing pile of bills and coins. And Tommy is down there with them, though he's really hard to spot. After continually being either blocked by adults or missed by the frame, he finally reappears by the basket when George picks up *The Adventures of Tom Sawyer*. Whew. We knew he could not possibly have been sent up to bed.

CLOSER LOOK: Clarence's inscription in *The Adventures of Tom Sawyer* reads:

> *Dear George:--*
>
> *Remember no man is a failure who has friends.*
> *Thanks for the wings!*
>
> *Love*
>
> *Clarence*

The book in which the inscription appears is a custom prop—there's no version of Twain's book that matches the cover artwork seen here.

MUSIC NOTES: Watch Zuzu as she struggles a bit with the words to "Auld Lang Syne." But in fairness to Karolyn Grimes, adults can't even remember the song's antiquated lines. Year after year people feel their way through this song without knowing what they're actually singing about. Well, in a nutshell, it's an old Scottish song that is meant to recall times gone by. *Auld lang syne* translates to "old long ago," which seems a touch redundant, but what do we know. There are several verses to the song, but here are the words we're accustomed to singing:

> *Should old acquaintance be forgot*
> *And never brought to mind?*
> *Should old acquaintance be forgot*
> *And days of auld lang syne?*
> *For auld lang syne, my dear*
> *For auld lang syne*
> *We'll take/drink a cup of kindness yet*
> *For auld lang syne.*

The message here? Let's all take a moment to remember the friends we've made through the years. Well, on this Christmas Eve, that is something George and his family will gladly do.

IT'S A WONDERFUL LIFE MUSIC

The soundtrack for *Wonderful Life* is comprised of popular songs as well as score cues by composer Dimitri Tiomkin. We've provided both lists for you. For both, we've included the scene in which a song appears. For the score cues, we've included cues that did not make it into the film and the scene in which they would have appeared.

Popular Songs

"Buffalo Gals" (unknown)—played throughout the film.

"Adeste Fidelis" (John Francis Wade)—played in the opening scene as George's friends and family are heard praying for him.

"Ave Maria" (Bach/Gounod)—played while angels Franklin and Joseph talk in heaven.

"Twinkle, Twinkle, Little Star" (unknown)—refrain played throughout the film.

"Collegiate" (Jaffe/Bonx)—the first song played by the band at the graduation dance.

"The Charleston" (Mack/Johnson)—played by the band at the graduation dance.

"My Wild Irish Rose" (Chauncey Olcott)—sung by Uncle Billy leaving Harry's "welcome home" party.

"Avalon" (Rose/Jolson)—played as George and his mother talk outside at Harry's "welcome home" party.

"Wedding March" (Felix Mendelssohn)—played during George and Mary's wedding send-off.

"Song of the Islands" (Charles E. King)—played on the phonograph on George and Mary's wedding night.

"I Love You Truly" (Carrie Jacobs-Bond)—sung by Bert and Ernie on George and Mary's wedding night.

"O Sole Mio" (Di Capua/Mazzucchi/Capurro)—played as the Martinis arrive at Bailey Park.

"This Is the Army Mr. Jones" (Irving Berlin)—played during the "war years" montage.

"Dankgebet" (unknown)—played during the "war years" montage for the church footage.

"When Johnny Comes Marching Home" (Patrick S. Gilmore, aka Louis Lambert)—played as Uncle Billy walks to the bank.

"Hark the Herald Angels Sing" (Felix Mendelssohn)—played by Janie on the piano, and sung by all in the film's final scene.

"Vieni, Vieni" (Kroger/Varna/Scotto)—the first song played at Martini's.

"Santa Lucia" (unknown)—the second song played at Martini's. Untitled Boogie Piano (Meade "Lux" Lewis)—played at Nick's.

"North America Meets South America" (Rodgers/Hart)—played as part of a medley as George walks through downtown Pottersville.

"Hallelujah" (Alfred Newman)—played as George runs through downtown and reunites with his family at home in the final scene.

"Auld Lang Syne" (unknown)—sung by all in the last scene.

Score Cues

"Main Title/Heaven/Ski Run"—first part used in the introduction; second part is used in the prayer scene and the scene in heaven; third part cut in full from the sledding scene.

"Death Telegram/Gower's Deliverance"—both parts cut in full from the poison capsules scenes.

"George and Dad"—cut in full from the Bailey family dinner table scene.

"Father's Death"—partially used in the scene where George learns that his father has had a stroke.

"Love Sequence"—cut in full from George and Mary's love scene.

"Wedding Cigars/George Lassos Stork"—first part cut in full from the end of the bank run scene; second part partially used in the scene where Mary tells George she's pregnant.

"Dilemma/Bank Crisis/Search for Money/Potter's Threat"—first two parts cut in full from the bank run scenes; third part partially used during the scene where George and Uncle Billy search for the bank deposit; fourth part cut in full from the scene where George asks Potter for a loan.

"Clarence's Arrival"—used in the scene where George arrives on the bridge contemplating suicide.

"George Is Unborn/Haunted House"—first part partially used in the scenes after Clarence grants George his wish that he'd never been born; second part used in the scene where George returns to his house in Pottersville.

"Pottersville Cemetery/Wrong Ma Bailey/Wrong Mary Hatch/The Prayer"—first part used for the cemetery scene; second part cut and replaced; third part used in the scene outside the library; fourth part used in the scene where George returns to the bridge.

"It's a Wonderful Life"—partially used during the final scenes; originally slated for George's run home through the end of the film.

PHOTOS

RKO's Encino Ranch backlot beginnings in 1930. Rectangular compound on lower right is actor Edward Everett Horton's ranch.

Encino Ranch in 1952. *Wonderful Life* set: (1) courthouse; (2) Potter's bank; (3) Building & Loan; (4) 320 Sycamore. Horton's ranch is lower right.

Encino Ranch entrance in 1948. In 1952 aerial photo, entrance was on lower left corner of property.

320 Sycamore in 1954, shortly before Encino Ranch was bulldozed and replaced with a subdivision.

320 Sycamore in 1942 from *The Magnificent Ambersons.* Note smaller size compared to house in *Wonderful Life* and in photo above. Sometime after filming wrapped, RKO moved the house to its residential set, called New England Street, which is where the house stood during *Wonderful Life* filming.

Encino Ranch, 1946. Ma Bailey's house on right; used for interior and exterior scenes. House on left visible in wedding send-off scene.

View down the street in front of Ma Bailey's house, looking toward 320 Sycamore and Mary Hatch's house. Arrow points to 320 Sycamore's turret. Hatch house is next door and visible at end of street.

George crashes car in between these two Encino Ranch structures. Homeowner who confronts George lives in house on right. Church on left is also visible during Ma Bailey's prayer at beginning of film.

House George and Mary walk past after the dance. Driveway has a gated entrance in *Wonderful Life.* Harry and Uncle Billy drive up this street, with house in background, as they find George.

View on Encino Ranch's New England Street set looking away from Hatch house. Ma Bailey's house is out of view on right side of street. Commercial building at far end is on Encino Ranch's Modern Street, which served as Bedford Falls' main street. Courthouse set used in *Wonderful Life* is three blocks down to the right from that commercial building.

Same block and side of street, looking opposite direction, back toward Hatch house (not visible).

Encino Ranch's Modern Street in 1937. Same block later used for Building & Loan in *Wonderful Life.* Street entrance to Building & Loan was below "Booksellers" sign; Anderson's store was to right of that, on first floor. Building & Loan was on second floor above Anderson's. Look for same point of view in *Wonderful Life* when young George and his pals see Potter.

Encino Ranch's Modern Street in 1935. Shows block used for Building & Loan, looking other direction. Building on near corner is garage in *Wonderful Life* and is visible as young George and his pals see Potter.

Encino Ranch's Modern Street in 1932, looking away from where set used for *Wonderful Life* courthouse stood. Building & Loan block is on left.

Modern Street in 1932, looking toward set used for *Wonderful Life* courthouse; courthouse structure visible at end of street.

Lamanda Park depot, Pasadena, CA, 1931. Palm trees forced tight shooting. Harry and Ruth got off train at spot even with top of ramp. George and Uncle Billy's talk and George and Ruth's talk occurred halfway between depot's right corner and tracks. Western Union sign hanging is visible in *Wonderful Life.*

Stan Kistler's photo of *Wonderful Life*'s Bedford Falls train station set, taken May 8, 1946. Larger Bedford Falls sign not visible in film; smaller one is. Bus stop sign is prop; not used in film. Filming activity in this photo is centered around the depot's ramp.

Entrance to Bailey Park. George actually heads the wrong direction here. In real life, Martini Castle is straight ahead, a dozen or so houses up on the left; arrow points to its location.

Modern-day view of view from entrance to Bailey Park.

The Martini Castle in *Wonderful Life.*

A modern-day view of the Martini Castle.

Sam Wainwright drives off in his Duesenberg. Scene filmed across the street from the Martini Castle.

Sam Wainwright's Duesenberg in its current home. Trunk is sitting on luggage rack, which is folded up in *Wonderful Life.*

Start of "The Charleston" contest in *Wonderful Life.* Filmed in Swim-Gym at Beverly Hills High School. Bunting is hanging from basketball backboard.

Virtually identical camera angle from scene in RKO Radio Picture's *The Bachelor and the Bobby-Soxer,* filmed in Swim-Gym shortly after *Wonderful Life.*

The last three men seen in possession of the loving cup from "The Charleston" contest: Harry Bailey, George Bailey and Cary Grant. Trophy's engraving reads: "Charleston Contest—1928—Bedford Falls High School."

(Above) George Bailey in his office during bank run scene, with trophy on cabinet. "Charleston" is visible on trophy.

(Left) Cary Grant in RKO Radio Picture's *The Bachelor and the Bobby-Soxer.* Trophy from *Wonderful Life* reused in that film; right half of "Charleston Contest" engraving is visible in this photo, including words "Contest" "Falls" and "School."

Jimmy Stewart photos, all visible in *Wonderful Life.* TOP LEFT: Jimmy on tricycle age 3 (Peter Bailey's desk in 1919; George and Mary's living room mantel on Christmas Eve). TOP RIGHT: Jimmy age 2 with his mother Elizabeth (Peter Bailey's desk; Bailey dining room night of dance). BOTTOM LEFT: Jimmy age 13 with sisters Mary and Virginia (George's living room work area). BOTTOM RIGHT: Jimmy's 1928 high school yearbook photo (Bailey dining room night of dance; George's living room work area).

ABOUT THE AUTHOR

Michael Willian is a writer, film buff, business executive and attorney. He is the author of a film guidebook for another American classic, *Casablanca,* titled, *The Scene-by-Scene Casablanca Film Guidebook.* Michael grew up in the Chicago area and calls Chicago home.

Author with *It's a Wonderful Life* actors at the 2019 *It's a Wonderful Life Festival,* Seneca Falls, New York. TOP LEFT: Karolyn Grimes (Zuzu Bailey). TOP RIGHT: Jimmy Hawkins (Tommy Bailey). LOWER LEFT: Jeanine Ann Roose (young Violet Bick). LOWER RIGHT: Carol Coombs (Janie Bailey).

Printed in Great Britain
by Amazon

31657228R00126